Living L ✔ P9-DXQ-814

CONVERSATIONAL
JAPANESE

REVISED AND UPDATED

The Living Language™ Series
Basic Courses on Cassette

Spanish*
French*
German*
Italian*
Japanese*
Portuguese (Continental)
Portuguese (Brazilian)
Advanced Spanish
Advanced French
Children's Spanish
Children's French
Russian
Hebrew
English for Spanish Speakers
English for French Speakers
English for Italian Speakers
English for German Speakers
English for Chinese Speakers

*Also available on Compact Disc

Living Language Plus®

Spanish
French
German
Italian

Living Language Traveltalk™

Spanish	*Russian*
French	*Japanese*
German	*Portuguese*
Italian	

Living Language Fast & Easy

Spanish	*Inglés/English for Spanish Speakers*
French	*Portuguese*
Italian	*Korean*
Japanese	*Mandarin Chinese*
German	*Hungarian*
Hebrew	*Arabic*
Russian	*Czech*
Polish	

Living Language™
CONVERSATIONAL
JAPANESE
REVISED AND UPDATED

Revised by Hiroko Storm, Ph.D.
University of Arizona

Based on the original by Ichiro Shirato
Assistant Professor of Japanese,
Lafayette College

CROWN PUBLISHERS, INC., NEW YORK

This work was previously published under the titles *Conversation Manual Japanese* and *Living Language™ Conversational Japanese* by Ichiro Shirato, based on the method devised by Ralph Weiman. Special thanks to Gladys Heldman.

Published by Crown Publishers, Inc., 201 East 50th Street, New York, New York 10022. Member of the Crown Publishing Group.

LIVING LANGUAGE and colophon are trademarks of Crown Publishers, Inc.

Random House, Inc. New York, Toronto, London, Sydney, Auckland

Crown is a trademark of Crown Publishers, Inc.

Manufactured in the United States of America

Library of Congress Catalog Card Number: 60-15399

ISBN 0-517-59066-2

10   9   8   7   6   5   4   3   2   1

1993 Revised and Updated Edition

CONTENTS

INTRODUCTION

Living Language™ Japanese makes it easy to learn how to speak, read, and write Japanese. This course is a thoroughly revised and updated version of *Living Japanese: The Complete Living Language Course®*. The same, highly effective method of language instruction is still used, but the content has been updated to reflect modern usage and the format has been clarified. In this course, the basic elements of the language have been carefully selected and condensed into forty short lessons. If you can study for about thirty minutes a day, you can master this course and learn to speak Japanese in a few weeks.

You'll learn Japanese the way you have learned English, starting with simple words and progressing to more complex phrases. Just listen and repeat after the native instructors on the recordings. To help you immerse yourself in the language, you'll hear only Japanese spoken. Hear it, say it, absorb it through use and repetition.

This *Living Language™ Conversational Japanese* manual provides English translations and brief explanations for each lesson. The first five lessons cover pronunciation, laying the foundation for learning the vocabulary, phrases, and grammar that are explained in the later chapters. If you already know a little Japanese, you can use the book as a phrasebook and a reference. In addition to the forty lessons, there is a summary of Japanese grammar, plus verb conjugations and a section on writing letters.

Also included in the course package is the *Living Language™ Japanese Dictionary*. It contains more than fifteen thousand entries, with many of the definitions illustrated by phrases and idiomatic expressions. More than one thousand of the most essential words are capitalized to make them easy to find. You can increase your vocabulary and range of expression just by browsing through the dictionary.

Practice your Japanese as much as possible. Even if you can't manage a trip abroad, watching Japanese movies, reading Japanese magazines, eating at Japanese restaurants, and talking with Japanese-speaking friends are enjoyable ways to help you reinforce what you have learned with *Living Language*™ *Japanese*. Now, let's begin. The following instructions will tell you what to do.

COURSE MATERIAL

1. Two 90-minute cassettes or three 60-minute compact discs.

2. *Living Language*™ *Conversational Japanese* manual. This book is designed for use with the recorded lessons, but it may also be used alone as a reference. It contains the following sections: basic Japanese in forty lessons, a summary of Japanese grammar, verb conjugations, and a section on letter writing.

3. *Living Language*™ *Japanese Dictionary*. The Japanese/English–English/Japanese dictionary contains more than fifteen thousand entries. Phrases and idiomatic expressions illustrate many of the definitions. More than one thousand of the most essential words are capitalized.

INSTRUCTIONS

1. Look at page 5. The words in **boldface** type are the ones you will hear on the recording.

2. Now read Lesson 1 all the way through. Note the points to listen for when you play the recording. The first word you will hear is **Ákira.**

3. Start the recording, listen carefully, and say the words aloud in the pauses provided. Go through the lesson once and don't worry if you can't pronounce everything correctly the first time around. Try it again and keep repeating the lesson until you are comfortable with it. The more often you listen and repeat, the longer you will remember the material.

4. Now go on to the next lesson. If you take a break between lessons, it's always good to review the previous lesson before starting a new one.

5. In the manual, there are two kinds of quizzes. With matching quizzes, you must select the English translation of the Japanese sentence. The other type requires you to fill in the blanks with the correct Japanese word chosen from the three given directly below the sentence. If you make any mistakes, reread the section.

6. Even after you have finished the forty lessons and scored 100 percent on the final quiz, keep practicing your Japanese by listening to the recordings and speaking with Japanese-speaking friends. For further study, try *Living Language Traveltalk™ Japanese.*

CONVERSATIONAL
JAPANESE

REVISED AND UPDATED

LESSON 1

DÁI ÍKKA

A. A PRELIMINARY NOTE

Japanese, as spoken by the majority of Japan's 120 million people, is the language you will be learning in this course. Not only can it be used throughout Japan, but also, to a limited extent, in Korea, Taiwan, and some parts of Southeast Asia.

Japanese is a language that is peculiarly original among the world's languages. Despite the fact that more than half the words in Japanese were borrowed from Chinese, the linguistic structure of Japanese is quite different from Chinese. And although Japanese grammar is amazingly similar to Korean, and although both languages share some vocabulary adopted from Chinese, the two languages differ from each other in all other respects.

There are several things you should know and remember to make your understanding of Japanese easier:

1. Japanese syllables can be classified into five kinds:

   a. a vowel by itself
   b. a consonant by itself
   c. a consonant + a vowel
   d. a semi-vowel + a vowel
   e. a consonant + *y* + a vowel

2. In Japanese, verbs, adjectives, copulas (linking words), and certain endings are inflected in a number of categories.

3. Japanese has many so-called "particles." They are used very frequently to show the grammatical relationship within a sentence of one word to another. Mastery of these particles is a key to the rapid learning of Japanese.

4. Punctuation is used in Japanese as it is in English. The use of punctuation marks in the Japanese writing system is relatively new, and rules governing punctuation usage have not yet been firmly established.

5. The word order of Japanese sentences differs from the word order of English sentences. In Japanese, verbs come at the end of a sentence, rather than following the subject and preceding the object, as they do in English.

6. Japanese has a complex system of "honorifics," words that reflect the relationship between the speakers and whom they are speaking about. Different words and word forms are used to indicate the degrees of politeness. This concept is similar to the French differentiation between "vous" and "tu," but in Japanese, there are more than a dozen ways to say "you." This book uses the most standard forms of the language, so that, unless otherwise indicated, each phrase can be said by both men and women in most situations without sounding too casual or too formal.

B. THE ALPHABET: THE LETTERS

All Japanese words and sentences in this course have been transcribed into Roman letters, and all the letters of the English alphabet (except for "l,"[1] "q," and "x") appear in the transcription. Note, however, that the letter "c" appears only in combination with "h" and that these two letters together (ch) are *always treated as one letter.*

A comprehensive list of signs and instructions in Japanese characters (including their English meanings) appears in Lesson 40. An explanation of the traditional Japanese writing system and a description of Japanese characters appear in the section called The Writing System. For a discussion of the Japanese Syllabary, see Lesson 5.

C. ACCENT

Regardless of their length, words *may* or *may not* be accented in Japanese. Consequently, it is possible for a word of one syllable to be accented or a word of several syllables to be unaccented. All words in this manual that do not carry an accent mark (´) are unaccented. In all cases, an accent mark denotes a drop in the pitch of the voice *directly after the accented syllable.* The degree of the drop does not matter, so long as it occurs. However, the more excited the speaker is, the greater may be the change in pitch.

Remember these points:

1. On an unaccented word, the pitch of the voice is held even except on the first syllable (where

---

[1] The sound of *l* is sometimes heard in the pronunciation of Japanese by Japanese nationals. But this sound is always interchangeable with the Japanese variety of *r*. For the sake of simplicity, all sounds that might sometimes be pronounced *l* are written throughout this course as *r*.

it is slightly lower) *no matter how long the word is.*

2. When a single-syllable word is accented, the drop in pitch occurs *after that word.*

3. In multisyllabic words having the accent on the first syllable, the pitch of the voice is dropped *directly after* that syllable and this lowered pitch is maintained for all the other syllables in that word.

4. For multisyllabic words having the accent on the second or any subsequent syllable, the same pitch is maintained for *all* the syllables *through the accented syllable* (with the exception of the first syllable, on which the pitch is slightly lowered); then the pitch is dropped.

5. The accent on certain words disappears when these words are placed next to another accented word. This accounts for the fact that words will on occasion carry an accent mark and at other times discard it.

6. Accent patterns vary more among different dialects than do grammatical patterns.

D. THE ALPHABET: THE SOUNDS

Many Japanese sounds are like English. Listen and repeat the following Japanese first names, and notice which sounds are similar and which are different:

Ákira	Haruo	Noboru
Áiko	Hídeko	Nóbuko
Átsuko	Isoo	Osamu
Chíeko	Ítoko	Rentaroo
Émiko	Jíroo	Ryuuichi
Éijiroo	Jún	Shinzoo
Fusao	Kíyoshi	Susumu
Fusáko	Kúniko	Tákashi
Gantaroo	Makoto	Téruko
Gíichi	Máriko	Úmeko

NOTE

1. Each sound is pronounced clearly and crisply; sounds are not slurred over as they often are in English.

2. Each syllable is spoken evenly for almost an equal length of time.

3. Some names or words have an accented syllable and some don't.

4. When a syllable is marked with an accent (´), the pitch of the voice is always lowered directly after that syllable.

E. Loan Words: English Words Used in Japanese

Now listen to and repeat the following words. These are some of the thousands of English "loan words" used in Japan. While the meanings of these loan words are the same as their English counterparts, notice how the Japanese spelling and pronunciation differ from the English:

ákusento	accent
amáchua	amateur
Amerika	America
báree	ballet
básu	bus
bátaa	butter
béru	bell
bóoto	rowboat
chokoréeto	chocolate
daiyamóndo	diamond
dánsu	dance
dezáato	dessert
dezáin	design
enameru	enamel
erebéetaa	elevator
esukaréetaa	escalator
furanneru	flannel
gáido	guide (traveler's)
gasorin	gasoline
garéeji	garage
górufu	golf
haihíiru	high heel
handobággu	handbag
herikóputaa	helicopter
hisutérii	hysteria, hysterics
hóosu	water hose
hoomushíkku	homesick
hóteru	hotel
infure	inflation
ínku	ink
interi	intelligentsia
jaanarísuto	journalist

jámu	jam, jelly
jázu	jazz
káppu	cup (trophy, measuring)
koppu	drinking glass
karee ráisu	curried rice
karéndaa	calendar
maagarin	margarine
máaketto	market
máaku	mark
modan	modern
náiron	nylon

LESSON 2

DÁI NÍKA

A. VOWELS

The following groups of words will give you some additional practice in spelling and pronunciation. Listen to the vowel sounds in each word.

1. The sound *a* is pronounced as in the English word "ah" or "father," but short and crisp:

hanásu	tell	**káta**	shoulder
akai	red	*wakái*	young

2. The sound *i* is pronounced like the "e" in the English word "keep," but short and crisp:

i	stomach	**ní**	two
kí	tree	*hí*	fire

3. The sound *u* is pronounced as in the English word "put," but spoken without rounding the lips:

ushi	cow, bull	**kutsú**	shoes
kushí	comb	*tsukue*	desk

4. The sound *e* is pronounced like the "a" in the English word "may," but without the final "y":

é	picture	**té**	hand
ke	hair	*mé*	eye

5. The sound *o* is pronounced as in the English word "go," but sharply cut off:

ó	tail	**otokó**	male
otó	sound	*sóto*	outside

B. VOWEL CLUSTERS

1. When two identical vowels such as *aa, ii, uu, ee,* or *oo* appear together, they form a sound twice as long as the single vowel. Compare the following pairs:

kádo	corner	**káado**	card
chízu	map	**chíizu**	cheese
sú	nest	**súu**	number
déta	came out	**déeta**	data
to	door	**tóo**	ten

Sometimes a pair of identical vowels is called a "long vowel" or a "double vowel,'' and it can be written as a single letter with a macron over it, e.g., *ā, ū, ē,* and *ō.* However, ''long'' or ''double'' *i* is usually written *ii*:

koohíi,	coffee	**kúuki,**	air
kōhii		*kūki*	
káaten,	curtain	*kéeki,*	cake
kāten		*kēki*	

2. In a succession of two or more different vowels, each vowel is pronounced clearly and distinctly, and each vowel is articulated for the same length of time:

ué	top	**akai**	red
tsukue	desk	**aói**	blue
chiisái	small	*aói úmi*	blue ocean
chiisái ié	small house	*aói kao*	pale face

The combination *ei* forms an exception to this rule, for in everyday speech *ei* is often pronounced like *ee:*

kéiko	practice	**Beikoku**	The United
(said		(said	States of
kéeko)		*Beekoku*)	America
séito	pupil,	*seinen*	youth
(said	student	(said	
séeto)		*seenen*)	

C. DEVOICED VOWELS

The vowels *i* and *u* are ''weak,'' ''devoiced'' vowels. Unless they are accented, they sometimes disappear altogether or are whispered in rapid conversation.

Devoicing usually occurs when these vowels are surrounded by such voiceless consonants as *ch, f, h, k, p,
s, sh, t,* and *ts;* or in a word immediately following
one of the voiceless consonants. In the following examples, the vowel with a circle underneath is a devoiced vowel:

kitté	postage stamp	**zéhi**	by all means
kutsúshita	socks	**sukkári**	entirely

However, the devoicing of vowels is not crucial. Unlike the case of single vowel vs. double vowel shown
in B-1 above, non-devoicing vs. devoicing does not
change the meaning.

LESSON 3

DÁI SÁNKA

A. CONSONANTS I

1. *B* is generally pronounced like the English
"b," but less explosively:

bentóo	box lunch	*binsen*	writing pad
kaban	briefcase	*obon*	tray

2. *Ch* is pronounced like the English "ch" in
"cheese":

ocha	tea	*uchi*	house
chótto	a little bit	*chúui*	caution

3. *D* is pronounced with the tip of the tongue

touching the back of the upper teeth and is less explosive than the English "d":

dáre	who	*densha*	streetcar
dóko	where	*kádo*	corner

4. *F* is usually pronounced by forcing the air out between the lips as though blowing out a candle:

fúne	ship	*furó*	bath
fukái	deep	*futatsu*	two

5. The Japanese *g* has two sounds:

a. At the beginning of a word, it is pronounced like the English "g" in "go":

gaikoku	foreign country	*genryóo*	raw material
gín	silver	*gó*	five

b. In the middle of a word, it usually has some nasal quality and sounds something like the "ng" of the English word "singer":

hagaki	postcard	*kagí*	key
káge	shadow	*kágu*	household furniture

6. The Japanese *h* has two sounds:

a. Before *a, e,* and *o,* it is pronounced like the English "h" in "high":

hái	yes	**hón**	book
hei	fence	*hóo*	cheek

b. Before *i* or *y,* it is pronounced like the English "h" in "hue":

higashi	earth	**hyakú**	one hundred
hirú	noon	*hyooshi*	rhythm

7. *J* is pronounced like the English "j" in "jeep":

jagaimo	potato	**shookáijoo**	letter of introduction
jibikí	dictionary	*júku*	cram school

8. *K* is pronounced like the English "k" in "kite":

kása	umbrella	**koya**	hut
késa	this morning	*kutsú*	shoes

9. *M* is pronounced like an English "m," but without tightening the lips as much:

máiasa	every morning	**míkan**	tangerine
mé	eye	*mushi*	bug

10. *N* has two sounds in Japanese:

a. *N* before *a, e, o,* and *u,* it is pronounced with the tip of the tongue touching the back of the upper teeth:

nashí	pear	**nódo**	throat
néko	cat	*numá*	marsh

b. Before *i* or *y*, it is pronounced like the "n" in the English word "news" (with the tip of the tongue touching the back of the lower teeth and the middle part of the tongue touching the roof of the mouth):

nikú	meat	**gyuunyuu**	cow's milk
nishi	west	*nyuuin*	hospitalization

11. *P* is pronounced like the English "p," but less explosively:

pán	bread	**pín**	pin
pén	pen	*sánpun*	three minutes

12. *R* is pronounced by first placing the tip of the tongue at the back of the upper teeth and then flapping it.[1]

ráigetsu	next month	**riku**	land
rénga	brick	*rokú*	six

LESSON 4

DÁI YÓNKA

A. CONSONANTS II

13. *S* is pronounced like the English "s" in "song," but with less hiss:

saká	slope	**sóra**	sky
sékai	world	*sú*	vinegar

---

[1] For more on the sound of *r*, refer to the footnote on page 3.

14. *Sh* resembles the English "sh" in "she":

shashin	photograph	**shooko**	proof
shichí	seven	*shúto*	capital city

15. *T* is pronounced with the tip of the tongue touching the back of the upper teeth and is less explosive than the English "t":

tamágo	egg	**té**	hand
takusan	a lot	*to*	door

16. *Ts* is pronounced like the English "ts" in "cats":

natsú	summer	*atsúi*	hot
tsunami	tidal wave	*tsutsúji*	azalea

17. *V* is pronounced like the English "v" in "vain." Note that the sound of *v* appears only in words borrowed from Occidental languages. Some Japanese do not use this sound at all but replace it with a *b*, as follows:

vaiorin	violin	**baiorin**	violin
véeru	veil	**béeru**	veil
viníiru	vinyl	*biníiru*	vinyl
révyuu	revue	*rébyuu*	revue

18. *Z* usually has two sounds in Japanese:

a. At the beginning of a word it has a sound similar to the English "ds" in "beds":

zaisei	finance	**zóo**	elephant
zeitakú	luxury	*zutto*	by far

b. In the middle of a word it is pronounced like the English "z" in "zero":

kaze	wind	*mizu*	water
suzume	sparrow	*kázoku*	family

Note that some Japanese mix the *dz* and *z* sounds described above without regard to the position of the letter in the word.

19. *P, t, k,* or *s* can be a syllable by itself.[1] To pronounce such a syllabic consonant, hold the tongue position abruptly for one beat before the next syllable is pronounced.

a. When a syllabic consonant (*p, t, k,* or *s*) is followed by the same consonant, they are called "double consonants" and the sound is doubled in length. Note the differences in pronunciation between the following pairs of words; the first member contains a single consonant and the second contains double consonants:

haka	tomb	**hakka**	peppermint
kasai	fire damage	**kassai**	applause
móto	formerly	*mótto*	more

b. Syllabic *t* can be followed by *ch* or *ts,* and *s* can be followed by *sh:*

itchi	agreement	**irasshái**	welcome
ittsuu	one letter	*késshin*	determination

[1] In words borrowed from Western languages (loan words), *d* or *g* can also be a syllable by itself.

20. The syllabic *n* represents another group of sounds which is independent from the *n* described above in item 10. In this manual, the syllabic *n* will be written like the ordinary *n*. Remember, however, that it differs in pronunciation from the ordinary *n* as follows:

a. It is always held as long as one full syllable.
b. Its own sound-value changes, depending on what follows.

(1) Before *n, t,* and *d,* it is pronounced like the English "n" in "pen":

anna	that sort of	**santoo**	third class
onná	female	*kóndo*	this time

(2) Before *m, p,* or *b,* it is pronounced like the English "m":

SPELLED	PRONOUNCED	
sánmai	**sámmai**	three sheets
shinpai	*shimpai*	worry
kanban	*kamban*	signboard

(3) Before a vowel or a semi-vowel (*y* or *w*), it is pronounced somewhat like the English *ng* in "singer," but without finishing the *g* sound and the preceding vowel is often nasalized.

gen'an[1]	original plan
tán'i	unit
hón'ya	bookstore
minwa	folklore

[1] Notice that an apostrophe is placed after a syllabic *n* when it precedes a vowel or *y*.

Note that in the following pairs of words, the first has an ordinary *n* and the second has a syllabic *n:*

taní	valley	**tán'i**	unit
zenin	approval	*zen'in*	all members

(4) Before *k, g,* and *s,* or when it is the final letter in a word, the syllabic *n* sounds somewhat like the English "ng" in "singer" described in (3) above:

kankei	relationship	*sénsei*	teacher
ningen	human be-ings	*san*	three
sén	one thousand	*kín*	gold

B. SEMI-VOWELS

21. *W* is pronounced somewhat like the English "w" in "want," but without rounding or protruding the lips:

wata-kushi[1]	I (formal)	**kawá**	river
watashi	(informal)	*uwagi*	jacket

22. *Y* occurs in two kinds of environments:

a. It occurs before a vowel (e.g., *ya, yu, yo*) and is pronounced like the English "y" in "yah":

yamá	mountain	**hayái**	fast
yóru	night	*fuyú*	winter

[1] The use of formal and informal forms is very complicated. It depends on the speaker and the particular situation. Women are more likely than men to use the formal form of the word.

b. It occurs between a consonant and a vowel. Then the consonant is palatalized (said with the tongue touching the palate):

kyaku	guest	**ryóodo**	territory
happyoo	announce-ment	*kyúu*	nine

LESSON 5

DÁI GÓKA

A. THE JAPANESE SYLLABARY

The traditional writing system used in Japan is based on two different types of symbols: "phonetic" and "ideographic." (See The Writing System for a detailed explanation.) The phonetic symbols are the Japanese equivalents of our alphabet and are called *kana*. Each *kana* symbol stands for a syllable.

These are the basic syllables represented in *kana:*[1]

a	ka	sa	ta	na	ha	ma	ya	ra	wa	n (syllabic)
i	ki	shi	chi	ni	hi	mi		ri		
u	ku	su	tsu	nu	fu	mu	yu	ru		
e	ke	se	te	ne	he	me		re		
o	ko	so	to	no	ho	mo	yo	ro	o[2]	

[1] For non-basic syllables, see The Writing System, page 380.
[2] These two *o* sounds are pronounced the same but their uses differ. For details, see The Writing System, page 380.

B. GENERAL SOUND EQUIVALENTS

1. Japanese *aa* = English "ar," "er," "ir," "or"

apáato	apartment	*sáakasu*	circus
pítchaa	pitcher (baseball)	*móotaa*	motor

2. Japanese *ee* = English "a"

géemu	game	*teeburu*	table
kéeki	cake	*kéeburu*	cable (car)

3. Japanse *oo* = English "o," "oā"

bóonasu	bonus	*hoomuran*	home run
bóoto	boat	*kóochi*	coach (athletic)

4. Japanese *ui* = English "ui," "wi"

kúizu	quiz (radio, TV program)	*uítto*	wit

5. Japanese *b* = English "v"

térebi	television	*sháberu*	shovel

6. Japanese *chi* = English "ti"

chíppu	tip	*chíimu*	team

7. Japanese *ji* = English "di"

rájio	radio	*jirénma*	dilemma
sutajio	studio (art, broadcasting, movie)		

8. Japanese *k* = English "c"

kákuteru	cocktail	*kámera*	camera
Amerika	America	*konsárutanto*	consultant

9. Japanese *kku* = English, "ack," "ock"

barákku	barrack
dókku	dock

10. Japanese *kki* = English "eck," "ick"

dékki	deck
sutékki	stick (walking)

11. Japanese *ru* — English "l," "rl"

hóteru	hotel	*káaru*	curl
booru	ball		

12. Japanese *suto* = English "st"

sutoráiki,	strike	*jaanarísuto*	journalist
or **suto**	(labor)		
pianísuto	pianist		

13. Japanese *tto* = English "t"

maakétto	market	*sokétto*	socket
pán-	pamphlet	*yótto*	yacht
furetto			

14. Japanese *tsu* = English "t"

jaketsu	jacket	*shátsu*	shirt
	(sweater)		
omuretsu	omelet		

15. Japanese *s* = English "th"

| **súriru** | thrill | *oosóritii* | authority |

C. MORE LOAN WORDS

As you have already observed, a great number of English words have been adopted by the Japanese and are in everyday use. The following is a list of some more loan words.

apáto	apartment house	*géemu*	game
		górira	gorilla
aribai	alibi	*gurúupu*	group
arufabétto	alphabet	*haamonika*	harmonica
arukooru	alcohol	*hoomúran*	homerun
asupírin	aspirin	*infuruénza*	influenza
bátto	bat (base-ball)	*iyáhoon*	earphone
		jíguzagu	zigzag
bóonasu	bonus	*jirénma*	dilemma
booru	ball	*károrii*	calorie
booi sukáuto	boy scout	*katarogu*	catalog
		kéeki	cake (Occidental)
búrashi	brush		
dáasu	dozen	*konkuríito*	concrete
dámu	dam	*kóoto*	coat
dainamáito	dynamite	*kóruku*	cork
dórama	drama	*kúupon*	coupon
dóru	dollar	*kúrabu*	club
emerárudo	emerald	*kuréyon*	crayon
épisoodo	episode	*kuríimu*	cream
feruto	felt	*kuríiningu*	cleaning
gaaru sukáuto	girl scout	*makaroni*	macaroni
		masukótto	mascot

massáaji	massage	*ríbon*	ribbon
mégahon	megaphone	*rokétto*	rocket
medaru	medal	*rómansu*	romance
ményuu	menu	*sáakasu*	circus
mémo	memo	*sáiren*	siren
móotaa	motor	*sakkárin*	saccharine
mótto	motto	*sandoítchi*	sandwich
neonsáin	neon sign	*sárarii*	salary
ónsu	ounce	*sháberu*	shovel
oosóritii	authority	*shoouíndoo*	show
ootóbai	motorcycle		window
	(auto-	*sokétto*	socket
	bicycle)	*sooséejii*	sausage
ootomíiru	oatmeal	*supái*	spy
Orinpíkku	Olympic	*supiido*	speed
	Games	*suríppa*	slipper
paasénto	percent	*sutereo*	stereo
pái	pie	*suutsu*	suitcase
painúppuru	pineapple	*kéesu*	
panfurétto	pamphlet	*taipuráitaa*	typewriter
panku	flat tire	*táiru*	tile
	(puncture)	*tákushii*	taxi
panorama	panorama	*tánku*	tank
párupu	pulp	*táoru*	towel
pasupooto	passport	*teeburu*	table
pianísuto	pianist	*tonneru*	tunnel
pokétto	pocket		(railroad)
raion	lion	*torákku*	truck
rajúumu	radium	*uéetoresu*	waitress
reenkóoto	raincoat	*uranyúumu*	uranium
résutoran	restaurant	*yótto*	yacht
	(Occi-	*yúumoa*	humor
	dental)		

Note that when a word from English is used in Japanese, not only is the *sound* of the word changed to harmonize with the Japanese sound system, but the *length* of the word may be cut, as in the following examples:

infure	inflation
panku	puncture (flat tire)
pasokon	personal computer
térebi	television

Notice that some words are used in a more restricted sense in Japanese than in English. Here are some more words borrowed from English that are used in a restricted or altered sense in Japanese:

JAPANESE FORM	WORD OF ORIGIN	BUT MEANS IN JAPANESE
barákku	barrack	shack; shabby-looking, flimsy wooden house
bíru *birudingu* }	building	Occidental-style concrete office building
bisukétto	biscuits	tea biscuits and cookies
dóa	door	Occidental-style door
dorámu	drum	drum (musical only; referring mainly to types used in jazz)
jámu	jam	jam and jelly
jaketsu	jacket	sweater
kápuu	cup	trophy, measuring cup
kónpasu	compass	compass (instrument for drawing circles)
mánshon	mansion	condominium (or high-class apartment)
míshin	machine	sewing machine
nóoto	note	notebook
paipu	pipe	pipe (for smoking)
ráitaa	lighter	cigarette lighter
sutóroo	straw	drinking straw

LESSON 6

DÁI RÓKKA

A. DAYS AND MONTHS

Getsuyóobi	Monday
Kayóobi	Tuesday
Suiyóobi	Wednesday
Mokuyóobi	Thursday
Kin'yóobi	Friday
Doyóobi	Saturday
Nichiyóobi	Sunday

Ichigatsu	January
Nigatsu	February
Sángatsu	March
Shigatsu	April
Gógatsu	May
Rokugatsu	June
Shichigatsu	July
Hachigatsu	August
Kúgatsu	September
Juugatsu	October
Juuichigatsu	November
Juunigatsu	December

B. NUMBERS 1–10

ichí	one
ní	two
san	three
shí, yón	four
gó	five
rokú	six

shichí, nána	seven
hachí	eight
kyúu, kú	nine
júu	ten

C. Colors

áo	blue
áka	red
kiiro	yellow
mídori	green
shíro	white
kúro	black
chairo	brown
nezumiiro, haiiro	gray

D. North, South, East, West

kitá	north	**higashí**	east
minami	south	**nishi**	west

QUIZ 1

Try matching the Japanese and English words in these two columns:

1.	*Nichiyóobi*	a.	Thursday
2.	*Hachigatsu*	b.	brown
3.	*Suiyóobi*	c.	ten
4.	*nezumiiro*	d.	Sunday
5.	*Mokuyóobi*	e.	red
6.	*kú*	f.	August
7.	*chairo*	g.	Monday
8.	*hachí*	h.	July
9.	*Shichigatsu*	i.	five
10.	*kiiro*	j.	white

11. *áka*   k. gray
12. *Getsuyóobi*   l. nine
13. *gó*   m. Wednesday
14. *shíro*   n. yellow
15. *júu*   o. eight

ANSWERS
1–d; 2–f; 3–m; 4–k; 5–a; 6–l; 7–b; 8–o; 9–h; 10–n;
11–e; 12–g; 13–i; 14–j; 15–c.

E. WORD STUDY

fuíto	feet
gáron	gallon
gúramu	gram
ínchi	inch
kiro meétoru	kilometer
máiru	mile
meetoru	meter
póndo	pound
ríttoru	liter
yáado	yard

LESSON 7

DÁI NANÁKA

A. GREETINGS

Now let's study some of the greetings you'll use
right from the start. The words in [brackets] are literal
translations.

Ohayoo gozaimásu.	Good morning.
Yamada-san[1]	Mr. Yamada
Yamada-san, ohayoo gozaimásu.	Good morning, Mr. Yamada.
Konnichi wá.	Good afternoon. [Good day.]
Konban wá.	Good evening.
Oyasumi nasái.	Good night (*said just before going to bed*).
Ogénki desu ka?	How are you? [Are you in good spirits?]
génki	well [good spirits]
Génki desu.	I am very well.
Arígatoo gozaimásu.	Thank you.
Okagesama de.	Thank you. [Due to your kind thought, am well.]
Onamae wa nán to osshaimásu ka?	What is your name?
Oname wa?	What is your name?
Yamada Masao to mooshimásu.[2]	My name is Yamada Masao.[2]
Yamada desu.	I am Yamada.
Watakushi no namae wa Yamada désu.	My name is Yamada.
Gomen nasái.	Excuse me. I'm sorry.
Íi desu.	That's all right.
yukkúri	slowly

---

[1] The suffix -*san* is used in Japanese as a term of respect meaning "Mr.," "Mrs.," "Miss," "Sir," or "Madam."

[2] Japanese people use their last names before their first names. Yamada, thus, is the last name of the person speaking. But for a Western name, even while speaking Japanese, the Western order is usually used.

Yukkúri hanáshite kudasái.	Please speak slowly.
dóozo	please
Dóozo yukkúri hanáshite kudasái.	Please speak slowly.
moo ichido	once more
Itte kudasái.	Please say [it].
Moo ichido itte kudasái.	Please repeat that. [Say it once more, please.]
Dóozo moo ichido itte kudasái.	Please repeat that. [Please once more say it.]
dóomo	very much [indeed!]
Dóomo arígatoo gozaimasu.	Thank you very much.
Dóo itashimáshite.	Not at all.
Arígatoo gozaimáshita.	Thank you (*for what you have done*).
Kochira kóso.	It was a pleasure. [It was my side (that should have thanked).]
Déwa ashita.	Till tomorrow. See you tomorrow. [Well, then, tomorrow.]
Déwa Doyóobi ni.	Till Saturday. See you Saturday. [Well, then, on Saturday.]
Déwa Getsuyóobi ni.	Till Monday. See you Monday.
Déwa Mokuyóobi ni.	Till Thursday. See you Thursday.
Déwa kónban.	Till this evening. See you this evening.

Déwa ashita no ban.	Till tomorrow evening. See you tomorrow evening.
Déwa raishuu.	Till next week. See you next week.
Déwa mata.	See you later. [Well, then, again.]
Déwa sono uchi ni.	See you sometime.
Sayonara.	Good-bye.

B. How's the Weather?

Kyóo no ténki wa doo desu ka?	How's the weather today? What's the weather like today?
Ii ténki desu.	It's nice weather.
Kyóo wa ténki ga warúi.	The weather is bad today.
Áme ga futté imásu.	It's raining.
Yuki ga futté imásu.	It's snowing.
Atsui desu.	It's hot.
Samui desu.	It's cold.
Suzushíi desu.	It's warm.

QUIZ 2

1. *Génki desu.*	a. Please speak.
2. *Konban wá.*	b. once more
3. *Hanáshite kudasái.*	c. It's hot.
4. *Arígatoo goa-zimásu.*	d. See you tomorrow.
5. *moo ichido*	e. How are you?
6. *Dóozo.*	f. I am very well.
7. *Atsui desu.*	g. slowly
8. *Déwa ashita.*	h. Thank you.
9. *Ogénki désu ka?*	i. Please.
10. *yukkúri*	j. Good evening.

ANSWERS
1–f; 2–j; 3–a; 4–h; 5–b; 6–i; 7–c; 8–d; 9–e; 10–g.

LESSON 8

DÁI HACHÍKA

A. DO YOU HAVE?

In the phrases below, you will see the particles *ka* and *ga*. Particles are an important part of basic grammar and will be studied in Lesson 11. For now, understand that different particles indicate the relationship between the words or parts of a phrase. For example, the particle *ka* is used at the end of an interrogative sentence and shows that what precedes it is a question. The particle *ga* is used to show that what precedes it is the grammatical subject of a verb. Also, note that there is usually no translation in Japanese for "some" or " any."

Arimásu ka?	Do you have . . . ? [Is there . . . ?]
mizu ga	some water (*as the subject of the verb*)
tabako ga	some (any) cigarettes
hí ga	a light
mátchi ga	some matches
sekken ga	some soap
kamí ga	some paper
Mizu ga[1] arimásu ka?	Do you have some water?
Tabako ga arimásu ka?	Do you have any cigarettes?

B. IN A RESTAURANT

asagóhan	breakfast
hirugóhan	lunch
bangóhan	supper
Irasshaimáse.	Welcome.
Náni o meshiagari-másu ka?	What would you like to eat?
Mísete kudasái.	Show me . . . , please.
Ményuu o mísete kudasái.	Show me a menu, please.
. . . kudasái.	I'd like [Please give me . . .]
Pán o kudasái.	I'd like some bread, please.

[1] Note that in the English equivalent, "water" is the object of "have," but *mizu* (water) is followed by the particle *ga* (the subject marker), as stated above. This holds true for the rest of the sentences in the section, too.

pán o	some bread
bátaa o	some butter
súupu o	some soup
nikú o	some meat
gyuuniku o	some beef
tamágo o	some eggs
yasai o	some vegetables
jagaimo o	some potatoes
sárada o	some salad
míruku o	some milk
wáin o	some wine
satóo o	some sugar
shió o	some salt
koshoó o	some pepper
yakizákana o	some broiled fish
miso shíru o	some bean soup
sashimí o	some sashimi (raw fish)
tenpura o	some tempura (fritter; fried food)
Motté kite kudasái . . .	Please bring me . . .
Súupu o motté kite kudasái.	Please bring me some soup.
tiisupúun o	a teaspoon
fóoku o	a fork
náifu o	a knife
napukin o	a napkin
sara o	a plate
kóppu o	a glass
. . . íppai kudasái.	I'd like [Please give me] a glass of . . .
. . . hitóbin kudasái.	I'd like [Please give me] a bottle of . . .
Mizu o íppai kudasái.	Please give me a glass of water.
ocha o íppai	a cup of tea

koohíi o íppai	a cup of coffee
wáin o ippon	a bottle of wine
biiru o ippon	a bottle of beer
tamágo a moo hitótsu	another egg
sore o sukóshi	a little of that
sore o moo sukóshi	a little more of that
pán o moo sukóshi	some more bread, a little more bread
nikú o mótto	some more meat
nikú o moo sukóshi	a little more meat
Denpyoo o motté kite kudasái.	The check, please.

QUIZ 3

1. *nikú o*	a.	please bring me
2. *bíiru o*	b.	matches
3. *arimásu ka?*	c.	please give me
4. *míruku o*	d.	meat
5. *bátaa o*	e.	some water
6. *kudasái*	f.	a light
7. *mátchi o*	g.	milk
8. *nikú o moo sukóshi*	h.	eggs
9. *motté kite kudasái*	i.	beer
10. *mizu o*	j.	the check
11. *hí o*	k.	Do you have . . .
12. *shió o*	l.	butter
13. *tamágo o*	m.	a cup of coffee
14. *koohíi o íppai*	n.	some more meat
15. *denpyoo o*	o.	salt

ANSWERS

1–d; 2–i; 3–k; 4–g; 5–l; 6–c; 7–b; 8–n; 9–a; 10–e; 11–f; 12–o; 13–h; 14–m; 15–j.

C. WORD STUDY

buráusu	blouse
hankáchi	handkerchief
nékutai	necktie
oobaakóoto	overcoat
séetaa	sweater
shátsu	shirt
sukáafu	scarf
sukáato	skirt
suríppu	slip

LESSON 9

DÁI KYÚUKA

This lesson and several of the following lessons are longer than the others. They contain the grammatical information you need to know from the start. Don't try to memorize anything; just read each section until you understand every point. Then, as you continue with the course, try to observe examples of the points mentioned. Refer back to these sections and to the Summary of Japanese Grammar at the back of the book as necessary. In this way you will eventually find that you have a good grasp of the basic features of Japanese grammar without any deliberate memorizing of "rules."

A. PRONOUNS

Personal pronouns are used much less frequently in Japanese than in English. The context clarifies what or who is being referred to or addressed. In addition, in Japanese there are more varieties of words that correspond to English pronouns. The list below will help you follow the sections to come, but be sure to study Section 12 of the Summary of Japanese Grammar for more information.

I	**watakushi**
you	**anáta**[1]
he/she	**anó hito**
he	**káre**
she	**kánojo**
we	**watakushítachi**
you (*pl.*)[2]	**anatagata**[1]
they	**anó hitotachi**

B. To Be or Not to Be

1. There is more than one way to say "is" in Japanese. A different word is used for this English verb in each of the following sentences:

Enpitsu désu.	It is a pencil.
Enpitsu ga arimásu.[3]	There is a pencil.
Nyuu Yóoku ni imasu.	He is in New York.

   a. When you say that one thing is equal to another, you use *desú*. Its meaning roughly corresponds to "am, is, are."
   b. When you are talking about something being located or situated in a place, use *ari-*

---

[1] *Anáta* and *anatagata* are usually to be avoided. It is more polite to use the person's name.

[2] Throughout this book *pl.* stands for "plural" and *sg.* stands for "singular."

[3] This sentence is ambiguous; it can also mean "(I) have a pencil." See Lessons 8 and 14 for phrases with "have."

másu if the thing referred to is inanimate, and

c. you use *imásu* if the thing referred to is animate.

Note that *désu* is called the *copula*. *Arimásu* and *imásu* are ordinary verbs and are inflected like other verbs, which you will begin to study in Lesson 10. Also, the negative of *desu* has its own particular forms; see below.

2. Study these examples with *désu, arimásu,* and *imásu:*

a. *Sore wa enpitsu desu.*
That is a pencil. (A equals B.)

b. *Soko ni enpitsu ga arimásu.*
There is a pencil there. (A—inanimate—is located at B.)

c. *Soko ni kodomo ga imásu.*
There is a child there. (A—animate—is located at B.)

a. *Sore wa tabako désu ka?*
Is that a cigarette?

b. *Tabako ga arimásu ka?*
Is there a cigarette?

c. *Yamada-san wa soko ni imásu ka?*
Is Mr. Yamada there?

a. *Shikágo wa ookíi machí desu.*
Chicago is a big city.

b. *Shikágo wa Irinoíshuu ni arimásu.*
Chicago is in the state of Illinois.

c. *Yamada-san wa Shikágo ni imásu.*
Mr. Yamada is in Chicago.

3. Listen for examples of these forms in the phrases below. Notice that the word or phrase which equals the element "A" (as used in the phrases above) is marked with the particle *wa* or *ga*. *Wa* is used when the emphasis in the sentence is not on "A." *Ga* is used to emphasize "A." The word or phrase equaling the element "B" always comes immediately before *désu*. (If no specific noun is used for "B," use *soo* in its place, for *désu* can never be used alone.)

Anáta wa Amerikájin desu ka?	Are you an American?
Hai, sóo desu.	Yes, I am. [Yes, am so.]
tatémono	building
taishíkan	embassy
Dóno tatémono ga Amerika Taishíkan desu ka?	Which building is the American Embassy?
Ano tatémono wa Amerika Taishíkan desu.	That building is the American Embassy.
Ano tatémono ga sóo desu.	That building is. [That building is so.]
Ano tatémono ga Amerika Taishíkan desu ka?	Is that building the American Embassy?
Hai, sóo desu.	Yes, it is. [Yes, is so.]
Súmisu-san wa Amerika Taishíkan ni imásu.	Mr. Smith is in the American Embassy.
Tanaka-san wa Tookyoo ni imásu.	Ms. Tanaka is in Tokyo.
Okinawa wa dóko ni arimásu ka?	Where is Okinawa?

Nippon to Taiwán no aida ni arimásu.	It is between Japan and Taiwan.
Dóno katá ga Tanaka-san désu ka?	Which person is Ms. Tanaka?
Watakushi ga Tanaka désu.	I am. [Am Tanaka.]
Watakushi ga sóo desu.	I am [so].
Sore wa tabako désu.	That is a cigarette.
Enpitsu ga arimásu ka?	Do you have a pencil? Is there a pencil?
Kodomo wa Tookyoo ni imásu.	The child is in Tokyo.
Tabako ga arimásu.	I have a cigarette. Therc is a cigarette.

C. DESU

1. Compare the following different forms of *desu* in the affirmative:

present or future	*A wa B desu.*	A is B.
past (or present perfect)	*A wa B deshita.*	A was B.
tentative	*A wa B deshoo.*	A is probably B.
tentative past	*A wa B datta deshoo.*	A was probably B.

2. The negative of the above are:

present or future	*A wa B* {*ja* / *dewa*}	*arimasén.*	A is not B.
	A wa B {*ja* / *dewa*}	*nái desu.*	

past	A wa B $\begin{Bmatrix} ja \\ dewa \end{Bmatrix}$	arimasén deshita.[1]	A was not B.
	A wa B $\begin{Bmatrix} ja \\ dewa \end{Bmatrix}$	nákatta desu.	
tentative	A wa B $\begin{Bmatrix} ja \\ dewa \end{Bmatrix}$	nái de- shoo.	A is prob- ably not B.
tentative past	A wa B $\begin{Bmatrix} ja \\ dewa \end{Bmatrix}$	nákatta deshoo.	A was probably not B.

Ja is a contraction of *dewa* that you will hear in conversation, while you are more likely to see *dewa* in written material. Their meaning is the same. Most of the examples in this book will use *ja*, since our focus is on conversational Japanese.

3. Study these examples with *desu* and its forms:

gakusei	student
Watakushi wa gakusei désu.	I'm a student.
kaisháin[2]	businessperson[2]
Watakushi wa kaisháin desu.	I'm a businessperson.
Watakushi wa Ameriká-jin desu.	I'm American.

---

[1] This form of the negative is not often heard in colloquial conversation as often as the second form, below. However, it is included here for reference, since some forms of adjectives follow this pattern, as you will see in Lesson 11.

[2] *Kaisháin* actually means "employee of a business firm." You will often hear *bijinesuman* for "businessman."

Kono tatémono wa Igirisu Taishíkan desu ka?	Is that building the British Embassy?
Igirisu Taishíkan ja arimasén.	It is not the British Embassy.
Watakushi wa gakusei ja arimasen.	I'm not a student.
Anó hito wa kaisháin ja arimasén.	He [that person] is not a businessperson.
Anó hito wa Nihonjín ja arimasén.	She [that person] is not Japanese.
Watakushi wa gakusei déshita.	I was a student.
senséi	teacher
Tanaka-san wa senséi deshita.	Ms. Tanaka was a teacher.
hóteru	hotel
Ano tatémono wa hóteru deshita.	That building was a hotel.
Káre wa gakusei ja arimasén deshita.	He was not a student.
Yamada-san wa kaisháin ja arimasén deshita.	Ms. Yamada was not a businessperson.
Amerika Taishíkan ja arimasén deshita.	That was not the American Embassy.
Kore wa hóteru deshoo.	This probably is a hotel.
Anó hito wa Amerikájin deshoo.	She probably is American.
Anó hito wa senséi ja nái deshoo.	He probably is not a teacher.
kuruma	car
Kuruma wa Nihonsei ja nái deshoo.	The car probably is not Japanese.

Igirusu Taishíkan ja nái deshoo.	That probably is the British Embassy.
Anó hito wa senséi ja nákatta deshoo.	He probably was not a teacher.
Kuruma wa Nihonsei ja nákatta deshoo.	The car probably was not Japanese.

QUIZ 4

1. *Tabako ga arimásu ka?*	a. Is this building the British Embassy?
2. *Watakushi wa gakusei ja arimasén.*	b. Mr. Yamada is a businessperson.
3. *Sore wa enpitsu desu.*	c. Ms. Tanaka was not a teacher.
4. *Kono tatémono wa Igirisu Taishíkan desu ka?*	d. It's a car.
5. *Tanaka-san wa senséi ja arimasén deshita.*	e. The child is in Tokyo.
6. *Nyuu Yóoku ni imásu.*	f. This probably is a hotel.
7. *Kuruma désu.*	g. Do you have a cigarette?
8. *Kore wa hóteru deshoo.*	h. I'm not a student.
9. *Kodomo wa Too-kyoo ni imásu.*	i. That is a pencil.
10. *Yamada-san wa kaisháin desu.*	j. I'm in New York.

ANSWERS

1–g; 2–h; 3–i; 4–a; 5–c; 6–j; 7–d; 8–f; 9–e; 10–b.

REVIEW QUIZ 1

Choose the correct Japanese equivalent for the English word or phrase:

1. five =
   a. *rokú*
   b. *shichí*
   c. *gó*

2. eight =
   a. *hachí*
   b. *kú*
   c. *shí*

3. Tuesday =
   a. *Suiyóobi*
   b. *Kayóobi*
   c. *Kin'yóobi*

4. Sunday =
   a. *Nichiyóobi*
   b. *Doyóobi*
   c. *Getsuyóobi*

5. March =
   a. *Sángatsu*
   b. *Kúgatsu*
   c. *Shigatsu*

6. June =
   a. *Shichigatsu*
   b. *Rokugatsu*
   c. *Gógatsu*

7. red =
   a. *áo*

    b. *kiiro*
    c. *áka*

8. green =
    a. *kiiro*
    b. *mídorií*
    c. *haiiro*

9. black =
    a. *kúro*
    b. *chairo*
    c. *shíro*

10. brown =
    a. *kúro*
    b. *áka*
    c. *chairo*

11. Good morning =
    a. *Ohayoo gozaimásu.*
    b. *Konban wá.*
    c. *Génki desu.*

12. I'm not a student. =
    a. *Kare wa Kaisháin desu.*
    b. *Watukushi wa gakusei ja arimasén.*
    c. *Igirisu Taishíkan ja arimasén.*

13. Thank you =
    a. *Itte kudasái.*
    b. *Arígatoo gozaimásu.*
    c. *Dóo itashimáshite.*

14. Please =
    a. *Hanáshite kudasái.*
    b. *Arígatoo gozaimásu.*
    c. *Dóozo.*

15. Good-bye =
    a. *Déwa ashita.*
    b. *Sayonara.*
    c. *Konnichi wá.*

16. car =
    a. *kuruma*
    b. *kaisháin*
    c. *kodomo*

17. She's probably American. =
    a. *Anó hito wa Amerikájin ja arimasén.*
    b. *Anó hito wa Amerikájin deshita.*
    c. *Anó hito wa Amerikájin deshoo.*

18. businessperson =
    a. *kaisháin*
    b. *hóteru*
    c. *kodomo*

19. There's a cigarette. =
    a. *Tabako ga arimásu.*
    b. *Tabako desu.*
    c. *Tabako ga imásu.*

20. He is in New York. =
    a. *Nyuu Yóoku ga arimásu.*
    b. *Nyuu Yóoku ni imásu.*
    c. *Nyuu Yóoku desu.*

ANSWERS
1–c; 2–a; 3–b; 4–a; 5–a; 6–b; 7–c; 8–b; 9–a; 10–c;
11–a; 12–b; 13–b; 14–c; 15–b; 16–a; 17–c; 18–a;
19–a; 20–b.

LESSON 10

DÁI JÍKKA

A. COMMON VERB FORMS

In Japanese, main verbs come at the end of a sentence (similar to *desu*). You will also see that Japanese verbs make no distinction between persons and numbers; the same forms are used for first, second, and third persons in both the singular and plural. And, as you have probably noticed, in Japanese it is the verb endings that determine tenses.[1]

1. I speak, I spoke, I'm speaking, etc.

Hanashimásu.	I speak. I will speak.
Hanashimáshita.	I spoke. I have spoken.
Hanashimashóo.	Let's talk. I think I'll talk.
Hanáshite imasu.	I am talking.
Hanáshite imáshita.	I was speaking.
Hanáshite kudasái.	Please speak.

NOTE

a. The endings denoting tense are:

present or future	(*hanashi*)*másu*
past (or present perfect)	(*hanashi*)*máshita*
tentative	(*hanashi*)*mashóo*
present progressive	(*hanáshi*)*te imasu*
past progressive	(*hanáshi*)*te imáshita*
polite request	(*hanáshi*)*te kudasái*

[1] You will learn more about verb forms in Lesson 12.

b. The same forms are used for singular and plural and for first, second, and third persons. The subject of a sentence does not have to be mentioned when the context clarifies who is speaking or what is being spoken about.

Hanashimásu.	I speak.
Hanashimásu.	You (*sg.*) speak.
Hanashimásu.	(S)he speaks.
Hanashimásu.	We speak.
Hanashimásu.	You (*pl.*) speak.
Hanashimásu.	They speak.

2. I don't speak, I didn't speak, I wasn't speaking, etc.

Hanashimasén.	I don't speak. I will not speak.
Hanashimasén deshita.	I didn't speak.
Hanáshite imasén.	I am not speaking.
Hanáshite imasén deshita.	I wasn't speaking.
Hanasánaide kudasái.	Please don't speak.

NOTE

a. The negative is formed as follows:

negative present or future	(*hanáshi*)*masén.*
negative past	(*hanáshi*)*masén deshita.*
negative present progressive	(*hanáshi*)*te imasén.*

negative past progressive	(*hanáshi*)*te imasen deshita.*
negative polite request	(*hanasá*)*naide kudasái.*

b. Note, again, that the subject of each of these sentences could be "I," "you," "(s)he," "we," or "they." "I" is arbitrarily used as the subject in the English translations.

3. Study these examples:

Tabemásu.	I eat. I will eat.
Tábete imasu.	I am eating.
Tabemáshita.	I ate.
Tábete imáshita.	I was eating.
Tábete kudasái.	Please eat.
Tabemashóo.	Let's eat.
Tabemasén.	I do not eat. I will not eat.
Tábete imasén.	I am not eating.
Tabemasén deshita.	I did not eat.
Tábete imasén deshita.	I was not eating.
Tabénaide kudasái.	Please don't eat.
Donna monó o tabemashita ka?	What sort of things did you eat?
Sukiyaki ya tenpura o tabemáshita.	We ate sukiyaki, tempura, and things like that.
koohíi	coffee
Koohíi o nomimásu.	I drink coffee.
ocha	tea
Ocha o nomimashóo.	Let's drink green tea.
Ocha o nomimáshita.	They drank green tea.

As the lessons proceed, you'll see more verbs in these forms and after a while you'll become more familiar

with them. Be sure to refer to Lesson 40 for more on
verbs, as well.

B. ASKING A QUESTION I

1. As we have seen, one way to ask a question is
to add the particle *ka* to the end of the sentence
and use either a rising or falling intonation.

Naraimásu.	You learn.
Naraimásu ka?	Do you learn?
Naraimáshita.	You learned. You have learned.
Naraimáshita ka?	Did you learn? Have you learned?
Narátte imasu.	You are learning.
Narátte imásu ka?	Are you learning?
Narátte imáshita.	You were learning.
Narátte imáshita ka?	Were you learning?

2. To ask a question with a negative, use the
particle *ka* in the same way:

Naraimasén ka?	Don't you learn?
Naraimasén deshita ka?	Didn't you learn?
Narátte imasén ka?	Aren't you learning?
Narátte imasén deshita ka?	Weren't you learning?

C. WHERE IS IT?

Chótto sumimasén.	Excuse me for a moment. [I am asking a question, but . . .]

dóko	where
arimásu	there is
Dóko ni arimásu ka?	Where is it?
Hóteru wa dóko ni arimásu ka?	Where is there a hotel?
resutoran	restaurant
Résutoran wa dóko ni arimásu ka?	Where is there a restaurant?
denwa	telephone
Denwa wa dóko ni arimásu ka?	Where is there a telephone?
uketsuke	reception desk
Uketsuke wa dóko ni arimásu ka?	Where is the reception desk?
éki	station
Éki wa dóko ni arimásu ka?	Where is the station?
yuubínkyoku	post office
Yuubínkyoku wa dóko ni arimásu ka?	Where is the post office?

D. HERE AND THERE

koko	here, this place
soko	there, that place (nearby)
asoko	there, that place over there (outside of immediate reach)
dóko	where, which place
Dóko desu ka?	Where is it? Which place is it?
kochira	this way
sochira	that way

achira	that way over there
dóchira	which way
Dóchira desu ka?	Which way is it?
Achira désu	It is over that way.
Kochira désu.	It's this way.
migi no hóo ni	to the right [in the direction of the right]
hidari no hóo ni	to the left [in the direction of the left]
Migi no hóo ni arimásu.	It's to the right. [It is in the direction . . .]
Hidari no hóo ni arimásu.	It's to the left.
Migi e magarimásu.	You turn right.
Hidari e magarimásu.	You turn left.
Massúgu ikimásu.	You go straight ahead.
Massúgu saki désu.	It's straight ahead.
Choodo hantaigawa désu.	It's directly opposite.
Kádo ni arimásu.	It's on the corner.
Koko ni arimasén.	It's not here.
Soko ni arimasén.	It's not there.
Asoko ni arimásu.	It's over there.
Koko ni imásu.	He is here.
Koko ni kite kudasái.	Come here, please.
Koko ni ite kudasái.	Stay here, please.
Soko de mátte ite kudasái.	Wait there, please.
Kochira e itte kudasái.	Go this way, please.
Achira e itte kudasái.	Go that way, please.
Soko ni dáre ga imásu ka?	Who's there?
Koko ni oite kudasái.	Put it here, please.
Soko ni oite kudasái.	Put it there, please.

E. NEAR AND FAR

Chikái desu.	It's near.
Koko kara chikái desu.	It's near here. [Near from here.]
Totemo chikái desu.	It's very near. It's quite close.
Mura no chikáku desu.[1]	It's near the village.
Michi no chikáku desu.	It's near the road.
Sonó hito no uchi no chikáku desu.	It's near his house.
Koko kara totemu chikái desu.	It's very near here.
tooi	far
Tooí desu ka?	Is it far?
Tooí desu.	It's far.
Tooku arimasén.	It's not far.
Koko kara tooí desu.	It's far from here.

QUIZ 5

1. *Denwa wa dóko ni arimásu ka?*	a. It's this way.
2. *Hanashimásu.*	b. It's to the right.
3. *Kochira désu.*	c. Turn left.
4. *Massúgu saki désu.*	d. It's directly opposite.
5. *Migi no hóo ni arimásu.*	e. It's straight ahead.
6. *Mura no chikáku desu.*	f. Where is there a telephone?
7. *Soko de mátte ite kudasái.*	g. He speaks.

[1] *chikáku:* nearby place (*a noun*).

8. *Kochira e itte kudasái.*
9. *Hidari e magarimásu.*
10. *Choodo hantaigawa désu.*
11. *Tooku arimasén.*
12. *Soko ni oite kudasái.*
13. *Koko ni arimasén.*
14. *Koko ni ite kudasái.*
15. *Soko ni dáre ga imásu ka?*
16. *Hóteru wa dóko ni arimásu ka?*
17. *Naraimáshita ka?*
18. *Tábete imasu.*
19. *Tabemashóo.*
20. *Koohíi nomimasu.*

h. It's near the village.
i. It's not here.
j. Stay here, please.
k. Wait there, please.
l. Go this way, please.
m. Who's there?
n. Put it there, please.
o. I'm eating.
p. Let's eat.
q. I drink coffee.
r. Where is there a hotel?
s. It's not far.
t. Did you learn?

ANSWERS
1–f; 2–g; 3–a; 4–e; 5–b; 6–h; 7–k; 8–l; 9–c; 10–d; 11–s; 12–n; 13–i; 14–j; 15–m; 16–r; 17–t; 18–o; 19–p; 20–q.

LESSON 11

DÁI JUUÍKKA

A. NOUNS AND NOUN PARTICLES

In Japanese, the form of a noun remains the same no matter where it appears in a sentence. Normally, every noun is followed by at least one "particle" when it is used in a sentence.[1] A particle, which is often not translatable, is the "tag" or "signpost" that tells what relation the word it accompanies has to another word or part of sentence. For instance, one particle may show that the noun it follows is the *subject* of the sentence, another may show that the noun it follows is the *object* of the sentence, and still another may show that the noun it follows is the *modifier of another noun.* Remember, however, that *all* particles must follow the words with which they are used.

Following is a list of important noun particles with a brief description of their use:[2]

1. *Wa* shows that the noun it follows is the "topic" of the sentence. Here the word "topic" is deliberately employed as a contrast to the word "subject," which we often use in grammar. A topic in Japanese—that is, a word or group of words that is followed by the particle *wa*—serves as advance notice of what the speaker will talk about. This practice of isolating a topic and setting it off with the particle *wa* is frequently used to start a sentence in Japanese, and can be compared to the occasional practice in English of beginning a sentence with "As for . . ." or "Speaking of . . ." For instance, in Japanese you would say:

   As for Mr. Yoshida, (he) came to this country again this year.
   Talking about this morning's *New York Times,* have (you) read (it)?

[1] There are some exceptions to this rule, but only a few.
[2] See the Summary of Japanese Grammar for a more complete list of particles and their uses.

Notice how a topic is first singled out and then followed by a simplified statement. Note also that a topic can be either an *implied subject* or an *implied object* of the verb, and that it may even specify a *time* or *place.*

Further examples with *wa:*

Kabukiza wa Tookyoo ni arimásu.	(The) Kabuki Theatre is in Tokyo. [As for the Kabuki Theatre, (it) is in Tokyo.]
Búnraku wa mimasén deshita.	I didn't see (the) Bunraku (Puppet Play). [As for Bunraku, I didn't see (it).]
Boardman-san wa Amerika e kaeri- máshita.	Speaking of Mr. Boardman, he returned to America.
Kinóo wa Tanaka-san no uchí e ikimáshita.	Speaking of yesterday, I went to Tanaka's house.

2. *Ga* shows that the noun it follows is both the grammatical subject of a verb and also an "emphatic" subject. In English, you place emphasis on a subject by raising your voice. In Japanese you can create the same emphasis, usually without raising the voice, by using the particle *ga.*

If you do *not* want to emphasize the subject, you can either introduce the subject with the topic-particle *wa* or avoid mentioning it altogether. In English you always mention the subject, except when using the imperative. In

Japanese you may omit specifically naming the subject when you feel that the person you are speaking to already knows what the subject is.

Watakushi ga ikimáshita.	I (not he) (*spoken with emphasis*) went. [(It) was I who went.]
Tanaka-san ga kimáshita.	*Ms. Tanaka (spoken with emphasis)* came.
Jikan ga arimasén.	There isn't *time.*

3. *O* shows that the noun it follows is *the thing acted on* by the verb. It roughly corresponds to the direct object of a transitive verb. Yet, the *O* also implies the notion of a place in which movements (transitions) such as "going," "coming," "passing," "walking," "running," "swimming," "flying," and "departing" take place.

Kippu o kaimáshita.	I bought some tickets.
Tegami o dashimáshita.	I sent a letter.
Ginza Dóori o arukimáshita.	We walked on Ginza Street.
Saka o hashirimáshita.	We ran on the slope.

4. *No* shows that the noun it follows modifies (i.e., explains, characterizes) another noun that comes after it. It is most frequently used for the possessive (''of ''):

Tookyoo no machí desu.	It is the city of Tokyo.

Yamada-san no uchí desu.	It is Mr. Yamada's house. [(It) is the house of Mr. Yamada.]
Tanaka-san no kodomo desu.	He is Ms. Tanaka's child. [He is the child of Ms. Tanaka.]

5. *Ni* is used in the following ways:

   a. The noun with *ni* may tell *where* a thing or person is (in the sense of being "in" or "at" a place):

Tanaka-san wa Tookyoo ni imásu.	Ms. Tanaka is in Tokyo.
Ginza wa Chuuóo-ku ni arimásu.	Ginza is in the Chuo ward (of Tokyo).

   b. The noun with *ni* may tell the *purpose* for which the action is performed (in the sense of "for" or "in order to"):

Nihón e benkyoo ni kimáshita.	I came to Japan to study.

   c. The noun with *ni* may tell the *person* or *thing* to which the action of the verb is directed (in the sense of "to," "from," or "of"):

Yamada-san ni agemáshita.	I gave it to Mr. Yamada.

d. The noun with *ni* may tell the *thing into which something changes* (there is usually no translation for this usage):

Tookyoo Dáigaku no gakusei ni narimáshita.

I became a student at [of] Tokyo University.

e. The noun with *ni* is the direction toward which a motion takes place ("to," "toward"):

Nára ni ikimáshita.

I went to Nara.

Amerika ni okurimáshita.

I sent it to America.

6. *De* signifies that the noun preceding it is:

a. the *place* of action ("at," "in"):

Kyóoto de kaimáshita.

I bought it in Kyoto.

b. the *means* of action ("by," "through"):

Hikóoki de ikimáshita.

I went by [means of a] plane.

c. the *limit* to which the predicate is restricted ("in," "within"):

Nihón de ichiban takái yamá desu.

It is the highest mountain in Japan. [Restricting ourselves to Japan, (it) is the highest mountain.]

7. *Kára* shows that the noun it follows is the *beginning point* in space or time of an action or state (''from,'' ''since''):

Amerika kara ki- **máshita.**	I came from America.
Nigatsú kara koko ni *súnde imasu.*	I have been living here since February.

8. *Máde* shows that the noun it follows is the *ending point* of an action or event (''up to,'' ''by,'' ''until''):

Hiroshima máde iki- **máshita.**	I went as far as Hiroshima.
Juugatsú made **Kyóoto ni imásu.**	I'll bc in Kyoto until October.

Kára and *máde* are often used together:

Tookyoo kára Osaka *máde ikimáshita.*	I went from Tokyo to Osaka.

9. *E* shows that the noun it follows is the *direction toward which* a motion takes place (''to,'' ''toward''). *E* and *ni* (in 5e above) are usually interchangeable.

Nara e ikimáshita.	I went to Nara.
Amerika e okurimáshita.	I sent it to America.

10. *To* shows that the preceding noun is one of the following:

a. a part of a complete list (''and''):

Tookyoo to Kyóoto to **Oosaka e ikimá-** **shita.**	I went to Tokyo, Kyoto, and Osaka. (These are the places I went to.)

Yamada-san to Tanaka-san to Takeda-san ga kimáshita.	Mr. Yamada, Ms. Tanaka, and Ms. Takeda came. (These are the people who came.)

    b. the one with whom the action of the verb is performed (''with''):

Kánai to ikimáshita.	I went with my wife.
Tanaka-san to hanashi-máshita.	I spoke with Mr. Tanaka.

    c. the thing into which something or somebody changes:

Ano tatemono wa Tanaka-san no monó to narimá-shita.	That building became Ms. Tanaka's (property).
Nihón no daihyoo to narimáshita.	She became the representative of Japan.
Daigíshi to narimásh-ita.	He became a member of Parliament.

Note that in this usage *to* is often interchangeable with *ni* (shown above).

    11. *Ya* shows, as *to* sometimes does, that the noun it follows is part of a list, but the fact that *ya* is used implies that the list is not a complete one:

Nikú ya pan ya sarada o tabemáshita.	I ate meat, bread, and salad (and some other things).

B. COMMON ADJECTIVE FORMS

There are two types of adjectives in Japanese: *i*-adjectives and *na-* adjectives.

12. *I*- adjectives
    I- adjectives all end in *-i*. They are used very much like verbs. They have their own forms for present, past, etc., and they have "plain" and "polite" forms, as do verbs (see Lesson 12).

    a. Below are some commonly used conjugations of the *i*- adjective *takai* (expensive):

Takái desu.	It is expensive. It will be expensive.
Tákakatta desu.	It was expensive.
Takái deshoo.	It probably is expensive.
Tákakatta deshoo.	It probably was expensive.
Tákaku arimasén. *Tákaku nái desu.*	It is not expensive.
Tákaku arimasén deshita. *Tákaku nákatta desu.*	It was not expensive.
Tákaku nái deshoo.	It probably is not expensive.
Tákaku nákatta deshoo.	It probably was not expensive.

    (1) Notice how the endings differ for affirmative and negative forms (parentheses set off the adjectival root "expensive" from the ending):

AFFIRMATIVE

present	*(taká) i desu*
past	*(táka) katta desu.*
tentative	*(taká) i deshoo.*
tentative past	*(táka) katta deshoo.*

NEGATIVE

present	*(táka) ku arimasén.*
	(táka) ku nái desu.
past	*(táka) ku arimasén deshita.*
	(táka) ku nákatta desu.
tentative	*(táka) ku nái deshoo.*
tentative past	*(táka) ku nákatta deshoo.*

(2) Notice how the same forms are used for both singular and plural, in all persons (I, you, he, she, it, we, you, they):

Takái desu.	It is expensive.
Takái desu.	They are expensive.
Tákakatta desu.	It was expensive.
Tákakatta desu.	They were expensive.
Kashikói desu.	You are wise.
Kashikói desu.	She is wise.

(3) Notice that the present negative and the past negative of *i-* adjectives have two forms. The *-ku nái* (present) and the *-ku nákatta* (past) forms are used more often in colloquial conversation:

Tákaku nái desu.	It is not expensive.
Hóteru wa tákaku ná-katta desu.	The hotel was not expensive.

See d. and f., below, as well.

h *I-* adjectives modifying a noun:

takái kuruma	expensive car
Takái kuruma désu.	It is an expensive car.
Takái kuruma ja nái desu.	It is not an expensive car.
ookíi	big
ookíi hóteru	big hotel
Ookíi hóteru deshita.	It was a big hotel.

    c. Sentences with present, affirmative *i-* adjectives:

Yasúi desu.	It's inexpensive/cheap.
Oishíi desu.	It's delicious/tasty.
Ookíi desu.	It's big.
Chiisái desu.	It's small.
Íi desu. Yói desu.[1]	It's good/nice.
Warúi desu.	It's bad.
Warúi ténki desu.	It's bad weather.
Ténki wa warúi desu.	The weather is bad.
Chiisái hón desu.	It's a small book.
Ookíi kuruma désu.	It's a big car.
Oishii koohíi desu.	It's delicious coffee.
Yasúi hón desu.	It's an inexpensive book.

    d. Sentences with present, negative *i-* adjectives:

Tákaku nái desu. } **Tákaku arimasén.** }	It is not expensive
Yóku nái desu. } **Yóku arimasén.** }	It is not good.

[1] Both *íi* and *yói* mean "good," but *íi* is more colloquial and more commonly used. However, conjugations, such as the negative or past, are based on *yói* and not *íi*.

omoshirói	interesting
Omoshíroku nái desu. ⎱ **Omoshíroku ari-** **masén.** ⎰	It is not interesting.
atarashíi	new
Ataráshiku nái desu. ⎱ *Ataráshiku ari-* *masén.* ⎰	It is not new.
furúi[1]	old
Fúruku nái desu. ⎱ *Fúruku arimasén.* ⎰	It is not old.
tooi	far
Tooku nái desu. ⎱ *Tooku arimasén.* ⎰	It is not far.
atsúi	hot
Átsuku nái desu. ⎱ *Átsuku arimasén.* ⎰	It is not hot.
Ténki wa wáruku nái **desu.**	The weather is not bad.
Kuruma wa yóku nái *desu.*	The car is not good.
Furúi kuruma wa **tákaku arimasén.**	The old cars are not expensive.

      e. Sentences with past, affirmative
         i- adjective:

Óokikatta desu.	It was big.
Átsukatta desu.	It was hot.
Ataráshikatta desu.	It was new.
Yókatta desu.	It was good.
Kuruma wa tákakatta **desu.**	The car was expensive.

---

[1] *Furúi*, "old," is used to describe inanimate things and not animate beings.

Heyá wa chíisakatta desu.	The room was small.
Ténki wa wárukatta desu ka.	Was the weather bad?

f. Sentences with past, negative *i-* adjectives:

Tákaku nákatta desu. **Tákaku arimasén deshita.**	It was not expensive.
Omoshíroku nákatta desu. *Omoshíroku arimasén deshita.*	It was not interesting.
Óokiku nákatta desu.	It was not big.
Kuruma wa óokiku nákatta desu.	The car was not big.
Koohíi wa oishiku nákatta desu.	The coffee was not tasty.
Hóteru wa yóku nákatta desu.	The hotel was not good.
Résutoran wa ataráshiku nákatta desu.	The restaurant was not new.

2. *Na-* adjectives

 Na- adjectives are used very much like nouns. Unlike *i-* adjectives, they do not inflect—that is, change their forms according to tense, etc. Instead, the copula *desu* that follows the *na-* adjectives conjugates.

 a. Below are some sentences with *na-* adjectives. Notice that the sentence patterns are just like those with nouns (see Lesson 9).

shízuka	quiet
Shízuka desu.	It is quiet.
Shízuka deshita.	It was quiet.
Shízuka deshoo.	It probably is quiet.
Shízuka datta deshoo.	It probably was quiet.
Shízuka {ja / dewa} arimasén. Shízuka {ja / de(wa)} nái desu.	It is not quiet.
Shízuka {ja / dewa} arimasén deshita. Shízuka {ja / de(wa)} nákatta desu.	It was not quiet.
Shízuka {ja / de(wa)} nái deshoo.	It probably is not quiet.
Shízuka {ja / de(wa)} nákatta deshoo.	It probably was not quiet.
kírei	pretty/clean
Kírei ja arimasén.	It is not pretty/clean.
fukuzatsu	complicated
Fukuzatsu ja arimasén.	It is not complicated.
Fukuzatsu de nákatta desu.	It was not complicated.
Kono mondai wa fukuzatsu désu.	This problem is complicated
Shigoto wa fukuzatsu ja nái desu.	The job is not complicated.
shínsetsu	kind
Yamada-san wa shínsetsu desu.	Mr. Yamada is kind.

Tanaka-san wa shínsetsu deshita.	Ms. Tanaka was kind.
kantan	simple/brief
Kantan déshita.	It was simple/brief.
Shigoto wa kantan déshita.	The job was simple.

b. *Na-* adjectives modifying a noun
   Na- adjectives are used with *na* before a noun:

shízuka na apáato	quiet apartment
kírei na shashin	pretty photograph
fukuzatsu na mondai	complicated problem
shínsetsu na senséi	kind teacher
taisetsu	important
taisetsu na monó	important thing
génki	healthy
génki na kodomo	healthy child
rippa	magnificent
rippa na tatémono	magnificent building
rakú	easy/comfortable
rakú na shigoto	easy task
Kantan na setsumei déshita.	It was a brief explanation.
Taisetsu na monó ja nái desu.	It is not an important thing.

QUIZ 6

1. Takái desu.	a. It's not a good car.
2. *Omoshíroku nái desu.*	b. It's delicious.
3. *Yói hóteru desu.*	c. It was good.

4. *Íi kuruma ja nái desu.*	d. It probably is expensive.
5. *Yókatta desu.*	e. It probably was expensive.
6. *Íi éiga deshita.*	f. It's a good hotel.
7. *Takái deshoo.*	g. It is pretty.
8. *Tákakatta deshoo.*	h. It is expensive.
9. *Oishíi desu.*	i. It's not interesting.
10. *Kírei desu.*	j. It was a good movie.

ANSWERS

1–h; 2–i; 3–f; 4–a; 5–c; 6–j; 7–d; 8–e; 9–b; 10–g.

LESSON 12

DÁI JUUNÍKA

A. PLAIN OR POLITE

For each of the forms of *i*- adjectives, verbs, and the copula used at the end of a sentence, there is an additional form called a "plain form." The forms we have seen at the end of a sentence are called "polite forms." The polite forms are derived from plain forms and are characterized by ending with *-désu* or *-másu* or a form derived from one of these. The plain form is usually used in the *middle* of a sentence, while the polite form is usually at the *end* of a sentence. However, the plain form, too, can be used at the end of a sentence, but only when the speaker is very familiar with and has a casual relationship to the person (s)he is speaking to. A husband, for example, may use this form with his wife, or a high-school boy with his classmates. But for anyone learning Japanese as a foreign language, it is best to use the polite form at the end of a sentence.

Dictionaries and glossaries usually list the plain present affirmative form of *i-* adjectives, verbs, and the copula. Here is a table showing the plain and polite present affirmative forms of some words that you have already seen:

PLAIN PRESENT AFFIRMATIVE	POLITE PRESENT AFFIRMATIVE	MEANING
	I- ADJECTIVES	
takái	*takái desu*	it is expensive
tooi	*tooí desu*	it is far
	VERBS	
hanásu	*hanashimásu*	I speak
kau	*kaimásu*	I buy
áru	*arimásu*	there is
tabéru	*tabemásu*	I eat
kúru	*kimásu*	I come
	COPULA	
da[1]	*désu*	A is B

To construct the polite present affirmative form of an *i-* adjective, add *désu* to the plain present affirmative.

Construct the polite present affirmative of a verb according to the rules set forth in the next section.

The polite present affirmative of the copula *da* is *désu.* Rarely, *dé arimásu* can also be used, but this form is considered very formal.

---

[1]*Na* or *no* is used in place of *da* in certain environments.

B. TO CONSTRUCT THE POLITE FORM OF A VERB

In order to construct the polite form of a verb from its plain present form, you must learn to identify the class or conjugation to which the verb belongs. To do so, you need to know the following basic facts:

1. The plain present affirmative form of all verbs ends in *-u.*

2. All verbs belong to one of three classes: *consonant, vowel,* or *irregular.* Consonant verbs make up the largest group and irregular verbs the smallest.

3. There are only two verbs that are really irregular, and they are the most common: *suru* [do] and *kúru* [come]. Although there are a few other verbs that are somewhat irregular, they are, basically, consonant verbs. Two examples are: *iku* [go] and *kudasáru* [give].

4. The vast majority of verbs that end in *-eru* or *-iru* are vowel verbs—for example, *tabéru* [eat] and *míru* [see]—so called because the base[1] (which remains unchanged most of the time) ends in a vowel. However, there are a few verbs that end in *-eru* or *-iru* that are not vowel verbs; for example: *kéru* [kick], *káeru* [return], *háiru* [enter]. Since the base of these verbs ends in *-r* (*ker-, kaér-, hair-,* respectively) they are classified as consonant verbs.

[1] The base of a vowel verb is that part remaining after the final *-ru* is dropped; i.e., *tabe(ru), mi(ru).*

5. All other verbs are consonant verbs, so called, because the base ends in a consonant.[1] Verbs that end in two vowels, such as *kau* [buy], or *iu,* which is *yuu* [say], are also included in this class because they add *-w* at the end of the base when appending an ending that begins with *-a;* e.g., *-anai* [not], *-areru* (*passive*), or *-aseru* (*causative*).

Once you can identify the class to which a given verb belongs, you can form the polite, present affirmative forms as follows:

I. Consonant Verbs

Add *-imásu* to the base, with two exceptions:

a. When the base ends in *s,* the letter is changed to *sh* before adding *-imásu.* For example: *hanásu* becomes *hanashimásu.*

b. When the base ends in *ts,* the latter is changed to *ch* before adding *-imásu.* For example: *tátsu* becomes *tachimásu.*

II. Vowel Verbs

Add *-masu* to the base.

III. Irregular Verbs

Learn the polite form of each individually.

---

[1] The base of a consonant verb is that part remaining after the final *u* has been dropped. For example: *dás*(*u*) [put out, send out], *ár*(*u*) [there is], *ka*(*w*)(*u*) [buy], *kák*(*u*) [write].

Note: In the following examples, the end of the base has been marked with a hyphen:

PLAIN PRESENT AFFIRMATIVE	POLITE PRESENT AFFIRMATIVE	MEANING
	CONSONANT VERBS	
kák-u	*kakimásu*	writes
kas-u	*kashimásu*	lends
máts-u	*machimásu*	waits
móts-u	*mochimásu*	holds
háir-u	*hairimásu*	enters
ka(w)-u	*kaimasu*	buys
	VOWEL VERBS	
tabé-ru	*tabemásu*	eat
tome-ru	*tomemásu*	stop
mí-ru	*mimásu*	see
okí-ru	*okimásu*	get up
	IRREGULAR VERBS	
suru	*shimásu*	do
kúru	*kimásu*	come

C. THE -*TE* AND -*TA* FORMS

When the -*te* form of a verb appears in a sentence, it signifies that one or more additional verbs will also appear in that sentence.

The -*te* form of a verb is used in such expressions as *hanáshite kudasái* [please speak] and *hanáshite imasu* [I'm speaking]. Although the verb in such a construction most often ends in -*te,* it can also end in -*tte* or -*de.* The way the -*te* form ends or the way it is formed from the plain, present, affirmative (which is the dictionary form), depends on (a) the *class of verb* to which it belongs, and (b) if it is a consonant verb, the *pronunciation of the last syllable* of the plain present.

The *-te* form is sometimes called a ''gerund,'' but unlike a proper gerund, is never used as a noun. (See page 75 for uses of the *-te* form.)

The *-ta* form is another way to refer to the plain past affirmative as opposed to the polite past affirmative. However, in the middle of a sentence, the *-ta* form is usually used in place of the polite form.

Remember that the polite past affirmative always ends in *-máshita,* whereas the *-ta* form can end not only in *-ta* but also in *-tta* or *-da.* The *-ta* form is derived from the plain present affirmative in exactly the same way as the *-te* form.

When when using either of these forms, be careful not to interchange the final *-e* and *-a.* Follow these instructions:

I. For Consonant Verbs

   a. When the last syllable of the plain present is *-u, -tsu,* or *-ru,* drop that syllable and add *-tte* or *-tta:*

PLAIN PRESENT AFFIRMATIVE	-TE FORM	-TA FORM	MEANING OF PLAIN PRESENT AFFIRMATIVE
kau	**katte**	**katta**	buy
omóu	*omótte*	*omótta*	think
mátsu	**mátte**	**mátta**	wait
mótsu	*mótte*	*mótta*	hold
okuru	**okutte**	**okutta**	send
tóru	*tótte*	*tótta*	take

   Note: To learn this rule it might be helpful to memorize the following fictitious word, which is made up by stringing together the three final syllables involved and the *-tta:*

u-tsu-ru-tta (*utsurutta*)

b. If the last syllable of the plain present affirmative is *-mu, -nu,* or *-bu,* drop it and replace it with *-nde* or *-nda.*

PLAIN PRESENT AFFIRMATIVE	-TE FORM	-TA FORM	MEANING OF PLAIN PRESENT AFFIRMATIVE
yómu	**yónde**	**yónda**	read
nómu	*nónde*	*nónda*	drink
shinu	**shinde**	**shinda**	die
yobu	**yonde**	**yonda**	call
tobu	*tonde*	*tonda*	fly

Mnemonic device: *mu-nu-bu-nda* (*munubunda*).

c. If the last syllable of the plain present affirmative is *-ku,* drop it and replace it with *-ite* or *-ita.* If the last syllable is *-gu,* drop it and replace it with *-ide* and *-ida.*

PLAIN PRESENT AFFIRMATIVE	-TE FORM	-TA FORM	MEANING OF PLAIN PRESENT AFFIRMATIVE
káku	**káite**	**káita**	write
saku	*saite*	*saita*	bloom
oyógu	**oyóide**	**oyóida**	swim
kagu	*kaide*	*kaida*	smells

Mnemonic device: *ku-gu-ita-ida* (*kuguita-ida*).

Note: *iku* [go] is one exception. Its *-te* and *-ta* forms are *itte* and *itta*, respectively.

d. When the last syllable of the plain present is *-su*, drop it and add *-shite* or *-shita*.

PLAIN PRESENT AFFIRMATIVE	-TE FORM	-TA FORM	MEANING OF PLAIN PRESENT AFFIRMATIVE
hanásu	**hanáshite**	**hanáshita**	speak
kasu	**kashite**	**kashita**	lend
hósu	*hóshite*	*hóshita*	dry
moyasu	*moyashite*	*moyashita*	burn

Mnemonic device: *su-shita* (*sushita*).

II. For Vowel Verbs

Simply drop the final syllable *-ru* and add *-te* or *-ta*.

PLAIN PRESENT AFFIRMATIVE	-TE FORM	-TA FORM	MEANING OF PLAIN PRESENT AFFIRMATIVE
tabéru	**tábete**	**tábeta**	eat
akeru	**akete**	**aketa**	open
míru	*míte*	*míta*	see
kiru	*kite*	*kita*	wear

III. For Irregular Verbs

PLAIN PRESENT AFFIRMATIVE	-TE FORM	-TA FORM	MEANING OF PLAIN PRESENT AFFIRMATIVE
suru	**shite**	**shita**	do
kúru	**kité**	**kitá**	come

D. Various Usages of the *-te* Form

The basic function of a *-te* form is to name an action or condition. It serves to show that the sentence is not complete. That is why, as a rule, it does not appear at the end of a sentence.

The *-te* form verb is used in many ways. Some of the more important follow:

1. When a sentence contains several different verbs, the *-te* form is usually used for all but the last.

Nippón e itte kaimáshita.	I bought it in Japan. [(I) went to Japan and bought it (there).]
Éiga o míte Ginza de góhan o tábete uchi e kaérimáshita.	I saw a movie, ate [my meal] on Ginza, and returned home.

Notice that the tense is expressed in *the terminal verb only* and not in the *-te* form verbs. In translation, however, the tense is expressed for the *-te* form verbs as well.

2. Sometimes the function of a *-te* form verb is merely to explain *how* the action of the following verb is performed:

Hashítte[1] ikimáshita.	He went running.
Isóide[2] kimáshita.	He came hurriedly.

---

[1] *hashíru* = run.
[2] *isógu* = hurry.

3. The phrase -*te imasu* is used to express an action going on or a state or condition resulting from an action that occurred in the past.

Áme ga futté imasu.	It is raining. [The rain is falling.]
Íma góhan o tábete imasu.	We are eating [the meal] now.
Okyaku sáma ga kité imasu.	We have a visitor. [(A) visitor came and is with us.]

4. The phrase -*te arimasu* is used to express a state or condition that is the result of the past action of a transitive verb. In English it is often translated by the passive voice.

Sore wa harátte arimasu.	That has been paid for. That is paid. [That is in the state of my having paid for it.]
Sono tegami wa moo káite arimasu.	That letter (you are speaking of) is already written. [The letter is already in the state of my having written it.]

5. The phrase -*te kudasai* is used to express a request and corresponds most closely to the imperative in English.

Kippo o katte kudasái.	Please buy a ticket.
Doyóobi ni kité kudasái.	Come on Saturday, please.

QUIZ 7

1. *Nippón e itte kaimáshita.*	a. He came hurriedly.
2. *Isóide kimáshita.*	b. I went to Japan and bought it there.
3. *Áme ga futté imásu.*	c. That letter is already written.
4. *Doyóobi ni kité kudasái.*	d. Come on Saturday, please.
5. *Hashítte ikimáshita.*	e. We have a visitor.
6. *Sono tegami wa moo káite arimásu.*	f. He went running.
7. *Okyaku sáma ga kité imasu.*	g. It is raining.
8. *Sore wa harátte arimasu.*	h. That has been paid for.
9. *Íma góhan o tábete imasu.*	i. We are eating now.
10. *Éiga o míte Ginza de góhan o tábete uchi e kaerimáshita.*	j. I saw a movie, ate on Ginza, and returned home.

ANSWERS
1–b; 2–a; 3–g; 4–d; 5–f; 6–c; 7–e; 8–h; 9–i; 10–j.

LESSON 13

DÁI JUUSÁNKA

A. MY, YOUR, HIS, HER, ETC.

There are no separate words for "my," "your," "his," "her," etc. To express the idea of these words, add the particle *no* to the words for "I," "you," "he," "she."

Watakushi no hón wa dóko ni arimásu ka?	Where is my book?
Anáta no hón wa dóko ni arimásu ka?	Where is your book?
Sonó hito no hón wa dóko ni arimásu ka?	Where is his/her [that person's] book?
Sonó hitotachi no hón wa dóko ni arimásu ka?	Where are their [those people's] books?
Anáta no tegami wa dóko ni arimásu ka?	Where is your letter?
Sonó hito no tegami wa dóko ni arimásu ka?	Where is his/her [that person's] letter?
Sonó hitotachi no tegami wa dóko ni arimásu ka?	Where are their [those people's] letters?

Sometimes the idea of "your" may be suggested by prefixing the noun referred to with *o-* or *go-*. In such cases, *anata no* [your] is usually not used. Notice that the nouns to which *o-* or *go-* can be added are limited in number.

Gokázoku[1] *wa?*	How about your family?

---

[1] *kázoku* = family.

Okuni[1] *wa dóchira*   Where are you from?
  desu ka?
Onamae[2] *wa nán desu*   What is your name?
  ka?

B. SOME COMPARISONS

Here are a few forms of comparisons. Refer to the
Summary of Japanese Grammar, Section 16, for more
information.

    1. more . . . than

Sono densha wa hayái   That train is fast.
desu.
Sono densha wa básu   That train is faster than
yori hayái desu.   the bus.
Sono kuruma wa   That car is new.
atarashíi desu.
Sono kuruma wa   That car is newer than
watashi no kuruma   my car.
yóri atarashíi desu.
Tanaka-san no heyá   Ms. Tanaka's room is
wa shízuka desu.   quiet.
Tanaka-san no heyá   Ms. Tanaka's room is
wa kono heyá yori   more quiet than this
shízuka desu.   room.

    2. the most . . .

Kono kuruma ga   This car is the newest.
ichiban atarashíi
desu.

[1] *kuni* = country, hometown.
[2] *namae* = name.

Watashi no shigoto ga ichiban rakú desu.	My job is the easiest.
Kono resutoran ga ichiban kírei desu.	This restaurant is the cleanest.
Kono mondai ga ichiban fukzatsu désu.	This problem is the most complicated.

3. not as (so) . . . as . . .

Tanaka-san wa Hárada-san hodo[1] séi ga tákaku arimasén.	Ms. Tanaka is not as tall as Ms. Harada.
Nára wa Kyóoto hodo óokiku arimasén.	Nara is not as big as Kyoto.
Watashi no heyá wa Tanaka-san no heyá hodo kírei ja arimasén.	My room is not as clean as Ms. Tanaka's room.
Kyóo no shikén wa máe no shikén hodo kantan déwa nákatta désu.	Today's test was not as simple as the previous test.

4. as . . . as possible

Dekiru dake kuwáshiku káite kudasái.	Please write it as detailed (with as much detail) as possible.
Dekiru dake kitsuku shímete kudasái.	Please tie it as tightly as possible.
Deriku dake háyaku shite kudasái.	Do it as soon as possible.

[1]*hodo* = not as . . . as

C. ASKING A QUESTION II

There are several ways to ask a question:

1. Add the particle *ka* at the end of a declarative sentence, and either raise the pitch of your voice at the end (i.e., use the "question-intonation"), or not, as you like.

2. Phrase the sentence like a declarative statement and use the question-intonation but do not use the particle *ka* at the end. This is a very informal usage.

3. When you ask a question that demands an answer, and the answer can be one of several alternatives, add *ka* to each of the alternatives you offer.

Kore désu ka?	Is it this?
Kore désu.	It's this.
Sore désu ka?	Is it that?
Kore désu ka sore désu ka?	Is it this or is it that?
Koko ni imásu ka?	Is he here?
Asoko ni imásu ka?	Is he over there?
Koko ni imásu ka asoko ni imásu ka?	Is he here or is he over there?
Dóko ni imásu ka?	Where is he?
Dóko desu ka?	Where is it? [Which place is (it)?]
Dáre desu ka?	Who is it?
Dónata[1] **desu ka?**	Who is it (*respect*)?

---

[1] *Dónata* is more polite than *dáre. Dónata* is called the "respect" form of *dare*. The respect form of words is used only when someone is talking about someone else in a more polite way. The "humble" form, as opposed to respect, is used to demote one's status.

Nán desu ka?	What is it?
Ítsu desu ka?	When is it?
Íkura desu ka?	How much is it?
Íkutsu desu ka?	How many? How old is he?
Náze desu ka?	Why is it?
Dóoshite[1] desu ka?	Why is it?
Dóo desu ka?	How is it?
Dóchira desu ka?	Which of the two is it? Which way is it?
Dóre desu ka?	Which is it (*used for more than two*)?
Dóno tatémono desu ka?	Which building is it?
Dóno hitó desu ka?	Which person is it?
Ikimashita ka?	Did you go?
Dáre ga ikimáshita ka?	Who went?
Náze ikimáshita ka?	Why did you go?
Ítsu ikimáshita ka?	When did you go?
Nán de ikimáshita ka?	How did you go? [By what means (of transportation) did (you) go?]
Dáre to ikimáshita ka?	With whom did you go?
Ítsu dáre to ikimáshita ka?	When and with whom did you go?
Dóoshite Tanaka-san to ikimáshita ka?	Why did you go with Ms. Tanaka?
Kabuki wa dóo deshita ka?	How was the Kabuki play?
Búnraku wa dóoshite mimasén deshita ka?	Why didn't you see the Bunraku (puppet play)?

[1] *Dóoshite* is less formal than *náze*.

Kabuki e dáre to iki-
máshita ka?

With whom did you go
to the Kabuki?

QUIZ 8

1. *Watakushi no hón
   wa dóko ni ari-
   másu ka?*

   a. Where is your
      book?

2. *Anáta no hón wa
   dóko ni arimásu
   ka?*

   b. What is your name?

3. *Sonó hitotachi no
   tegami wa dóko ni
   arimásu ka?*

   c. That train is not as
      fast as this train.

4. *Onamae wa nán
   desu ka?*

   d. Which building is
      it?

5. *Sono kishá wa
   kono kishá hodo
   háyaka arimasén.*

   e. Where are their
      [those people's]
      letters?

6. *Kono jidóosha no
   hóo ga ano ji-
   dóosha yori at-
   arashíi desu.*

   f. Where is my book?

7. *Dóno tatémono
   desu ka?*

   g. When is it?

8. *Deriku dake háy-
   aku shite kudasái.*

   h. This car is newer
      than that one.

9. *Kore désu ka?*

   i. Do it as soon as
      possible.

10. *Ítsu desu ka?*

    j. Is it this?

ANSWERS
1–f; 2–a; 3–e; 4–b; 5–c; 6–h; 7–d; 8–i; 9–j; 10–g.

D. WORD STUDY

aisukuríimu	ice cream
bifuteki	beefsteak
chíizu	cheese
kecháppu	catsup
mayonéezu	mayonnaise
omuretsu	omelet
sárada	salad
sóosu	sauce (Worcestershire)
súupu	soup
tóosuto	toast

LESSON 14

DÁI JUUYÓNKA

A. TO HAVE AND HAVE NOT

1. I (you, he, she . . .) have.

Mótte imasu.[1]
- I have. [Am holding.]
- You have. [Are holding.]
- He has. [Is holding.]
- They have. [Are holding.]

2. I (you, he, she . . .) don't have.

Mótte imasén.	I don't have. You don't have, etc.
Nani mo mótte imasén.	I have nothing. I don't have anything.
Okane o mótte imasu.	I have money.

[1] Another expression for "have" was introduced in Lesson 8.

Okane o juubún mótte imasu.	I have enough money.
Okane o sukóshi mo mótte imasén.	I don't have any money. [I don't have even a little bit of money.]

3. Do I (you, he, she . . .) have?

Mótte imásu ka?	Do I have (it)?

4. Don't I (you, he, she . . .) have?

Mótte imasén ka?	Don't I have (it)?
Okane o mótte imásu ka?	Does he have (any) money?
Okane o juubún mótte imásu ka?	Does he have enough money?
Enpitsu o mótte imásu ka?	Do you have a pencil?
Pén o mótte imásu ka?	Do you have a pen?
Okane o juubún mótte imasén ka?	Don't you have enough money?
Enpitsu o mótte imasén ka?	Don't you have a pencil?
Pén o mótte imasén ka?	Don't you have a pen?

5. I (you, he, she . . .) have to have.

Mótte inákereba narimasén.	I have to have (it). [If (I) don't have (it), it won't do.]

6. Do I (you, he, she . . .) have to have?

Mótte inákereba nari-masén ka?   Do I have to have (it)?

7. I (you, he, she . . .) don't have to have.

Mótte inákute mo íi desu.   I don't have to have (it). [Even if (I) don't have (it), I will be all right.]

8. Don't I (you, he, she . . .) have to have?

Mótte inákute mo íi desu ka?   Don't I have to have it?

Pasupóoto o mótte inákereba nari-masén.   You have to have a passport.

Kippu o mótte in-ákereba narimasén.   You have to have a ticket.

Shookáijoo o mótte inákereba nari-masén.   You have to have a letter of introduction.

Pasupóoto o mótte inákereba nari-masén ka?   Do you have to have a passport?

Kippu o mótte in-ákereba narimasén ka?   Do you have to have a ticket?

Shookáijoo o mótte inákereba narimasén ka?   Do you have to have a letter of introduction?

Pasupóoto o mótte inákute mo íi desu.   You don't have to have a passport.

Kippu o mótte in-ákute mo íi desu.   You don't have to have a ticket.

Shookáijoo o mótte inákute mo íi desu.	You don't have to have a letter of introduction.
Pasupóoto o mótte inákute mo íi desu ka?	Don't I have to have a passport? [Is it all right (to go) even if I don't have a passport?]

9. I (you, he, she . . .) may have it.

Mótte iru ká mo shiremasén.	I may have (it). [I cannot tell if I have (it).]

10. I (you, he, she . . .) may not have it.

Mótte inái ká mo shiremasén.	I may not have (it).
Okane o mótte iru ká mo shiremasén.	He may have (some) money.
Kippu o mótte iru ká mo shiremasén.	He may have the ticket.
Okane o mótte inái ká mo shiremasén.	He may not have any money.
Kippu o mótte inái ká mo shiremasén.	He may not have the ticket.

B. ALSO

mo	also, too
watakushi mo	I also, I too
anáta mo	you also
anó hito mo	(s)he also
watakushitachi mo	we also

anátatachi mo   you also
ano hitótachi mo   they also
Ano hitótachi mo kimásu.   They are coming too.
Watakushi mo kimásu.   I'm coming too.

QUIZ 9

1. *Oishíi desu.*   a. He may have a ticket.

2. *Atarashíi desu.*   b. I don't have any money.

3. *Nán desu ka?*   c. You don't have to have a ticket.

4. *Dóno tatémono desu ka?*   d. You have to have a passport.

5. *Okane o juubún mótte imasu.*   e. I have enough money.

6. *Enpitsu o mótte imásu ka?*   f. It's delicious.

7. *Pasupóoto o mótte inákereba narimasén.*   g. Which building is it?

8. *Okane o sukoshi mo mótte imasén.*   h. It's new.

9. *Kippu o mótte inákute mo íi desu.*   i. Do you have a pencil?

10. *Kippu o mótte iru ká mo shiremasén.*   j. What is it?

ANSWERS
1–f; 2–h; 3–j; 4–g; 5–e; 6–i; 7–d; 8–b; 9–c; 10–a.

C. WORD STUDY

buráusu	blouse
máfuraa	muffler
nékutai	necktie
oobaakóoto	overcoat
séetaa	sweater
shátsu	shirt
sukáafu	scarf
sukáato	skirt
suríppu	slip

LESSON 15

DÁI JUUGÓKA

A. I HAVE BEEN TO . . .

**Hakone e itta kotó[1]
ga arimásu.**

I have been to Hakone.
[(I) have the experience of having gone to Hakone.]

Taiwán e itta kotó ga arimásu.

I have been to Taiwan.

Nihon ryóori o tábeta kotó ga arimásu.

I have eaten Japanese cooking. [(I) have had the experience of eating Japanese cooking.]

Kabuki o míta kotó ga arimásu.

I have seen (the) Kabuki.

[1] *kotó* = act, event, experience.

B. SOMETIMES I GO . . .

Hakone e iku kotó ga arimásu.	Sometimes I go to Hakone. [The act of my going to Hakone exists.]
Taiwán e iku kotó ga arimásu.	Sometimes I go to Taiwan.
Nihon ryóori o tabéru kotó ga arimásu.	Sometimes I eat Japanese cooking.
Kabuki o míru kotó ga arimásu.	Sometimes I see Kabuki plays.

C. I CAN, I AM ABLE TO . . .

Ashitá wa Hakone e iku kotó ga dekimásu.	Tomorrow I can go to Hakone. [The act of my going to Hakone tomorrow is possible.]
Rainen wa Taiwán e iku kotó ga dekimásu.	Next year I can go to Taiwan.
Nihon ryóori o tabéru kotó ga dekimásu.	I can eat Japanese cooking.
Nyuu Yóoku de Kabuki o míru kotó ga dekimáshita.	I could see the Kabuki in New York.

D. I'VE DECIDED TO . . .

Ashitá wa Hakone e iku kóto ni shimáshita.	I've decided to go to Hakone tomorrow.

Rainen wa Taiwán e iku kóto ni shimásh-ita.	I've decided to go to Taiwan next year.
Nihon ryóori o tabéru kotó ni shimáshita.	I've decided to have [eat] Japanese cooking.
Kabuki o míru kotó ni shimáshita.	We've decided to see the Kabuki plays.

QUIZ 10

1. *Sore desu ka?*

    a. We've decided to see the Kabuki plays.

2. *Dóko ni imásu ka?*

    b. Please do it as soon as possible.

3. *Ookíi deshoo.*

    c. I have seen (the) Kabuki.

4. *Ítsu desu ka?*

    d. Why didn't you see the Bunraku?

5. *Dáre to ikimáshita ka?*

    e. That one isn't as big as this one.

6. *Ookiku arimasén deshita.*

    f. I was able to eat Japanese cooking.

7. *Kabuki wa dóo deshita ka?*

    g. When is it?

8. *Ítsu ikimáshita ka?*

    h. It is probably big.

9. *Dáre ga ikimáshita ka?*

    i. Where is he?

10. *Sore wa kore hodo óokiku arimasén.*

    j. Is it that?

11. *Kabuki o míta kotó ga arimásu.*

    k. It wasn't big.

12. *Nihon ryoori o tabéru kotó ga de-kimáshita.*

    l. When did you go?

13. *Dekiru dake há-*   m. Who went?
    yaku shite kudasái.
14. *Búnraku wa dóo*   n. With whom did
    shite mimasén   you go?
    deshita ka?
15. *Kabuki o míru kotó*   o. How was the Ka-
    ni shimáshita.   buki play?

ANSWERS
1–j; 2–i; 3–h; 4–g; 5–n; 6–k; 7–o; 8–l; 9–m; 10–e;
11–c; 12–f; 13–b; 14–d; 15–a.

LESSON 16

DÁI JUURÓKKA

A. DO YOU SPEAK JAPANESE?

Nihongo ga dekimásu   Do you speak Japa-
ka?   nese? [Is Japanese
                               possible?]

Iie, dekimasén.   No, I don't speak Japa-
                               nese.

  hetá desu.   speak poorly [be
                                 poor (in skill)]

  taihen hetá desu   speak very poorly
                                 [be very poor]

Taihen hetá desu.   I (speak) very poorly.
  sukóshi   a little
Hái, sukóshi deki-   Yes, I speak a little.
másu.
  honno sukóshi   just a little
Honno sukóshi deki-   I speak just a little.
másu.

amari . . . dekimasén	not much (*used with a negative verb*)
wázuka daké	just a little
Wakarimásu ka?	Do you understand (it)?
Iie, wakarimasén.	No, I don't understand (it).
Amari yóku wakarimasén.	I don't understand (it) very well.
Nihongo wa amari yóku wakarimasén.	I don't understand Japanese very well.
Hai, wakarimásu.	Yes, I understand.
Hai, sukóshi wakarimásu.	Yes, I understand a little.
Yomemásu[1] ga[2] hanasemasén.	I can read but I can't speak.
Wakarimásu ka?	Do you understand?
Sukóshi mo wakarimasén.	Not at all.
Yóku wakarimasén.	I don't understand very well.
Káite kudasái.	Write it, please.
Dóo kakimásu ka?	How do you write it?
Sono kotobá wa shirimasén.	I don't know that word.
Sore wa Nihongo de dóo iimásu ka?	How do you say that in Japanese?
"Thank you" wa Nihongo de dóo iimásu ka?	How do you say, "Thank you," in Japanese?

---

[1] *Yomemásu* = can read; *hanasemásu* = can speak. These examples present a way of saying "can . . ." different from the one introduced in Section C of Lesson 15. See also Section D of Lesson 40 and Section 31 of the Summary of Japanese Grammar.

[2] *ga* = but.

B. PLEASE SPEAK A LITTLE SLOWER

Yukkúri hanáshite kudasáreba . . .	If you speak slowly (for me) . . .
Yukkúri hanáshite kudasáreba wakarimásu.	If you speak slowly, I'll be able to understand you.
Yukkúri hanáshite kudasái.	Please speak slowly.
Nán to osshaimáshita ka?	What did you say?
Dóo yuu ími desu ka?	What do you mean?
. . . kudasaimasén ka?	Would you not . . . ?
hanásu	speak
mótto yukkúri	slower
Mótto yukkúri hanáshite kudasaimasén ka?	Would you please speak slower? [Would you not speak . . .]
dóozo	please
Dóozo mótto yukkúri hanáshite kudasaimasén ka?	Would you mind speaking a little slower, please?
Moo ichido itte kudasaimasén ka?	Would you please say (that) again?

C. THANKS!

Arígatoo.	Thanks.
Dóomo arígatoo gozaimásu.	Thank you very much.
Dóo itashimáshite.	Don't mention it.
Arígatoo gozaimásu.	Thanks. [(I) thank (you).]
Dóo itashimáshite.	Not at all.

Gomennasái.	Excuse me.
Dóozo.	Certainly. [Please (go ahead).]
Dóozo osaki ni.	Go ahead!
Sumimasén. Nán to osshaimáshita ka?	Pardon? What did you say?
Déwa mata.	See you soon.
Déwa nochihodo.	See you later.
Déwa kónban.	See you this evening.

QUIZ 11

1. *Káite kudasái.*	a. I don't speak Japanese.
2. *Nihongo wa deki-masén.*	b. Just a little.
3. *Nihongo wa yóku wakarimasén.*	c. Do you understand?
4. *Wakarimásu ka?*	d. I don't understand Japanese very well.
5. *Honno sukóshi.*	e. Write it down, please.
6. *Moo ichido itte kudasaimasén ka?*	f. How do you write it?
7. *"Thank you" wa Nihongo de dóo iimasu ka?*	g. I don't know that word.
8. *Dóo yuu ími desu ka?*	h. How do you say, "Thank you," in Japanese?
9. *Dóo kakimásu ka?*	i. What do you mean?
10. *Sono kotobá wa shirimasén.*	j. Would you please say that again?

ANSWERS
1–e; 2–a; 3–d; 4–c; 5–b; 6–j; 7–h; 8–i; 9–f; 10–g.

D. WORD STUDY

bánana	banana
karifuráwaa	cauliflower
kyábetsu	cabbage
méron	melon
orénji	orange
páseri	parsley
remon	lemon
rétasu	lettuce
sérori	celery
tómato	tomato

LESSON 17

DÁI JUUNANÁKA

A. THIS AND THAT

1. *Kono* This

kono hón	this book
konó hito	this person
kono hóteru	this hotel
kono tegami	this letter
kono hanashí	this story

2. *Sono* That

Sono refers to a thing or place that is nearby.

sono hón	that book
sono hí	that day
sono kotobá	that word
sonó hito	that person

sono hóteru   that   hotel
sono tegami   that   letter

    3. *Ano*   That

      Ano refers to something outside of imme-
      diate reach.

ano uchi   that house (over there)
ano kí   that tree (over there)
ano néko   that cat (over there)

    The distinction among *kono, sono,* and *ano* holds
true with the distinction among *kore, sore,* and *are,*
respectively. The difference between the *kono-sono-
ano* series and the *kore-sore-are* series below is that a
member of the former series must be followed by a
noun (e.g., *kono hón* [this book]), and a member of
the latter series cannot be followed by a noun.

    4. *Kore*   This

Kore wa doo yuu ími   What does this mean?
  desu ka?
Kore wa watakushi   This is mine.
  nó desu.

    5. *Sore*   That

Sore désu.   That's it. It's that.
Sore o tótte kudasai.   Please pick that one.
Sore wa íi kangáe   That is a good idea.
  desu ne.
Kore mo sore mo   Both this one and that
  damé desu.   one are no good.

6. *Are* That

Are désu.	It's that (over there).
Are ja arimasén.	It isn't that. That's not it.
Are o kudasái.	Give me that (over there), please.
Kore wa watakushi nó desu; are wa anáta no désu.	This one is mine; that one (over there) is yours.

QUIZ 12

1. *Are wa anáta no desu ka?*	a. What does this mean?
2. *Kore wa dóo yuu ími desu ka?*	b. It isn't that.
3. *Are o kudasái.*	c. That is mine.
4. *Ano hón o kudasái.*	d. This one is mine; that one is yours.
5. *Sore désu.*	e. This is mine.
6. *Kore wa watakushi nó desu.*	f. Give me that, please.
7. *Are désu.*	g. It's that.
8. *Sore wa watkushi nó desu.*	h. Please give me that one (over there).
9. *Kore wa watakushi nó desu; are wa anáta no desu.*	i. It's that.
10. *Are ja arimasén.*	j. Is that yours?

ANSWERS

1–j; 2–a; 3–f; 4–h; 5–g; 6–e; 7–i; 8–c; 9–d; 10–b.

B. NOT

Yóku arimasén.	It's not good.
Wáruku arimasén.	It's not bad.
Sore ja arimasén.	It's not that.
Koko ni arimasén.	It's not here.
Amari takusán de náku.	Not too much.
Amari háyaku náku.	Not too fast.
Máda desu.	Not yet. [It's yet (to come).]
Sukóshi mo . . . masén.	Not at all (*with a negative predicate*).
Sukóshi mo jikan ga arimasén.	I don't have any time.
Dóo suru ka shirimasén.	I don't know how to do it.
Ítsu ka shirimasén.	I don't know when.
Dóko ka shirimasén.	I don't know where.
Nani mo shirimasén.	I don't know anything.
Nani mo iimasén déshita.	He didn't say anything.
Nani mo arimasén.	Nothing. [There is nothing.]
Nani mo mótte imasén.	I don't have anything.
Kesshite.	Never (*with a negative predicate*).
Kesshite kimasén.	She never comes.
Dáre ga kimáshita ka?	Who came?
. . . Dare mo kimasén déshita.	. . . Nobody came.
Dáre mo miemasén.	I don't see anyone. [No one is in sight.]

Móo soko e ikimasén.	I don't go there anymore.
Móo kimasén.	She doesn't come anymore.
Hyakuen shika arimasén.	I have only a hundred yen. [(I) don't have but a hundred yen.]
Ichijíkan shika arimasén.	You have only one hour.
Tóo shika mótte imasén.	He has only ten of them.

C. ISN'T IT, AREN'T YOU? ETC.

Hontoo désu ne?	It's true, isn't it?
Kimásu ne?	You are coming, aren't you?
Juubún mótte imásu ne?	You have enough of it, don't you?
Sukóshi mo mótte imasén ne?	You don't have any of it, do you?
Sansei désu ne?	You agree, don't you?

QUIZ 13

1. *Sore ja arimasén.*	a. I don't see anyone.
2. *Ítsu ka shirimasén.*	b. I have only a hundred yen.
3. *Sukóshi mo jikan ga arimasén.*	c. You have only one hour.
4. *Nani mo arimasén.*	d. You are coming, aren't you?
5. *Kimásu ne?*	e. You don't have any of it, do you?
6. *Ichijíkan shika arimasén.*	f. It's not that.

7. *Dáre mo mie-*
   masén.
8. *Hyakuen shika ari-*
   masén.
9. *Sukóshi mo mótte*
   imasén ne?
10. *Nani mo iimasén*
    déshita.

g. I don't have any time.

h. I don't know when.

i. He didn't say any-
   thing.

j. Nothing.

ANSWERS
1–f; 2–h; 3–g; 4–j; 5–d; 6–c; 7–a; 8–b; 9–e; 10–i.

D. WORD STUDY

baree bóoru	volleyball
basuketto bóoru	basketball
bókushingu	boxing
górufu	golf
háikingu	hiking
pínpon	Ping-Pong (table tennis)
résuringu	wrestling
sukéeto	skating
sukíi	ski, skiing
ténisu	tennis

LESSON 18

DÁI JUUHACHÍKA

A. IT'S ME (I), ETC.

Watakushi désu.	It's me (I).
Anáta desu.	It's you.
Anó hito desu.	It's him/her (he/she).
Watakushítachi desu.	It's us.

B. IT'S MINE, ETC.

Notice that when a noun appears together with *no* but the combination is not followed by another noun, it often means, literally, "a thing pertaining to (that noun)." For example:

watakushi no	a thing pertaining to me; my thing; mine
Watakushi no desu.	It's mine.
Anáta[1] no desu.	It's yours.
Anó hito no desu.	It's his (hers).
Watakushítachi no desu.	It's ours.
Anatagáta no desu.	It's yours (*plural*).
Anó hitotachi nó desu.	It's theirs.

C. ABOUT ME, ETC.

Anáta no kotó o hanáshite irú no desu.[2]	I'm talking about you. [(I'm) talking of things pertaining to you.]
Watakushi no kotó o hanáshite irú no desu ne?	You are talking about me, aren't you? [. . . that's what it is, isn't it?]

---

[1] It is more polite to use the person's name, rather than the personal pronoun "you" (*anáta, anatagata*). If you want to say "it's yours" and you are speaking to Mr. Yamada, you would say *Yamada-san no desu.*

[2] Notice that when the sequence *no desu* (or *n desu*) immediately follows a predicate, it means, "That's what it is," or, "It's a fact that," and the predicate itself is usually in the plain form.

D. To Me, Etc.

Watakushi ni kudasái.	Give it to me, please.
Watakushítachi ni kudasái.	Give it to us, please.
Watakushi ni kudasaimáshita.	She gave it to me.
Watakushítachi ni kudasaimáshita.	She gave it to us.

E. The Modifiers

In Japanese, a modifier *always* precedes the word modified, whether the modifier is a single word, a phrase, or a clause. An adjective that modifies a noun is always placed before the noun, and an adverb that modifies a verb is always placed before the verb. Even a long clause, which in English would follow the noun, precedes it in Japanese. In fact, the very act of placing a clause before a noun makes it a modifier of that noun.

Here are some examples:

ié	a house
akai	it is red (*plain*)
akai ié	a red house
yáne	a roof
Yáne ga akai.	The roof is red.
yáne ga akai ié ⎫ **yáne no akai ié** ⎭	the house whose roof is red [the-roof-is-red house]
Yáne no akai ié ni súnde imasu.	He lives in a house with a red roof.
hito	a person
súnde imasu	he lives [is residing]
súnde iru	he lives (*plain*)

súnde iru hito	the person who lives (there)
sono ié ni súnde iru hito	the person who lives in that house
yáne no akai ié ni súnde iru hito	the person who lives in the house with a red roof
Ano yáne no akai ié ni súnde iru híto ga kyónen Amerika kara kitá hito desu.	The person who lives in that house with a red roof is the person who came from America last year.

F. THE NOUN-MAKER *No*

In addition to the particle *no* that follows a noun and links it to another noun, there is a "noun-maker" *no* which appears only *after* a clause. (As you have already seen, a clause *can* be a single adjective or a verb or a series of words ending in an adjective or verb.) This *no* makes a noun out of the clause and is usually translated "one who," "one which," "the act of doing," "the time when," or "the place where."

Akái no o kudasái.	Please give me one which is red. Please give me a red one.
Akaku nái no o kudasái.	Give me one which is not red, please.
Yáne ga akái no ga watakushi no ié desu.	The one (house) with a red roof is my house. [The-roof-is-red one (house) is my house.]
Tabemáshita.	I ate.

Tábeta.	I ate (*plain*).
sakana	fish
Tábeta no wa sakana déshita.	The food [thing] that I ate was fish.
Sakana o tábeta.	I ate fish (*plain*).
Sakan o tábeta no wa kinóo deshita.	It was yesterday that I ate fish. [The day that (I) ate fish was yesterday.]

QUIZ 14

1. *Watakushi nó desu.*
2. *Tábeta no wa sakana déshita.*
3. *Anáta no kotó o hanáshite irú no desu.*
4. *Anatagáta no desu.*
5. *Watakushítachi ni kudasái.*
6. *Watakushi ni kudasaimáshita.*
7. *Yáne no akai ié ni súnde imasu.*
8. *Akaku nái no o kudasái.*
9. *Akái no o kudasái.*
10. *Sakana o tábeta no wa kinóo deshita.*

a. It was yesterday that I ate fish.
b. Give me one which is not red, please.
c. Give it to us, please.
d. Give me one which is red, please.
e. He lives in a house with a red roof.
f. It's yours.
g. He gave it to me.
h. The food that I ate was fish.
i. It's mine.
j. I'm talking about you.

ANSWERS

1–i; 2–h; 3–j; 4–f; 5–c; 6–g; 7–e; 8–b; 9–d; 10–a.

LESSON 19

DÁI JUUKYÚUKA

A. HELLO, HOW ARE YOU?

Konnichi wá.	Hello. Good afternoon.
Ohayoo gozaimásu.	Good morning.
Ogénki desu ka?	How are you?
Okagesama de génki desu.	Very well, thanks. [Thanks to your thinking of me . . .]
Bestu ni kawari arimasén.	So so. [No special change.]
Anáta wa?	And how are you? [And you?]
Dóo ni ka yatte orimásu.	Not bad.
Okagesama de dóo ni ka yatte orimásu.	Not bad, thanks.

B. I'D LIKE YOU TO MEET . . .

Sákata-san o goshookai itashimásu.	Allow me to present Ms. Sakata. [May (I) introduce Ms. Sakata.]
Hajimemáshite.	Glad to meet you. [It is a pleasure to meet you.]
Sákata desu. Dóozo yoroshiku.	I am Sakata. Glad to meet you.
Dóozo yoroshiku.	Glad to meet you.

C. WHAT'S NEW?

Konnichi wá.	Hello.
Ogénki desu ka?	How are you?
Okage sama de.	Fine, thanks.
Kawatta kotó wa arimasén ka?	What's new?
Betsu ni arimasén.	Nothing much. [There isn't anything especially.]
Nisánnichi shitára denwa o kákete kudasái.	Call me one of these days, please.
Wasurenáide kudasái.	Please don't forget.
Kashikomarimáshita.	I'll certainly do so.
Daijóobu desu ne?	Are you sure? You're sure?
Daijóobu desu.	Sure!

D. SEE YOU SOON!

Déwa mata.	See you soon. [Well, then, again.]
Getsuyóobi ni ome ni kakarimásu.	See you on Monday.
Isshúukan shitára ome ni kakarimásu.	I'll see you in a week.
Nishúukan shitára ome ni kakarimásu.	I'll see you in two weeks.
Kin'yóobi no yóru ome ni kakarimásu.	I'll see you Friday night.
Kono Mokuyóobi ni ome ni kakarimásu.	I'll see you this coming Thursday.

**Kono Mokuyóobi no
ban hachíji ni ome
ni kakarimásu.**

I'll see you this coming
Thursday at eight
o'clock in the even-
ing. [This coming
Thursday evening at
eight o'clock (I'll)
see you.]

**Kón'ya ome ni kaka-
rimásu.**

I'll see you tonight.

QUIZ 15

1. *Ogénki desu ka?*
2. *Ashita ome ni
kakarimásu.*
3. *Dóozo yoroshiku.*
4. *Kawatta kotó wa
arimasén ka?*
5. *Mokuyóobi ni ome
ni kakarimásu.*
6. *Okagesama de.*
7. *Betsu ni arimasén.*
8. *Konnichi wá.*
9. *Dóo ni ka yatte
orimásu.*
10. *Betsu ni kawari
arimasén.*
11. *Isshúukan shitára
ome ni kakarimásu.*
12. *Nisánnichi shitára
denwa o kákete
kudasái.*
13. *Déwa mata.*

a. So so.
b. Very well, thanks.
c. Not too bad.
d. How are you?
e. I'll see you tomor-
row.
f. I'm happy to know
you.
g. What's new?
h. I'll see you on
Thursday.
i. Good afternoon.
Hello.
j. Nothing much.
k. Allow me ... (I
would like to intro-
duce ...)
l. Call me one of
these days, please.
m. See you Monday.

14. *Goshookai itashi-*   n. See you soon.
   másu.
15. *Getsuyóobi ni ome*   o. See you in a week.
   ni kakarimásu.

ANSWERS
1–d; 2–e; 3–f; 4–g; 5–h; 6–b; 7–j; 8–i; 9–c; 10–a;
11–o; 12–l; 13–n; 14–k; 15–m.

LESSON 20

DÁI NÍJIKKA

A. HAVE YOU TWO MET?

Kono katá o gozónji desu ka?	Do you know my friend [this person]?
Iie, kyoo hajímete ome ni kakarimásu.	No, I don't think so. [Am meeting him for the first time today.]
Iie, kore máde ome ni kakátta kotó wa arimasén.	No, I haven't had the pleasure of meeting [this person].
Máe kara gozónji desu ne?	I believe you already know one another.
Hái, máe kara zonjiágete orimásu.	Yes, we've already met. [Have known him from before.]
Iie, zonjiágete orimasén.	No, I don't believe we've met before. [No, (I) don't know (the gentleman.)]

B. GLAD TO HAVE MET YOU

Hajimemashite.	Glad to meet you. [It's a pleasure to meet you.]
Ome ni kakárete yókatta desu.	Glad to have met you. [Has been good fortune (for me) to have been able to see you.]
Mata zéhi oai shitái to omoimásu.	Hope to see you soon.
Dóozo yoroshiku.	Same here.
Moo ichido sono uchi ni hi o kimete oai shimashóo.	Let's get together again one of these days.
Arígatoo gozaimásu.	Fine. [Thank you.]
Watakushi no júusho to denwa bángoo wa omochi deshóo ka?	Do you have my address and telephone number?
Iie, mótte orimasén.	No, I don't.
Itadakemásu ka?	Let me have it. [Can I have it?]
Banchi wa Bunkyóo-ku Oiwaké-chóo[1] ni-choome[2] juugo bánchi desu.	My address is 15 2-choome, Oiwake-choo, Bunkyo-ku.

[1] *Chóo* is a word for "street" or "block," and is sometimes added to the name proper, as in *Oiwaké-choa.*
[2] *Choome* is a word for "street." *Me* in "*choome*" signifies that the street is an ordinal (e.g., *Ginza yon choome* = Ginza Fourth Street).

Denwa bángoo wa san yón hachi sán no roku yón roku sán ban desu.	My telephone number is 3483-6463.
Jimúsho no banchi mo itadakemásu ka?	Give me your office address, too. [Can I have . . .]
Okaki shimashóo. Ginza yon choome no ni bánchi desu.	I'll write it for you. It's 2 Ginza Fourth Street.
Ása wa kuji máe deshitara uchi ni orimásu.	You can get me at home before nine in the morning. [If it is before nine (I'll) be at home.]
Sono áto wa jimúsho no hóo ni orimásu.	Otherwise [afterward] at the office.
Aa sóo desu ka. Déwa, táshika ni gorenraku shimásu.	Good. I'll be sure to get in touch with you.
Déwa shitsúrei shimásu. Odénwa o omachi shite orimásu.	Good-bye. [And] (I) shall be waiting for your phone call.
Déwa mata.	See you soon.

QUIZ 16

1. *Iie, kyoo hajímete ome ni kakarimásu.*	a. Yes, we've already met.
2. *Hái, máe kara zonjiágete orimásu.*	b. No, I haven't had the pleasure of meeting (this person).
3. *Iie, mótte orimasén. Itadakemásu ka?*	c. No, not yet. [I am meeting him for the first time today.]

4. *Jimúsho no banchi mo itadakemásu ka?*

d. Glad to have met you.

5. *Déwa mata.*

e. I hope to see you soon.

6. *Aa sóo desu ka. Déwa táshika ni gorenraku shimásu.*

f. Give me your office address, too.

7. *Watakushi no júusho to denwa bángoo wa omochi deshóo ka?*

g. No, let me have it.

8. *Iie, ome ni kakátta kotó wa arimasén.*

h. Do you have my address and telephone number?

9. *Mata zéhi oai shitái to omoimásu.*

i. Good. I will be sure to get in touch with you.

10. *Ome ni kakárete yókatta desu.*

j. See you soon.

ANSWERS

1–c; 2–a; 3–g; 4–f; 5–j; 6–i; 7–h; 8–b; 9–e; 10–d.

C. WORD STUDY

baiorin	violin
furúuto	flute
gítaa	guitar
háapu	harp
kurarinétto	clarinet
mandorin	mandolin
paipu órugan	pipe organ
piano	piano
sakísofon	saxophone
chéro	cello

REVIEW QUIZ 2

1. *Dóozo moo sukóshi yukkúri* _____ (speak) *ku-dasaimásen ka?*
   a. *káite*
   b. *hanáshite*
   c. *kákete*

2. *Dóozo* _____ (slowly) *hanáshite kudasái.*
   a. *hakkíri*
   b. *yóku*
   c. *yukkúri*

3. *Kodomo* _____ (direction-particle) *hón o yari-máshita.*
   a. *ga*
   b. *ni*
   c. *no*

4. *Yamada-san ni tegami* _____ (object-particle) *kakimáshita.*
   a. *o*
   b. *ga*
   c. *no*

5. *Sonna ni* _____ (far) *arimasén.*
   a. *tooku*
   b. *chikaku*
   c. *tákaku*

6. *Anó hito* _____ (topic-particle) *kodomo ni okane o yarimáshita.*
   a. *o*
   b. *wa*
   c. *to*

7. *Watakushi wa jimúsho ni* _____ (am).
    a. *désu.*
    b. *imásu.*
    c. *arimásu.*

8. _____ (Late) *kimáshita.*
    a. *Háyaku*
    b. *Tooku*
    c. *Osoku*

9. *Sono hón wa dóko ni* _____ (is) *ka?*
    a. *imásu*
    b. *arimásu*
    c. *désu*

10. *Koppu o* _____ (bring) *kudasái.*
    a. *katte*
    b. *tótte*
    c. *mótte kite*

11. *Sore wa* _____ (easy) *desu.*
    a. *yasashíi*
    b. *muzukashíi*
    c. *ookíi*

12. *Kodomo no* _____ (room) *desu.*
    a. *monó*
    b. *heyá*
    c. *hón*

13. *Okane ga* _____ (there isn't).
    a. *arimasén.*
    b. *imasén.*
    c. *kimasén.*

14. *Tabako o* _____ (have) *imásu ka?*
    a. *míte*

    b. *káite*
    c. *mótte*

15. *Nihongo wa yóku* _____ (don't understand).
    a. *wakarimasén.*
    b. *kakemasén.*
    c. *shimasén.*

16. *Dóo mo* _____ (thank) *gozaimásu.*
    a. *osamuu*
    b. *arígatoo*
    c. *otakoo*

17. _____ (Here) *ni imásu ka?*
    a. *Dóko*
    b. *Soko*
    c. *Koko*

18. _____ (Letter) *wa dekimáshita ka?*
    a. *Tegami*
    b. *Shitaku*
    c. *Benkyoo*

19. *Sore wa* _____ (yesterday) *deshita ka?*
    a. *kón'ya*
    b. *hontoo*
    c. *kinóo*

20. _____ (A little) *wakarimásu.*
    a. *Yóku*
    b. *Takusan*
    c. *Sukóshi*

ANSWERS
1–b; 2–c; 3–b; 4–a; 5–a; 6–b; 7–b; 8–c; 9–b; 10–c;
11–a; 12–b; 13–a; 14–c; 15–a; 16–b; 17–c; 18–a;
19–c; 20–c.

LESSON 21

DÁI NÍJUU ÍKKA

A. NUMBERS

1. One, Two, Three
   For one to ten only, there are two sets of numbers.

ichí	one
ní	two
san	three
shí, yón	four
gó	five
rokú	six
shichí, nána	seven
hachí	eight
kú, kyúu	nine
júu	ten

hitótsu	one
futatsu	two
mittsú	three
yottsú	four
itsútsu	five
muttsú	six
nanátsu	seven
yattsú	eight
kokónotsu	nine
tóo	ten

juuichí	eleven
juuní	twelve
júusan	thirteen

juushí, juuyón	fourteen
júugo	fifteen
juurokú	sixteen
juushichí, juunána	seventeen
juuhachí	eighteen
júuku	nineteen
níjuu	twenty
níjuu ichí	twenty-one
níjuu ní	twenty-two
níjuu san	twenty-three
sánjuu	thirty
sánjuu ichí	thirty-one
sánjuu ní	thirty-two
sánjuu san	thirty-three
yónjuu, shijúu	forty
yónjuu ichí	forty-one
yónjuu ní	forty-two
yónjuu san	forty-three
gojúu	fifty
gojuu ichí	fifty-one
gojuu ní	fifty-two
gojuu san	fifty-three
rokujúu	sixty
rokujuu ichí	sixty-one
rokujuu ní	sixty-two
rokujuu san	sixty-three
nanájuu, shichijúu	seventy
nanájuu ichí	seventy-one
nanájuu ní	seventy-two
nanájuu san	seventy-three
hachijúu	eighty
hachijuu ichí	eighty-one
hachijuu ní	eighty-two
hachijuu san	eighty-three

kyúujuu	ninety
kyúujuu ichí	ninety-one
kyúujuu ní	ninety-two
kyúujuu san	ninety-three

B. MORE NUMBERS

hyakú	one hundred
hyaku ichí	one hundred and one
hyaku ní	one hundred and two
hyaku san	one hundred and three
hyaku níjuu	one hundred and twenty
hyaku níjuu ichí	one hundred and twenty-one
hyaku sánjuu	one hundred and thirty
hyaku yónjuu, hyaku shijúu	one hundred and forty
hyaku gojúu	one hundred and fifty
hyaku rokujúu	one hundred and sixty
hyaku nanájúu	one hundred and seventy
hyaku nanájuu ichí	one hundred and seventy-one
hyaku hachijúu	one hundred and eighty
hyaku kyúujuu	one hundred and ninety
hyaku kyúujuu hachí	one hundred and ninety-eight
hyaku kyúujuu kú	one hundred and ninety-nine
nihyaku	two hundred
sánbyaku[1]níjuu shí	three hundred and twenty-four

[1] Notice the *b* in *sánbyaku*, the *p* in *happyaku* (page 119), and the *z* in *sanzén* (page 119). See Section 4 of the Summary of Japanese Grammar.

happyaku nanájuu gó	eight hundred and seventy-five
sén	one thousand
sén ichí	one thousand and one
sén ní	one thousand and two
sén san	one thousand and three
ichi mán	ten thousand
juu mán	one hundred thousand
hyaku mán	one million
sanzén sánbyaku sán- juu san	three thousand three hundred and thirty-three

C. PRONUNCIATION OF NUMBERS BEFORE CERTAIN COUNTERS

The pronunciation of numbers often differs before "counters" beginning with certain consonants. "Counters" are words like "sheet" in "ten sheets of paper" or "cup" in "ten cups of water." Most things have to be counted with a counter in Japanese.

Before a counter beginning with *h, f, k, s, sh, t, chi,* or *ts,* the pronunciation of the *ichí* [one], *hachí* [eight], and *júu* [ten] usually changes. When a counter begins with *h* or *f,* the *h* or *f* changes to *p.* Before a counter beginning with *h, f,* or *k,* the numbers *rokú* [six] and *hyakú* [one hundred] also change form. Following are some examples of these changes in form:

COUNTER: *-FUN*	MINUTE
ichí, íppun	one, one minute
rokú, róppun	six, six minutes

hachí, háppun (or) **hachífun**	eight, eight minutes
júu, júppun (or) **jíppun**	ten, ten minutes
hyaku, hyáppun	one hundred, one hundred minutes

COUNTER: *-KEN*	HOUSE
ichí, íkken	one, one house
rokú, rókken	six, six houses
hachí, hákken (or) **hachíken**	eight, eight houses
júu, júkken (or) **jíkken**	ten, ten houses
hyakú, hyákken	one hundred, one hundred houses

COUNTER: *-SATSU*	VOLUME
ichí, issatsu	one, one volume
hachí, hassatsu	eight, eight volumes
júu, jussatsu (or) **jissatsu**	ten, ten volumes

COUNTER: *-TEN*	POINT
ichí, ittén	one, one point
hachí, hattén	eight, eight points
júu, juttén (or) **jittén**	ten, ten points

D. First, Second, Third

dái ichí[1]	first
dái ní	second
dái san	third
dái yón	fourth

[1] When *dái* precedes a numeral, it shows that the number which follows is an ordinal. Occasionally, an ordinal is used without *dái*.

dái gó	fifth
dái rokú	sixth
dái nána	seventh
dái hachí	eighth
dái kyúu	ninth
dái júu	tenth
Dái Ichíji Taisen	World War I
dái ní maku	the second act
sán too	the third class
yón kai	the fourth floor
dái gó ka	the fifth lesson
dái rokkái	the sixth time
dái naná shuu	the seventh week
hachikagetsume[1]	the eighth month
dái kyuu nen	the ninth year
dái júu	the tenth
juuichi ninmé no hito	the eleventh person
dái juuní shoo	the twelfth chapter
juusan nichimé	the thirteenth day
juuyon séiki	the fourteenth century
juugo kenmé no uchi	the fifteenth door, the fifteenth house
juuroku banmé no fúne	the sixteenth boat
juushichi choome *juunana choome* }	the seventeenth street
dái juuháppan	the eighteenth edition
juuku banmé no kuruma	the nineteenth car
nijikkenmé no ié	the twentieth house

QUIZ 17

1. *rókkiro*
2. *yón kai*
3. *jíppun*

a. the third class
b. the eighth month
c. the ninth year

---

[1] *-me* is another way to indicate an ordinal number.

4. *sántoo*	d. six kilometers
5. *juuyon séiki*	e. the fourth floor
6. *juuichi ninmé no hito*	f. ten minutes
7. *dái gó ka*	g. the eleventh person
8. *hachikagetsumé*	h. the thirteenth day
9. *juusan nichimé*	i. the fifth lesson
10. *dái kyúunen*	j. the fourteenth century

ANSWERS
1–d; 2–e; 3–f; 4–a; 5–j; 6–g; 7–i; 8–b; 9–h; 10–c.

E. TWO AND TWO

Ichí to ní de san ni narimásu. — Two and one are [become] three.

Ní tasu ichí wa san désu. — Two and [plus] one are three.

Ní to ní wa yón desu. — Two and two are four.

Ní tasu ní wa yón desu. — Two and [plus] two are four.

Yón to san wa shichí desu. — Four and three are seven.

Yón tasu san wa shichí desu. — Four and [plus] three are seven.

Gó to ní de shichí ni narimásu. — Five and two are [become] seven.

Gó tasu ní wa shichí desu. — Five and [plus] two are seven.

Shichí to ichí de hachí ni narimásu. — Seven and one are [become] eight.

Shichí tasu ichí wa hachí desu. — Seven and [plus] one are eight.

LESSON 22

DÁI NÍJUU NÍKA

A. IT COSTS . . .

Kore wa . . . shimásu.	This costs . . .
Kore wa gosen en shimásu.	This costs five thousand yen.
Kono nóoto wa gohyaku gojúu en shimásu.	This notebook costs five hundred fifty yen.
Kono booshi wa gosen en shimáshita.	This hat cost me five thousand yen.
Kono dóresuni ichi mán gosen en haraimáshita.	I paid fifteen thousand yen for this dress.
Kono kuruma o sanbyakumán en de kaimáshita.	I bought this car for three million yen.
Ichi ríttoru nisén en desu.	It's two thousand yen a liter.
Ichi meetoru nihyaku gojúu en desu.	That costs two hundred fifty yen a meter.
Sén nihyakú en shimásu.	The price is twelve hundred yen. It costs twelve hundred yen.
Hitótsu gojúu en desu.	They cost fifty yen a piece.

B. THE TELEPHONE NUMBER IS . . .

Watakushi no denwa bángoo wa san yón hachi sán no san róku yon hachí ban desu.	My telephone number is 3483-3648.

San sán san yón no goo níi[1] **san rokú ban ni kákete míte kudasai.**	Try number 3334-5236.
Denwa bángoo ga kawarimáshita. Íma no wa san níi roku yón no nii níi nii yón ban desu.	My telephone number has been changed; it's now 3264-2224.
Denwa wa san kyúu nii níi no san sán rei naná ban desu.	Their phone number is 3922-3307.

C. MY ADDRESS IS . . .

Yoyogi ni-choome juunana bánchi ni súnde imasu.	I live at 17, 12-chome (street), Yoyogi.
Yamada-san wa dóko ni súnde imásu ka?	Where does Mr. Yamada live? [Where is Mr. Yamada residing?]
Kono machí ni súnde imasu.	He lives in this town.
Asakusa san-choome yon bánchi ni súnde imasu.	She lives at 4, 3-chome, Asakusa.
Ikebúkuro yon-choome juuni bánchi desu.	Our address is 12, 4-chome, Ikebukuro.
Ogikubo go-choome nihyaku rokujuu san bánchi ni súnde imasu.	We live at 263, 5-chome, Ogikubo.

---

[1] When giving phone numbers, numerals with one syllable can be pronounced with long vowels: *goo* and *níi*.

**Heya no bangóo wa
yónjuu ní desu.**

My room number is
42.

D. SOME DATES

**Amerika wa sén yón-
hyaku kyúujuu ní
nen ni hakken sare-
máshita.**

America was discov-
ered in 1492.

**Sén happyaku kyúu-
juu ichí nen ni oko-
rimáshita.**

It happened in 1891.

*Sén kyúuhyaku juuní
nen ni umaremásh-
ita.*

I was born in 1912.

*Nyuu Yóoku no Sekai
hakuránkai wa sén
kyúuhyaku sánjuu
kyúu nen ni arimásh-
ita.*

The New York World's
Fair took place in
1939.

*Kore wa mina sén
kyúuhyaku
hachijúu ni
okorimáshita.*

All this happened in
1980.

*Watakushi wa sen
kyúuhyaku kyúujuu
nen ni wa Tookyoo
ni imáshita.*

I was in Tokyo in
1990.

QUIZ 18

1. *Kore wa gosen en
shimásu.*

2. *Denwa bángoo wa
san nána nii kyúu
no san sán rei nana
ban desu.*

a. This costs five thou-
sand yen.

b. I bought this car for
five million yen.

3. *Kono kuruma o go-*
   hyakumán en de
   kaimáshita.

4. *Watakushi wa sén*
   kyúuhyaku kyúujuu
   nen ni Tookyoo ni
   imáshita.

5. *Sore wa hitótsu*
   gojúu en desu.

c. Their phone number
   is 3729-3307.

d. They cost fifty yen
   apiece.

e. I was in Tokyo in
   1990.

ANSWERS
1–a; 2–c; 3–b; 4–e; 5–d.

LESSON 23

DÁI NÍJUU SÁNKA

A. WHAT TIME IS IT?

Nánji desu ka?	What time is it?
Nánji ka oshiete ku- **dasaimasén ka?**	Do you have the time, please?
Ichíji desu.	It's one o'clock.
Níji desu.	It's two o'clock.
Sánji desu.	It's three o'clock.
Yóji desu.	It's four o'clock.
Góji desu.	It's five o'clock.
Rokúji desu.	It's six o'clock.
Shichíji desu.	It's seven o'clock.
Hachíji desu.	It's eight o'clock.
Kúji desu.	It's nine o'clock.
Júuji desu.	It's ten o'clock.
Juuichíji desu.	It's eleven o'clock.
Juuníji desu.	It's noon. It's twelve o'clock.

Gógo ichíji desu.	It's 1:00 p.m.
Gógo níji desu.	It's 2:00 p.m.
Gógo sánji desu.	It's 3:00 p.m.
Gógo yóji desu.	It's 4:00 p.m.
Gógo góji desu.	It's 5:00 p.m.
Gógo rokúji desu.	It's 6:00 p.m.
Gógo shichíji desu.	It's 7:00 p.m.
Gógo hachíji desu.	It's 8:00 p.m.
Gógo kúji desu.	It's 9:00 p.m.
Gógo júuji desu.	It's 10:00 p.m.
Gógo juuichíji desu.	It's 11:00 p.m.
Gógo juuníji desu.	It's 12:00 p.m.
Yóru no juuníji desu.	It's midnight.

B. THE TIME IS NOW . . .

byóo	second
fún, pún	minute
ji	hour
Níji júu gófun desu.	It's two fifteen.
Níji juu gofún sugí desu.	It's a quarter after two.
Níji juu gofún máe desu.	It's a quarter to two.
Sánji yónjuu gófun desu.	It's three forty-five.
Niji-hán desu.	It's half-past two.
Níji sánjippun desu.	It's two thirty.
Góji nijippun máe desu.	It's twenty to five.
Kúji sánjuu gófun desu.	It's nine thirty-five.
Shóogo desu.	It's noon.
Juuníji gofún máe desu.	It's five to twelve.

Juuníji gofún sugí desu.	It's five past twelve.
Gózen ichíji desu.	It's one o'clock in the morning.
Goji góro desu.	It's about five.
Shichiji góro desu.	It's about seven.
Juuichíji sukóshi máe desu.	It's almost eleven.
Máda rokuji-hán desu.	It's only half-past six.
Goji sugí desu.	It's after five.

C. WHEN WILL YOU COME?

Ítsu oide ni narimásu ka?	When will you come (*respect*)? What time will you come?
Sánji ni soko e iki-másu.	I'll be there at three o'clock.
Sánji nijuppún máe ni kimáshita.	She came at twenty to three.
Gógo níji ni kimásu.	He'll come at 2:00 p.m.
Kúji níjuu gofun góro ni soko e ikimásu.	We'll be there about nine twenty-five.
Kónban no juuji-hán ni káette kimásu.	He'll be back at ten thirty this evening.
Hachíji juu gofun góro ni soko de ome ni kakari-mashóo.	I'll see you there about eight fifteen.
Rokúji ni aimásu.	We'll meet at six.
Yóji ni dekakemásu.	I'm going out at four o'clock.

Shichíji to hachíji no aida ni kité kudasái.	Come between seven and eight, please.
Yóru no rokúji ni kimásu.	He'll come at six in the evening.
Kónban júuji ni kité kudasái.	Come at ten o'clock tonight, please.
Densha wa shichíji níjuu sánpun ni tsukimásu.	The train arrives at seven twenty-three.
Densha wa kúji yónjippun ni demásu.	The train leaves at nine forty.

D. IT'S TIME

Jikan désu.	It's time.
Sore o suru jikan désu.	It's time to do it. [(It) is to-do-it time.]
Déru jikan désu.	It's time to leave.
Uchi e káeru jikan désu.	It's time to go home.
Jikan ga arimásu.	I have time.
Juubún jikan ga arimásu.	I have enough time.
Jikan ga arimasén.	I don't have the time.
Dono kurai nágaku soko ni iru tsumori désu ka?	How long do you intend to stay here?
Dono kurai nágaku koko ni imáshita ka?	How long have you been here?
Jikan no muda o shite imásu.	He's wasting his time.
Suru jikan o agete kudasái.	Give her time to do it, please.

Kimono o kikaéru aida dake mátte kudasái.

Just give me enough time to change my clothes. [Please wait just for the duration that I am changing clothes.]

Tokidoki kimásu.

He comes from time to time.

QUIZ 19

1. *Niji-hán desu.*
2. *Níji júu gófun desu.*
3. *Jikan désu.*
4. *Jikan no muda o shite imásu.*
5. *Soko de hachíji juu gofun góro ni ome ni kakarimásu.*
6. *Densha wa shichíji níjuu sánpun ni tsukimásu.*
7. *Kónban júuji ni kité kudasái.*
8. *Gózen ichíji desu.*
9. *Kúji níjuu gofun góro ni soko e ikimásu.*
10. *Níji ni kimásu.*

a. I'll see you there about eight fifteen.
b. The train arrives at seven twenty-three.
c. He's wasting his time.
d. Come at ten o'clock this evening, please.
e. It's one o'clock in the morning.
f. He'll come at 2:00.
g. We'll be there about nine twenty-five.
h. It's two fifteen. It's a quarter after two.
i. It's half-past two. It's two thirty.
j. It's time.

ANSWERS
1–i; 2–h; 3–j; 4–c; 5–a; 6–b; 7–d; 8–e; 9–g; 10–f.

E. WORD STUDY

anpaia	umpire
baaténdaa	bartender
dezáinaa	designer
konsárutant	consultant
enjínia	engineer
manéejaa	manager
sararíiman	salaried man
seerusúman	salesman
supónsaa	sponsor
taipísuto	typist

LESSON 24

DÁI NÍJUU YÓNKA

A. AGO

máe	ago
ichijíkan máe	an hour ago
nijíkan máe	two hours ago
sanjíkan máe	three hours ago
ichinichi máe	a day ago
futsuka máe	two days ago
sanshúukan máe	three weeks ago
gokágetsu máe	five months ago
gonen máe	five years ago
júunen máe	ten years ago
zutto máe	a long time ago
kánari máe	a rather long time ago, quite a long time ago
sukóshi máe	a short time ago

B. MORNING, NOON, AND NIGHT

ása	morning
hirú \ shóogo ∫	noon
gógo	afternoon
ban	evening
yóru	night
hi	the day
shúu	the week
isshúukan	a week
nishúukan	two weeks
tsukí	month
toshí	year
kinóo	yesterday
kyóo	today
ashita	tomorrow
ototói	the day before yesterday
tsugí no hi	the next day
asátte	the day after tomorrow
íma	now
súgu	in a moment, soon
késa	this morning
kinoo no ása	yesterday morning
ashita no ása	tomorrow morning
kyóo no gógo	this afternoon [today's afternoon]
kinoo no gógo	yesterday afternoon
ashita no gógo	tomorrow afternoon
kónban	this evening, tonight
kinoo no ban \ sakúban ∫	yesterday evening
ashita no ban	tomorrow evening

kinoo no yóru ⎫ sakúya ⎬ yuube ⎭	last night
ashita no yóru	tomorrow night

C. This Week, Next Month, etc.

konshuu	this week
senshuu	last week
raishuu	next week
saraishuu	in two weeks, the week after next
kongetsu	this month
séngetsu	last month
ráigetsu	next month
saraigetsu	the month after next
senséngetsu	two months ago, the month before last
kotoshi	this year
kyónen ⎫ sakunen ⎭	last year
rainen	next year
sarainen	in two years, the year after next
issakunen ⎫ otótoshi ⎭	the year before last
ása	in the morning
ban	in the evening
hiru góro	around noon
yuushokugo	after dinner (the evening meal)
shuumatsu	at the end of the week
getsumatsu	at the end of the month
konshuu no owari góro ni	toward the end of the week
ichijíkan máe	an hour ago

juu gohun ínai ni	in a quarter of an hour
sono uchi ni	one of these days
Sono uchi ni ome ni kakarimásu.	See you one of these days.
máinichi	everyday
ichinichi juu	all day (long)
hitoban juu	all night (long)
Ása kara ban máde hatarakimásu.	He works from morning to night.
Kyóo wa nánnichi desu ka?	What's the date?

D. EXPRESSIONS OF PAST, PRESENT, AND FUTURE

PAST	PRESENT	FUTURE
tsúi sákki a moment ago	**íma** now	**súgu ato de** in a moment
kinoo no asa yesterday morning	**késa** this morning	**ashita no ása** tomorrow morning
kinoo no gógo yesterday afternoon	**kyóo no gógo** this afternoon	**ashita no gógo** tomorrow afternoon
sakúban yesterday evening	**kónban** this evening	**ashita no ban** tomorrow evening
sakúya last night	**kón'ya** tonight	**ashita no yóru** tomorrow night
senshuu last week	**konshuu** this week	**raishuu** next week
séngetsu last month	**kongetsu** this month	**ráigetsu** next month
sakunen last year	**kotoshi** this year	**rainen** next year

LESSON 25

DÁI NÍJUU GÓKA

A. DAYS OF THE WEEK

Getsuyóobi	Monday
Kayóobi	Tuesday
Suiyóobi	Wednesday
Mokuyóobi	Thursday
Kin'yóobi	Friday
Doyóobi	Saturday
Nichiyóobi	Sunday

B. DAYS OF THE MONTH

In Japanese, each day of the month has a name, and these, except for the word for the first day, are also used to count the *number* of days.[1] For example, *futsuka*, ''second day,'' can also mean ''two days''; whereas, to count ''one day,'' you say *ichinichi*.

tsuitachí	first day (of the month)
futsuka	second day
mikka	third day
yokka	fourth day
itsuka	fifth day
muika	sixth day
nanoka, nanuka	seventh day
yooka	eighth day
kokonoka	ninth day
tooka	tenth day

---

[1] For counters, see Section 11 of the Summary of Japanese Grammar.

juuichinichí	eleventh day
juuninichí	twelfth day
juusánnichi	thirteenth day
júuyokka	fourteenth day
juugónichi	fifteenth day
juurokunichí	sixteenth day
juushichinichí	seventeenth day
juuhachinichí	eighteenth day
juukúnichi	nineteenth day
hatsuka	twentieth day
níjuu ichinichí	twenty-first day
níjuu ninichí	twenty-second day
níjuu sánnichi	twenty-third day
níjuu yokka	twenty-fourth day
níjuu gónichi	twenty-fifth day
níjuu rokunichí	twenty-sixth day
níjuu shichinichí	twenty-seventh day
níjuu hachinichi	twenty-eighth day
níjuu kúnichi	twenty-ninth day
sanjúunichi	thirtieth day
sánjuuichinichí	thirty-first day

C. WHAT'S THE DATE TODAY?

Kyóo wa nánnichi desu ka?	What's the date today?
Doyóobi wa nánnichi desu ka?	What will be the date Saturday? [As for Saturday, what is the date?]
Kyóo wa tooka désu.	Today's the tenth.
Kyóo wa hatsuka désu.	Today's the twentieth.

Kyóo wa Kayóobi desu ka Suiyóobi desu ka?

Is today Tuesday or Wednesday?

Kyóo wa Suiyóobi desu.

Today's Wednesday.

Kyóo wa Getsuyóobi desu.

Today's Monday.

Raishuu no Doyóobi ni kité kudasái.

Come next Saturday, please.

Raishuu no Kayóobi ni tachimásu.

She's leaving next Tuesday.

Senshuu no Getsuyóobi ni tsukimáshita.

She arrived last Monday. [She arrived last week's Monday.]

Raishuu no Getsuyóobi ni tsukimásu.

She's arriving next Monday.

Soko ni mikka imáshita.

I was there three days.

Soko ni ichinichí shika imasén deshita.

I was there only one day. [(I) wasn't there any more than one day.]

QUIZ 20

1. *ototói*
2. *kyóo*

3. *gógo*
4. *tsúi sákki*
5. *ashita no gógo*
6. *kyóo no gógo*
7. *asátte*
8. *Jikan o muda ni shite imásu.*

a. afternoon
b. day before yesterday
c. today
d. day after tomorrow
e. a moment ago
f. tomorrow afternoon
g. all night long
h. He's wasting his time.

9. *hitoban juu*	i. this afternoon
10. *Dono kurai nágaku koko ni imáshita ka?*	j. How long have you been here?
11. *raishuu*	k. the month after next
12. *senshuu*	l. the week before last
13. *sensénshuu*	m. next week
14. *saraigetsu*	n. the year before last
15. *otótoshi*	o. last week
16. *Jikan désu*	p. It's time to go home.
17. *Jikan ga arimásu.*	q. tomorrow night
18. *Uchi e káeru jikan désu.*	r. this evening
19. *ashita no yóru*	s. It's time.
20. *kónban*	t. I have time.

ANSWERS
1–b; 2–c; 3–a; 4–e; 5–f; 6–i; 7–d; 8–h; 9–g; 10–j; 11–m; 12–o; 13–l; 14–k; 15–n; 16–s; 17–t; 18–p; 19–q; 20–r.

D. Months of the Year

Ichigatsu	January
Nigatsu	February
Sángatsu	March
Shigatsu	April
Gógatsu	May
Rokugatsu	June
Shichigatsu	July
Hachigatsu	August

Kúgatsu	September
Juugatsu	October
Juuichigatsu	November
Juuinigatsu	December

Kyoo wa Rokugatsu tsuitachí desu.
Today is the first of June.

Watakushi wa Shigatsu juuninichí ni umaremáshita.
I was born on April twelfth.

Imootó wa Gógatsu itsuka ni umaremáshita.
My sister was born on May fifth.

Watakushi no tanjóobi wa Nigatsu futsuka désu.
My birthday is February second.

Shichigatsu júuyokka ni kimásu.
I'll come on the fourteenth of July.

Gakkoo wa Kúgatsu hatsuka ni hajimarimásu.
School begins on the twentieth of September.

Sángatsu níjuu ninichí ni kaerimásu.
I'll be back on March twenty-second.

Juuichigatsu juuichinichí wa yasumí desu.
November eleventh is a holiday.

Shichigatsu mikka ni tachimásu.
She's leaving on July third.

Tegami wa Rokugatsu muika zuke désu.
The letter is dated June sixth.

Gógatsu juuichinichí ni otazune shimásu.
We'll come to see you on May eleventh.

Kyóo wa sén kyúuhyaku kyúujun nínen Gógatsu itsuka désu.
Today is May fifth, 1992.

E. THE SEASONS

háru	spring
natsú	summer
áki	autumn
fuyú	winter
fuyú ni	in winter
natsú ni	in summer
áki ni	in autumn, in fall
háru ni	in spring

QUIZ 21

1. *Kyóo wa nan'yóobi desu ka?*
2. *Sono uchi ni ome ni kakarimásu.*
3. *ichinichi juu*
4. *natsú ni.*
5. *júugo fun de*
6. *Raishuu no Getsuyóobi ni tsukimásu.*
7. *Kyóo wa Getsuyóobi desu.*
8. *Raishuu no Doyóobi ni kité kudasái.*
9. *fuyú*
10. *Nichiyóobi*
11. *Kyoo wa hatsuka désu.*
12. *Doyóobi wa nánnichi desu ka?*

a. Sunday
b. in a quarter of an hour
c. See you one of these days.
d. all day
e. What's today?
f. in the summer
g. winter
h. What's the date Saturday?
i. Today's the twentieth.
j. Today's Monday.
k. Come next Saturday, please.
l. He'll arrive next Monday.

13. *Shichigatsu no júuyokka ni kimásu.*

m. The letter is dated June sixth.

14. *Kyóo wa Rokugatsu no tsuitachí desu.*

n. I'll come on the fourteenth of July.

15. *Tegami wa Rokugatsu muika zuke désu.*

o. Today is the first of June.

ANSWERS

1–e; 2–c; 3–d; 4–f; 5–b; 6–l; 7–j; 8–k; 9–g; 10–a; 11–i; 12–h; 13–n; 14–o; 15–m.

LESSON 26

DÁI NÍJUU RÓKKA

A. *Iku* To Go[1]

1. I go, I don't go.

PLAIN	POLITE	
iku	**ikimásu**	I, you, we, they go; he, she goes[1]
itta	**ikimáshita**	I went
itte	**itte**	I go and ...
ikanai	**ikimasén**	I don't go
ikitái	**ikitái desu**	I wish to go
ikéba } **ittára** }		if I go

[1] Remember that in Japanese the same forms are used for first, second, and third persons in both the singular and plural.

ikanákereba } **ikanákattara** }		if I don't go
ittári[2]		sometimes I go
ikóo	**ikimashóo**	I think I'll go. Let's go.
iké		Go! (*sharp command*)

2. Study these phrases with forms of *iku*:

Kodomótachi wa dóko e ikimásu ka?	Where are the children going?
Doobutsúen e ikimásu.	They are going to the zoo.
Kinóo wa dóko e ikimáshita ka?	Where did you go yesterday?
Úmi e ikimáshita.	I went to the beach [sea].
Kono kishá wa dóko made ikimásu ka?	How far does this train go?
Kóobe máde ikimásu.	It goes as far as Kobe.

3. Some common expressions with *iku*:

Itte kudasái!	Please go!
Ikanáide kudasái.	Please don't go.
Yukkúri itte kudasái.	Go slowly, please.
Itte sagashite kudasái.	Go look for it, please. [Go and look for (it), please.]
Soko e ikanákereba narimasén.	We have to go there. [If (I) don't go, (it) won't do.]

---

[2] See footnote 1, page 141.

Itté wa ikemasén.	You must not go.
Ikanákute mo íi desu.	We don't have to go. [Even if (we) don't go (it) will be all right.]
Itté mo ikanákute mo íi desu.	It doesn't matter whether we go or not. [Even if (we) go, even if we don't go, (it) will be all right.]
Itté mo íi desu.	You may go. You have my permission to go. [Even if (you) go (it) will be all right.]
Ikitái desu ga iku kotó ga dekimasén.	I want to go but I can't [go].
Itta kotó ga arimásu.	I have been there.
Itta kotó wa arimasén.	I have never been there.
Iku kotó ga arimásu.	I sometimes go.

4. Verb particles with *iku*:

Soko e iku to[1] kau kotó ga dekimásu.	If you go there, you can buy (them).
Ashita ikú to[2] iimáshita.	I said I would go tomorrow.
Ittá keredomo[3] áu kotó ga dekimasén deshita.	I went, but couldn't meet her.

[1] *to* = if, when.
[2] *to* marks the end of a quote.
[3] *keredomo* = but.

Kinóo wa ikimáshita ga[1] kyóo wa ikimasén.

I went yesterday, but I am not going today.

Tákushii de ittá kara[2] ma ni aimáshita.

I went by taxi and so I was able to make it.

Tookyoo e itté kara[3] Kyooto e ikimáshita.

I went to Tokyo and then [after that] I went to Kyoto. After I went to Tokyo, I went to Kyoto.

Áme ga futtá node[4] ikimasén deshita.

It rained and so [because of that fact] I didn't go.

Hiroshima e ikimáshita shi[5] Nagásaki é mo ikimashita.

I went to Hiroshima and, in addition [not only that], I even went to Nagasaki.

Hanashinágara[6] ikimashóo.

Let's go as we talk.

Nichiyóobi ni wa Enoshima e ittári Hakone e ittári[7] shimásu.

On Sundays I sometimes go to Enoshima and sometimes [go] to Hakone.

---

[1] *ga* (particle) = but.

[2] *kara* (when it follows a sentence-ending form) = and so, and therefore, because of that.

[3] *kara* (when it follows a *-te* form) = and after that, and subsequently.

[4] *node* = and because of that fact, the situation being what it is.

[5] *shi* = and not only that, and in addition to that.

[6] *-nágara* = as, while (denotes simultaneous actions by the same subject).

[7] *-tári . . . -tári* when followed by *suru* = sometimes do A, sometimes do B; do such things as A and B.

B. A Few Action Phrases

Abunai!	Watch out! [(It) is dangerous!]
Ki o tsukéte kudasái!	Be careful! Pay attention!
Háyaku itte kudasái.	Please go fast.
Mótto háyaku itte kudasái.	Please go faster.
Sonna ni háyaku ikanáide kudasái.	Do not go so fast, please.
Anmari háyaku ikanáide kudasái.	Don't go too fast, please.
Mótto yukkúri itte kudasái.	Go slower, please.
Mótto háyaku kité kudasái.	Please come sooner.
Mótto osoku kité kudasái.	Please come later.
Isóide kudasái.	Please hurry up.
Isogánaide kudasái.	Please don't hurry.
Isóide imasu.	I'm in a hurry.
Isóide imasén.	I'm not in a hurry.
Dóozo goyukkúri.	Take your time.
Chótto mátte kudasái.	Just a minute!
Súgu mairimásu.[1]	I'm coming right away.

C. Word Study

bíiru	beer
júusu	juice
kákuteru	cocktail
kókoa	cocoa
koohíi	coffee

[1] *mairu* (humble verb) = come, go.

míruku	milk
shanpén	champagne
sóoda	soda
uísukii	whiskey
yoogúruto	yogurt

D. *Shinbun Uriba De*

Kyaku: **Japan Táimuzu o kudasái. Komakái okane o mótte inái n desu ga, sen en de tótte moraemásu ka?**

Ten'in: **Ashitá de kékkoo desu.**

Kyaku: **Démo kón'ya kuruma ka nan ka ni hikarete shinde shimattára dóo shimásu?**

Ten'in: **Kamaisén. Táishita kotó ja arimasén kara.**

At the Newstand

Customer: Give me the *Japan Times,* please. However, I don't have any small change. Can you give me change for one thousand yen?

Dealer: Pay me tomorrow.

Customer: But suppose I get run over by a car or something tonight?

Dealer: So what! It wouldn't be a great loss.

NOTE

tótte moraemásu ka = can I have you take it (from)?

Ashitá de kékkoo desu. = Tomorrow will do.

hikarete shinde shimattára: hikareru is a passive form of *hiku* [run over]; *shinde shimau* = (and) die [end up in death]; *-tára* = if, suppose.

kara = and so, and therefore (when used after a sentence-ending form of a verb or an adjective).

LESSON 27

DÁI NÍJUU NANÁKA

A. THEY SAY THAT . . .

-sóo desu	They say that . . . It's said that . . . People say that . . . I understand that . . . I hear . . .
Soko wa taihen kírei da sóo desu.[1]	They say that the place is very pretty.
Sore wa hontoo da sóo desu.	They say that it is true.
Yamada-san no piano wa taihen yókatta sóo desu.	People say that Mr. Yamada played the piano very well. [Talking about Mr. Yamada's piano (-playing), it was very good, so I hear.]
Tanaka-san wa kinoo Yokohama ni tsúita soo desu.	I understand that Ms. Tanaka arrived in Yokohama yesterday.
Tanaka-san wa kinoo kónakatta soo desu.	I understand that Ms. Tanaka did not come yesterday.
Tanaka-san wa íma Tookyoo ni inai sóo desu.	I hear that Ms. Tanaka is not in Tokyo now.

[1] Notice that the predicate appearing before *sóo desu* is in the plain form.

Takeda-san wa rainen Amerika e iku sóo desu.	I hear that Mr. Takeda will be going to America next year.

B. I HAVE TO, I MUST . . .

Góhan o tabéna-kereba narimasén.	I must eat [my meal].
Kisóku o yóku oboénakereba narimasén.	You have to remember the regulations well.
Isogánakereba narimasén.	I have to hurry.
Yukkúri arukánakereba narimasén.	You must walk slowly.
Nihongo de hanasá-nakereba narimasén.	You have to speak Japanese.
Nihón de kawanákereba narimasén.	I have to buy it in Japan.
Yamada-san ni awánakereba narimasén.	I have to see Mr. Yamada.
Yamada-san ni denwa o kakénakereba narimasén.	I have to telephone Mr. Yamada.
Keikan ni kikanákereba narimasén.	I have to ask a police-man.
Tookyoo e kuruma de ikanákereba narimasén deshita.	I had to go to Tokyo by car.

Éki de Yamada-san ni awánakereba narimasén deshita.

I had to see Mr. Yamada at the station.

Éki kara Yamada-san ni denwa o kakénakereba narimasén deshita.

I had to phone Mr. Yamada from the station.

Béru o narashite hito ga déte kuru no o matánakereba narimasén deshita.

I had to ring the bell and wait for someone to answer.

To ga shimátte itá node soko ni tátte mátte inákereba narimasén deshita.

The door was closed, so I had to stand there and wait.

Okane o mótte inákatta node karinákereba narimasén deshita.

I had no money, (and) so I had to borrow (some).

C. SOMETHING TO DRINK

Mizu ga hoshíi desu.

I want some water. [Water is wanted.]

Mizu ga hoshíi desu ka?

Do you want some water? [Is water wanted?]

Mizu wa hóshiku arimasén.

I don't want any water.

Ocha wa ikága desu ka?

How about some green tea?

Koohíi wa ikága desu ka?

How about some coffee?

Kuríimu wa ikága desu ka?

How about some cream?

Osatoo wa ikága desu ka?	How about some sugar?
Kuríimu wa dono kurai iremashóo ka?	How much cream shall I put in?
Osatoo wa dono kurai iremashóo ka?	How much sugar shall I put in?
Ocha wa dono kurai kaimashóo ka?	How much green tea shall I buy?
Koohíi wa dono kurai kaimashóo ka?	How much coffee shall I buy?
Dónna ocha o kaimashóo ka?	What sort of green tea shall we buy?
Dónna koohíi o kaimashóo ka?	What sort of coffee shall we buy?
Dóno koohíi o kaimashóo ka?	Which coffee shall we buy?
Dóno koohíi ga hoshíi desu ka?	Which coffee do you want?
Dónna koohíi ga sukí desu ka?	What sort of coffee do you like?
Dóno koohíi ga ichiban sukí desu ka?	Which coffee do you like best?
Dóno koohíi ga ichiban hoshíi desu ka?	Which coffee do you want most?

QUIZ 22

1. *Tookyoo e kuruma de ikanákereba narimasén deshita.*
2. *Ocha wa ikága desu ka?*
3. *Isogánakereba narimasén.*
4. *Yukkúri arukánakereba narimasén.*
5. *To ga shimátte itá node soko ni tátte mátte inákereba narimasén deshita.*
6. *Yamada-san ni denwa o kakénakereba narimasén.*

7. *Okane ga nákatta node karinákereba narimasén deshita.*
8. *Góhan o tabénakereba narimasén.*
9. *Keikan ni kikanákereba narimasén deshita.*
10. *Éki de Yamada-san ni awánakereba narimasén deshita.*

a. I have to hurry.
b. You have to walk slowly.
c. I had to go to Tokyo by car.
d. How about some green tea?
e. I have to phone Mr. Yamada.
f. The door was closed, so I had to stand there and wait.
g. I must eat.
h. I had no money, so I had to borrow some.
i. I had to see Mr. Yamada at the station.
j. I had to ask a policeman.

ANSWERS
1–c; 2–d; 3–a; 4–b; 5–f; 6–e; 7–h; 8–g; 9–j; 10–i.

D. WORD STUDY

fírutaa	filter
fóokasu	focus
fuirumu	film
furasshu ranpu	flash lamp
kámera	camera
néga	negative
rénzu	lens
serufu táimaa	self-timer
sháttaa	shutter
suraido	slide

LESSON 28

DÁI NÍJUU HACHÍKA

A. A LITTLE AND A LOT

Sukóshi.	A little.
Sukóshi desu ka takusán desu ka?	A lot or a little. [Is (it) a little or is (it) a lot?]
Honno sukóshi.	Just a little.
Sukoshi zútsu.	Little by little.
Moo sukóshi kudasái.	A little bit more. [Give (me) a little bit more.]
Sukóshi shika hana-shimasén.	He doesn't talk much. [(He) doesn't talk except a little.]
Sukóshi hoshíi desu ka takusan hoshíi desu ka?	Do you want a little or a lot of it?
Sukóshi koko de yasúnde ikimashóo.	Let's rest here a little and (then) go.
Sukóshi kudasái.	Give me a little of it, please.
Sukóshi mizu o kudasái.	Give me a little water, please.
Honno sukóshi daké desu.	It's only a very little bit.
Nihongo wa sukóshi shika dekimasén.	I speak very little Japanese. [(I) can't speak Japanese except a little.]
takusan	a lot, much
Okane wa takusan arimasén.	I don't have much money.

Jikan wa takusan arimasén.	I don't have much time.

B. Too Much

amari	too
amari takusan	too much
Amari takusán desu. **Amari oosugimásu.**	It's too much.
Amari takusan ja arimasén.	It's not too much.
Amari atsusugimásu.	It's too hot.
Amari samusugimásu.	It's too cold.
Amari mizu ga oosugimásu.	There is too much water.

C. More or Less

tashoo	more or less
óokute mo	at the most
sukunákute mo	at the least
mótto mótto	more and more
mótto mótto sukunáku	less and less
moo rokubai	six times more
mótto háyaku	earlier (*adv.*)
mótto osoku *mótto áto de*	later (*adv.*)
mótto átsuku	hotter
Mótto átsuku shite kudasái.	Please make it hotter.
mótto tákaku	more expensive
Mótto tákaku narimáshita.	It became more expensive.
Moo arimasén.	There is no more of it. There is no more of it left.

Sore íjoo desu.	It's more than that.
Sore íka desu.	It's less than that.
Ichiban omoshirói hón desu.	This is the most interesting book.
Anó hito wa oníisan yori sé ga takái desu.	He is taller than his older brother.
Watakushi hodo sé ga tákaku arimasén.	She isn't as tall as I.
Watakushi yóri hikúi desu.	She is shorter than I.

D. Enough and Some More

juubún	enough
Juubún desu ka?	Is it enough?
Juubún desu.	It's enough.
Juubún ja arimasén.	It's not enough.
Juubún ookíi desu.	It's large enough.
Okane wa juubún mótte imásu ka?	Do you have enough money?
mótto	some more
Mótto desu ka?	(Do you want) some more?
moo sukóshi	a little more
Mizu o moo íppai kudasái.	Give me another glass of water, please.
Pán o moo sukóshi kudasái.	Please give me some/a little more bread.
Nikú o moo sukóshi kudasái.	Please give me some/a little more meat.
mótto mótto	much more, lots more
Moo ichido kité kudasái.	Come again [visit us once more], please.
Moo ichido itte kudasái.	Say it again [once more], please.

Moo ichido kuri-
káeshite kudasái.

Please repeat it [Repeat
it once more . . .].

QUIZ 23

1. *Sukóshi hoshíi*
   desu ka takusan
   hoshíi desu ka?

a. I can speak little
   English.

2. *Eigo wa sukóshi*
   shika
   hanasemasén.

b. It became more ex-
   pensive.

3. *Amari atsusugi-*
   másu.

c. She is not as tall
   as I.

4. *Amari mizu ga*
   oosugimásu.

d. He doesn't talk
   much.

5. *Mótto tákaku nari-*
   máshita.

e. I don't have much
   money.

6. *Watakushi hodo sé*
   ga tákaku
   arimasén.

f. There is too much
   water.

7. *Okane wa juubún*
   mótte imásu ka?

g. Do you want a little
   or do you want a
   lot?

8. *Moo ichido itte*
   kudasái.

h. It's too hot.

9. *Okane wa takusan*
   arimásen.

i. Do you have
   enough money?

10. *Sukóshi shika*
    hanashimasén.

j. Say it again, please.

ANSWERS
1–g; 2–a; 3–h; 4–f; 5–b; 6–c; 7–i; 8–j; 9–e; 10–d.

LESSON 29

DÁI NÍJUU KYÚUKA

A. I WANT TO . . .

When you want to *have* something you say *ga hoshii desu*. When you want to *do* something, you use *o* (for the object) plus a pre-*masu* form plus *tai desu*.

The combination of a pre-*masu* plus *tai* acts exactly like an *i-* adjective. The item involved in the action that you want to perform is normally marked by *o*, but the use of *ga* is acceptable in limited cases. Usually, *ga* can be used with daily actions, such as "eat" or "drink."

Nomitái desu.	I want to drink it.
Tabetái desu.	I want to eat it.
Kaitái desu.	I want to buy it.
Mitái desu.	I want to see it.
Nomitáku arimasén.	I don't want to drink it.
Tabetáku arimasén.	I don't want to eat it.
Kaitaku arimasén.	I don't want to buy it.
Mitáku arimasén.	I don't want to see it.
Koohíi o nomitái desu.	I'd like some coffee. [(I) want to drink coffee.]
Kudámono o tabetái desu.	I'd like some fruit. [(I) want to eat fruit.]
Kutsú o kaitái desu.	I want to buy (a pair of) shoes.
Éiga o mitái desu.	I want to see a movie.
Koohíi o nomitáku narimáshita.	I want to drink coffee now (though I didn't before). [(I) became desirous of drinking coffee.]

Kudámono o tabetáku narimáshita.	I want to eat fruit now. [I became desirous of . . .]
Kutsú o kaitaku narimáshita.	I want to buy shoes now. [I became desirous of . . .]
Éiga o mitáku narimáshita.	I want to see a movie now. [I became desirous of . . .]

B. I INTEND TO . . .

Iku tsumori désu.	I intend to go.
Ryokoo suru tsumori désu.	I intend to travel.
Benkyoo suru tsumori désu.	I intend to study.
Kekkon suru tsumori désu.	I intend to marry.
Iku tsumori désu ka?	Do you intend to go?
Iku tsumori déshita ka?	Did you intend to go?
Iku tsumori ja arimasén ka?	Don't you intend to go?
Iku tsumori ja arimasén deshita ka?	Didn't you intend to go?
Ryokoo suru tsumori déshita ga shimasén deshita.	I (had) intended to travel, but didn't.
Ryokoo suru tsumori déshita ga dekimasén deshita.	I (had) intended to travel, but couldn't.
Ryokoo suru tsumori déshita ga akiramemáshita.	I (had) intended to travel, but I gave it up [the idea].

*Ryokoo suru tsumori
déshita ga dekíru
ka doo ka
wakarimasén.*

I (had) intended to
travel, but I can't tell
(now) if I can or
not.

C. IT IS SUPPOSED TO . . .

Kúru hazu désu.

It is supposed to come.

*Tegami ga kúru hazu
désu.*

A letter is supposed to
come.

*Tomodachi ga kúru
hazu désu.*

A friend of mine is
supposed to come.

*Denwa ga áru hazu
désu.*

There is supposed to be
a telephone. He is
supposed to have a
telephone.

Shiranai hazu désu.

He is not supposed to
know it.

Kitá hazu désu.

It is supposed to have
come.

**Tegami o uketotta
hazu désu.**

He is supposed to have
received a letter.

**Tomodachi ga
shiraseta hazu désu.**

My friend is supposed
to have notified (him
about it).

**Tomodachi kara
denwa ga átta hazu
désu.**

There is supposed to
have been a phone
call from a friend of
mine.

**Minna yónda hazu
désu.**

He is supposed to have
read all of it.

**Minna dékite iru hazu
désu.**

Everything is supposed
to have been done.

D. SOMETHING, EVERYTHING, NOTHING

náni = what
náni ka[1] = something
nán de mo (used with affirmative) = everything, anything at all
nani mo (used with negative) = nothing, not anything

Náni ka kaimáshita ka?	Did you buy something?
Dáre ka kimáshita ka?	Did someone come?
Ítsu ka ikimashóo.	Let's go sometime.
Dóko ka de kikimáshita.	I heard it somewhere.
Nán de mo kaimáshita.	I bought everything.
Dáre de mo hairemásu.	Anybody at all can enter.
Ítsu de mo ikimásu.	I go anytime.
Dóko de mo kaemásu.	You can buy it at any place.
Nani mo kaimasén deshita.	I didn't buy anything.
Dare mo kimasén deshita.	Nobody came.
Ítsu mo imasén deshita.	He wasn't there at any time. He was always absent.
Doko mo mimasén deshita.	I didn't see any place.

[1] See Section 23 of the Summary of Japanese Grammar for uses of question words with particles.

Náni ka tsumetai monó o nomimashóo.

Let's drink something cold.

Dáre ka Nihongo no yóku dekíru hitó ni kikimashóo.

Let's ask someone who can speak Japanese well.

Ítsu ka anmari isogáshiku nái tóki ni ikimashóo.

Let's go there when we are not too busy.

Dóko ka mótto shízuka na tokoró e ikimashóo.

Let's go somewhere quieter.

Náni o míte mo kaitaku narimásu.[1]

Whatever I see, I [get to] want to buy.

Dáre ga kité mo kyóo wa au kotó ga dekimasén.

No matter who comes [Whoever may come], I can't meet her/him today.

Ítsu itté mo anó hito wa jimúsho ni imasén deshita.

No matter when I went to his office, he wasn't there. [Whenever (I) went, he wasn't at his office.]

Dóko e itté mo Eigo no dekíru hitó ga imáshita.

Wherever I went, there was someone who could speak English.

QUIZ 24

1. *Kaitái desu.*

a. Everything is supposed to have been done.

2. *Iku tsumori désu.*

b. I didn't buy anything.

---

[1] Note the construction: The interrogative plus the *-te* form plus *mo* = "-ever" plus the verb.

3. *Kúru hazu désu.*

4. *Náni ka kaimáshita ka?*

5. *Kaitaku arimasén.*

6. *Ryokoo suru tsumori désu.*

7. *Dóko ka de kikimáshita.*

8. *Kitá hazu désu.*

9. *Dáre de mo hairemásu.*

10. *Dáre ka Nihongo no yóku dekíru hitó ni kikimashóo.*

11. *Ryokoo suru tsumori ja arimasén deshita.*

12. *Nani mo kaimasén deshita.*

13. *Minna dékite iru hazu désu.*

14. *Dare mo kimasén deshita.*

15. *Náni ka tsumetai monó o nomimashóo.*

c. Let's drink something cold.

d. Nobody came.

e. I didn't intend to travel.

f. Anybody at all can enter.

g. Let's ask someone who can speak Japanese well.

h. Did you buy something?

i. It is supposed to come.

j. I intend to travel.

k. I don't want to buy it.

l. I intend to go.

m. I want to buy it.

n. I heard it somewhere.

o. It is supposed to have come.

ANSWERS
1–m; 2–l; 3–i; 4–h; 5–k; 6–j; 7–n; 8–o; 9–f; 10–g; 11–e; 12–b; 13–a; 14–d; 15–c.

E. WORD STUDY

kuraimákkusu	climax
kyásuto	cast
rabushíin	love scene
rokéishon	location
shíin	scene
shinario	scenario
sukuríin	screen
sutáa	star
sutajio	studio
táitoru	title

LESSON 30

DÁI SANJUKKA

A. OF COURSE! IT'S A PITY! IT DOESN'T MATTER!

Mochíron desu.	Of course. Certainly.
Shoochi itashimáshita.	Fine! [(I) have understood.]
Sóo desu ka?	Indeed? Is that so?
Soo omoimásu.	I think so.
Soo omoimasén.	I don't think so.
Tanaka-san désu ka?	Are you Ms. Tanaka?
Hái, sóo desu.	Yes, I am. [Am so.]
tábun	perhaps, probably
Tábun sóo deshoo.	I suppose so. Probably it is so.
Tábun sóo ja nái deshoo.	I suppose not. Probably it is not so.

Sóo da to íi to omoimásu.	I hope so. [If (it) is so it would be good, that way (I) think.]
Sóo ja nái to íi to omoimásu.	I hope not. [If (it) is not so it would be good, that way (I) think.]
Táshika ni sóo desu.	Certainly. [Certainly (it) is so.]
Táshika ni sóo ja arimasén.	Certainly not. [Certainly (it) is not so.]
Okinodóku desu.	It's a pity! It's a shame! She has my sympathy.
Sore wa baai ni yorimásu.	That depends [on the occasion].
Kamaimasén.	That's nothing. That's not important. That doesn't matter. [(I) don't mind.]
Zenzen kamaimasén.	That doesn't matter at all.
Gotsugoo ga yoróshi-kereba.	If you have no objections. If it doesn't inconvenience you. [If (it) is convenient.]
Dóchira de mo kékkoo desu.	I don't care. It's all the same to me. [Either will do.]

QUIZ 25

1. *Soo omoimásu.*
2. *Mochíron desu.*
3. *Tábun sóo deshoo.*

a. It's a pity.
b. I suppose not.
c. I hope so.

4. *Shoochi itashi-* *máshita.*	d. If you have no objections.
5. *Sóo da to íi to omoimásu.*	e. I don't care. Either will do.
6. *Tábun sóo ja nái to omoimásu.*	f. Certainly it is so.
7. *Táshika ni sóo desu.*	g. I think so.
8. *Okinodóku desu.*	h. Agreed!
9. *Gotsugoo ga yoróshikereba.*	i. Of course.
10. *Dóchira de mo kékkoo desu.*	j. I suppose so.

ANSWERS
1–g; 2–i; 3–j; 4–h; 5–c; 6–b; 7–f; 8–a; 9–d; 10–e.

B. THE SAME

onaji	same
Onaji monó desu.	It's the same thing (*a tangible article*).
Onaji kotó desu.	It's the same thing (*abstract*).
Kore wa onaji ja arimasén.	This isn't the same. These aren't the same.
dóoji ni } **onaji tokí ni**	at the same time
onaji shunkan ni	at the same moment
onaji machí ni	in the same town

C. ALREADY

móo	already

móo mukoo ni itte imásu.	He is already there. [(He) is already in the state of having gone there.]
Móo shite shimai-máshita.	He has already done that. [(He) has already done that and (it) is all finished.]
Móo dáshite shimai-máshita ka?	Has he sent it already?
Móo sumásete shimai-máshita ka?	Have you finished already?

D. WORD STUDY

abunóomaru	abnormal
cháamingu	charming
derikéeto	delicate
éreganto	elegant
kuráshikku	classic
modan	modern
nóomaru	normal
ríberaru	liberal
senchiméntaru	sentimental
yuníiku	unique

LESSON 31

DÁI SÁNJUU ÍKKA

A. I LIKE IT, IT'S GOOD

Sukí desu.	I like it. [That's (my) favorite.]

Nihon ryóori ga sukí desu.	I like Japanese cooking.
Kodomo ga sukí desu.	I like children.
Hón o yómu kotó ga sukí desu.	I like reading books.
Oyógu kotó ga sukí desu.	I like swimming.
Kékkoo desu.	Good! It's good.
Kono wáin wa kékkoo desu.	This wine is good.
Kono nikú wa kékkoo desu.	This meat is good.
Kékkoo na oténki desu ne.	The weather is fine, isn't it?
Mótto ikága desu ka?	How about some more?
Moo kékkoo desu.	No, thanks, I'm fully satisfied.
Taihen kékkoo desu.	It's very good.
Subarashíi desu.	It's wonderful.
Mígoto desu.	It's admirable.
Kanzen désu.	It's perfect.
Taihen ki ni iri-máshita.	I'm very pleased with it. I like it very much.
Taihen íi hitó desu.	He's very nice. [(He) is a very good person.]
Taihen kanji no íi hitó desu.	He's very pleasant.
Dóomo goshínsetsu sama.	You're very kind. That's very kind of you.

B. I Don't Like It, It's Bad

Sukí ja arimasén.	I don't like it. It's not good. [That's not (my) favorite.]
Sakana wa sukí ja arimasén.	I don't like fish. [Fish is not (my) favorite.]
Kirai désu.	I dislike it.
Sakana wa kirai désu.	I dislike fish.
Yamada-san wa kirai désu.[1]	I dislike Mr. Yamada.
Yóku nái desu.	It's not good.
Amari kékkoo ja arimasén.	It's not very good.
Warúi desu.	It's bad.
Mazúi desu.	It tastes bad.
Kanshin dekimasén.	It's not good. [I can't admire it.]
Hón o yómu kotó wa sukí ja arimasén.	I don't like reading books.
Hón o yómu kotó wa kirai désu.	I dislike reading books.

QUIZ 26

1. *Taihen kékkoo desu.*   a. He's very nice.
2. *Kanshin dekimasén.*   b. It's perfect.
3. *Subarashíi desu.*   c. I'm very pleased with it.
4. *Kanzen désu.*   d. I dislike fish.

---

[1] Note that this same sentence can also mean "Mr. Yamada dislikes it."

5. *Taihen ki ni irimáshita.*	e. He's very pleasant.
6. *Sakana wa kirai désu.*	f. It tastes bad.
7. *Dóomo goshínsetsu sama.*	g. You're very kind.
8. *Mazúi desu.*	h. It's wonderful.
9. *Taihen kanji no íi hitó desu.*	i. It's very good.
10. *Taihen íi hitó desu.*	j. It's not good.

ANSWERS
1–j; 2–i; 3–h; 4–b; 5–c; 6–d; 7–g; 8–f; 9–e; 10–a.

REVIEW QUIZ 3

1. *San tasu ní wa* _____ (five) *desu.*
   a. *gó*
   b. *rokú*
   c. *hachí*

2. _____ (Last week) *kaerimáshita.*
   a. *Séngetsu*
   b. *Senshuu*
   c. *Sakúban*

3. *Kyoo wa* _____ (Monday) *desu.*
   a. *Getsuyóobi*
   b. *Doyóobi*
   c. *Suiyóobi*

4. _____ (Must hurry) *narimasén.*
   a. *Ikanákereba narimasén.*
   b. *Isogánakereba narimasén.*
   c. *Oboénakereba narimasén.*

5. *Koohíi ga* _____ (want) *desu.*
   a. *hoshíi*
   b. *sukí*
   c. *yóku nái*

6. Ginkoo e _____ (am going).
   a. *haraimásu.*
   b. *kashimásu.*
   c. *ikimásu.*

7. _____ (Sugar) *wa ikága desu ka?*
   a. *Osatoo*
   b. *Ocha*
   c. *Mizu*

8. *Okane o* _____ (a little) *kashite kudasái.*
   a. *sukóshi*
   b. *takusan*
   c. *nisen en*

9. *Okane o* _____ (much) *mótte imasu.*
   a. *sukóshi*
   b. *takusan*
   c. *sukoshi mo*

10. _____ (More) *arimásu.*
    a. *Sukóshi*
    b. *Mótto*
    c. *Moo sukóshi*

11. _____ (Enough) *arimasén.*
    a. *Nani mo*
    b. *Takusan*
    c. *Juubún*

12. _____ (Expensive) *desu.*
    a. *Yasúi*

h *Takái*

c. *Hikúi*

13. *Sore wa kore* _____ (as) *oishiku arimasén.*
    a. *wa*
    b. *hodo*
    c. *mo*

14. _____ (All) *yónde shimaimáshita.*
    a. *Hanbun*
    b. *Sukóshi*
    c. *Minna*

15. _____ (Anybody) *hairemásu.*
    a. *Dáre de mo*
    b. *Dáre ga*
    c. *Dáre ka*

16. *Soo* _____ (don't think).
    a. *hurimasén.*
    b. *omoimasén.*
    c. *kaimasén.*

17. *Iku* _____ (intend to) *désu.*
    a. *hazu*
    b. *tsumori*
    c. *yóo*

18. _____ (Nothing) *kaimasén deshita.*
    a. *Dare mo*
    b. *Nani mo*
    c. *Dore mo*

19. *Dóre de mo* _____ (same).
    a. *onaji desu.*

    b. *chigaimásu.*
    c. *hoshíi desu.*

20. _____ (Already) *sumásete shimaimáshita ka?*
    a. *Mótto mótto*
    b. *Mótto*
    c. *Móo*

ANSWERS
1–a; 2–b; 3–a; 4–b; 5–a; 6–c; 7–a; 8–a; 9–b; 10–b;
11–c; 12–b; 13–b; 14–c; 15–a; 16–b; 17–b; 18–b;
19–a; 20–c.

C. WORD STUDY

bakkumíraa	rearview mirror (of a car)
bánpaa	bumper
buréeki	brake
énjin	engine
gasorin	gasoline
gíya	gear
handoru	handle (of a tool), steering wheel
heddoráito	headlight
kurátchi	clutch
taiya	tire

D. WARAIBANASHI

Tanaka-san to Yamada-san ga résutoran e itte bifuteki o chuumon shimáshita. Shibáraku tátte bifuteki ga kimáshita. Hitókire wa óokikute hitótsu wa chiisákatta no desu. Tanaka-san wa súgu ookíi hoo o torimáshita. Sore o míte Yamada-san wa okorimáshita. Soshite "Nán to reigi no nái hitó daroo. Hito yóri saki ni tóru tokí wa chiisái hoo o tóru mon da" to iimáshita.

Kore o kiite Tanaka-san wa: "Anáta ga watashi dáttara dóo shimásu ka?" to tazunemáshita.

"Mochíron chiisái hoo o torimásu yo!" to Yamada-san wa kotaemáshita.

Tanaka-san wa: "Sóre gorannasái, mónku wa nái hazu ja arimasén ka? Chiisái hoo o anáta ga, morattá n da kara," to iimáshita.

A Funny Story

Tanaka and Yamada went to a restaurant and ordered steak. A few minutes later the steaks arrived. One piece was large and one piece was small. Tanaka took the large piece. Yamada was furious and said to him: "What bad manners you have! Don't you know that since you were the first to help yourself you should have taken the smaller piece?"

Tanaka answered: "If you were in my place, which piece would you have taken?"

"The smaller one, of course," said Yamada.

"Well, then," Tanaka answered, "what are you complaining about? You've got it, haven't you?"

NOTE

waraibánashi: "a story to laugh"
chuumon shimáshita: ordered
shibáraku tátte: after a short while
okórimáshita: got furious
soshite: and
Nán to . . . daroo: What a . . . !
reigi: manners
shiranai: (negative of *shiru*): don't know
. . . monó da: that's what one should do; that's an accepted way to do
dáttara: if (you) were

torimásu yo: yo is an emphatic particle corre-
    sponding to an exclamation mark.
mónku: complaint
nái hazu désu: there is supposed to be not; there
    isn't supposed to be

LESSON 32

DÁI SÁNJUU NÍKA

A. WHO? WHAT? WHEN? ETC.

dóno	which, . . . ?
Dóno hon desu ka?	Which book is it?
Dóno tegami desu ka?	Which letter is it?
dóre	which one?
ítsu	when?
dáre	who?
náni, nán	what?
náze, dóoshite	why?
dóko	where?
íkura	how much?
dóo, dóoshite	how?

    1. *Náni, Nán*   What?

Náni o shite imásu ka?	What are you doing?
Náni ga hoshíi desu ka?	What do you want? What would you like?
Kore kara náni o shitái desu ka?	What do you want to do now?
Náni o sagashite imásu ka?	What are you looking for?

Náni is used instead of *nán* when the word
that follows it is *desu, to* (with a verb *iu*
[say], etc.), *no*, or a counter.

Onamae wa nán desu ka?	What's your name?
Kono machi no namae wa nán desu ka?	What's the name of this town?
Kono toori no namae wa nán desu ka?	What's the name of this street?
Nán to iimashóo ka?	What shall we say?
Nán to osshaimáshita ka?	What did she say (*extra polite*)?
Nán to iu machí desu ka?	What is the name of the town? [What is the town called?]
Nán no hón desu ka?	What book is it?
Kore wa nán no é desu ka?	What picture is this?
Kyóo wa nánnichi desu ka?	What's today?
Nángatsu desu ka?	What month is it?
Nánji desu ka?	What time? [What hour is it?]

2. *Dóre*   Which one?

Dóre desu ka?	Which one is it?
Dóre ga anáta no hón desu ka?	Which is your book?
Watakushi nó wa dóre desu ka?	Which is mine?
Dóre ga íi hoo desu ka?	Which is the better one?
Dóre ga hoshíi desu ka?	Which one do you want?

Dóre ga tadashíi desu ka?   Which one is right?

3. *Ítsu*   When?

Ítsu desu ka?	When is it?
Ítsu made desu ka?	Until when is (it)?
Ítsu kimásu ka?	When are you coming?
Ítsu oide ni narimásu ka?	When are you coming (*respect*)?
Ítsu tachimásu ka?	When are you leaving?
Ítsu otachi ni narimásu ka?	When are you leaving (*respect*)?

4. *Dáre*   Who?

Dáre desu ka?	⎰Who is it? ⎱Who are you?
Dónata desu ka?	Who are you (*respect*)?
Dáre ga sore o shitte imásu ka?	Who knows that?
Dáre ga watakushítachi to ikimásu ka?	Who is coming with us?
Dáre no desu ka?	Whose is it?
Dáre no tamé desu ka?	Who(m) is it for? [Whose sake is it?]
Dáre ni hanáshite imásu ka?	Who(m) are you talking to?
Dáre no kotó o hanáshite imásu ka?	Who(m) are you speaking about? [Whose matters are you speaking?]
Dáre to kimásu ka?	Who(m) are you coming with?
Dáre ni aitái desu ka?	Who(m) do you want to see?

Dónata ni oai ni naritái desu ka?	Who(m) do you want to see (*respect*)?
Dáre o sagashite imásu ka?	Who(m) are you looking for?
Dónata o sagashite irasshaimásu ka?	Who(m) are you looking for (*respect*)?

5. *Náze, Dóoshite*   Why?

Náze desu ka?	Why is it?
Dóoshite desu ka?	Why is it?
Dóoshite damé desu ka?	Why not? [Why is it no good?]
Náze sonna kotó o iú n desu ka?	Why do you say that [such a thing]?
Dóoshite sonna kotó o shitá n desu ka?	Why did he do such a thing?

6. *Dóo, Dóoshite*   How?

Dóo desu ka?	How is it?
Dóo shimásu ka?	How do you do it?
Dóo iu ími desu ka?	What do you mean?
Nihongo de kono kotobá wa dóo kakimásu ka?	How do you write this word in Japanese?
Sore wa Eigo de dóo iimásu ka?	How do you say that in English?
"Thanks" wa Nihongo de dóo iimásu ka?	How do you say "thanks" in Japanese?
Dóo shita n desu ka?	How did it happen?
Dóo shitara íi n desu ka?	How does one go about it?
Dóo sureba íi n desu ka?	How does one go about it?

Sore wa dóo shite tsukurimásu ka?	How's it made? [Acting how do you make (it)?]
Sore wa dóoshite tsukurimáshita ka?	How did you make it?
Soko é wa dóo ikimásu ka?	How do you go there?
Dóo shimashóo ka?	What's to be done? What can one do? [How shall we do?]
Sono futatsú wa dóo chigaimásu ka?	What is the difference between the two? [As for the two, how do they differ?]

QUIZ 27

1. *Dóno hon desu ka?*
2. *Nán to iimáshita ka?*
3. *Náni o sagashite imásu ka?*
4. *Dóno tegami desu ka?*
5. *Onamae wa nán desu ka?*
6. *Náni o shite imásu ka?*
7. *Kyóo wa nánnichi desu ka?*
8. *Náni ga hoshíi desu ka?*
9. *Nángatsu desu ka?*
10. *Kono toori no namae wa nán desu ka?*

a. How is it?
b. What is the difference between the two?
c. Why did he do such a thing?
d. Who are you looking for?
e. Why is it?
f. How do you go there?
g. Until when?
h. Which one do you want?
i. What is the name of the street?
j. What do you want to do now?

11. *Kore kuru náni o*   k. What time is it?
    shitái desu ka?
12. *Nánji desu ka?*   l. What do you want/
                               would you like?
13. *Sono futatsú wa*   m. What month is it?
    dóo chigaimásu
    ka?
14. *Dóoshite desu ka?*   n. Which letter?
15. *Dóre ga hoshíi*   o. What is your
    desu ka?   name?
16. *Ítsu made desu ka?*   p. What are you look-
                               ing for?
17. *Dónata o sagashite*   q. What's today?
    irasshaimásu ka?
18. *Dóoshite sonna*   r. What are you do-
    kóto o shitá n desu   ing?
    ka?
19. *Dóo desu ka?*   s. Which book is it?
20. *Soko é wa dóo*   t. What did you say?
    ikimásu ka?

ANSWERS
1–s; 2–t; 3–p; 4–n; 5–o; 6–r; 7–q; 8–l; 9–m; 10–i;
11–j; 12–k; 13–b; 14–e; 15–h; 16–g; 17–d; 18–c;
19–a; 20–f.

B. WORD STUDY

akademíkku	academic
ekizochíkku	exotic
gurotésuku	grotesque
nóoburu	noble
pedanchíkku	pedantic
romanchíkku	romantic
senséeshonaru	sensational

C. How Much?

Nedan wa?	The price? How much is this?
Nedan wa íkura desu ka?	What's the price?
Íkura?	How much?
Íkura desu ka?	How much is it? How much do you want for it?
Zénbu de íkura desu ka?	How much for everything? How much does it all cost?
Hitótsu íkura desu ka?	How much each?

D. How Many?

Íkutsu?	How many?
Íkutsu nokótte imásu ka?	How many are left?
Íkutsu mótte imásu ka?	How many of them do you have?
Nánnin desu ka?	How many persons?
Nanjíkan?	How many hours?
Nándo?	How many times?
Dono kurai désu ka?	How much time?
Dono kurai nagái desu ka?	How long?
Soko e ikú ni wa dono kurai jíkan ga kakarimásu ka?	How long [how much time] does it take to get there?

QUIZ 28

1. *Íkutsu arimásu ka?*   a. How many persons?

2. *Íkura desu ka?*   b. How much for ev-
                                           erything?

3. *Íkutsu nokótte*   c. How long does it
   imasu ka?   take to get there?

4. *Nedan wa íkura*   d. How much each?
   desu ka?

5. *Dono kurai nagái*   e. What's the price?
   desu ka?

6. *Zénbu de íkura*   f. How much is it?
   desu ka?

7. *Nánnin desu ka?*   g. How many are left?

8. *Íkutsu mótte imásu* h. How long is it?
   ka?

9. *Hitótsu íkura desu* i. How many of them
   ka?   do you have?

10. *Soko e ikú ni wa*   j. How many are
    dono kurai jikan   there?
    ga karimásu ka?

ANSWERS
1–j; 2–f; 3–g; 4–e; 5–h; 6–b; 7–a; 8–i; 9–d; 10–c.

LESSON 33

DÁI SÁNJUU SÁNKA

A. SOME, SOMEONE, SOMETHING[1]

íkura ka no   some (*an indeterminate
                                     amount of*)

íkutsu ka no   some (*an indeterminate
                                      number of*)

---

[1] See Lesson 29-F and Section 23 of the Summary of Japanese
Grammar for more information.

íkura ka no okane	some money
íkura ka no híyoo	some expense
íkura ka no jikan	some time
Íkura ka no jikan ga kakarimásu.	It takes some time.
Íkura ka no okane ga irimásu.	We need some money.
Íkutsu ka no kotobá o shitte imásu.	I know some words.
nánnin ka no	some (*an indeterminate number of persons*)
Nánnin ka no hitó ni kikimáshita.	I have asked a number of persons.
Nánnin ka kité imásu.	Several people are here.
náni ka	something, anything (*not a specific thing*)
náni ka atarashíi monó	something new, anything new
náni ka kaitai monó	something you want to buy, anything you want to buy
Náni ka kaitai monó ga arimásu ka?	Do you have anything you want to buy?
Náni ka kikitai kotó ga arimásu ka?	Do you have anything you want to ask?
Náni ka kudasái.	Give me something, please.
Náni ka káku monó o kudasái.	Give me something to write with, please.
Náni ka ochimáshita.	Something fell down.
Náni ka kaimáshita.	She bought something.
Náni ka shirimasén.	I don't know what it is.
dáre ka	someone
Dáre ka sore no dekíru hitó ga imásu ka?	Is there anyone who can do it?

Dáre ka Eigo no yóku dekíru hitó ga imásu ka?	Is there anyone who can speak English well?
áru hito	someone
Áru hito ga hoshíi to itte imásu.	Someone (a certain person who shall be nameless) says that she wants to have it.
áru tokoro	someplace
Áru tokoro e iki-máshita.	He went someplace.
ítsu ka	sometime
Ítsu ka kité kudasái.	Please come sometime.
Ítsu ka ikimashóo.	Let's go there some-time.
tokidoki	sometimes, occasion-ally
Sonó hito ni tokidoki aimásu.	I see him sometimes.
Soko de tokidoki gó-han o tabemásu.	I eat [my meal] there sometimes.

B. ONCE, TWICE

-do, -kai	a time
ichido, ikkái	once, one time
nido, nikái	twice, two times
maido, maikai	every time, each time
kóndo	this time, this coming time
dái ikkái	the first time
Dái ikkái wa sen kyúuhyaku kyúujuu déshita.	The first time was (in) 1990.
hajímete	for the first time

Hajímete ikimáshita.	I went there for the first time.
tsugí	the next time, the next item, the next number, etc.
kono máe	last time
betsu no tóki	another time, another occasion
mata	again
moo ichido	once more

C. Up to

máde	up to
ima máde	up to now
soko máde	up to there
owari máde	(up) to the end
éki made	up to the station
kónban made	up to this evening
ashitá made	up till tomorrow
Getsuyóobi made	up to Monday

D. I Need It, It's Necessary

Irimásu.	I need it.
Kore wa irimasén.	She doesn't need this one.
Náni ka irimásu ka?	Do you need anything?
Nani mo irimasén.	I don't need anything.
Zenzen irimasén.	I don't need it at all.
Zéhi oai shinákereba narimasén.	It's absolutely necessary that I see you.
Anó hito ni hanasá-nakereba narimasén.	I have to tell him.

Háyaku uchi e káette kónakereba narimasén.	I must come home early.
Hontoo dá to iu kotó o mitomenákereba narimasén.	One must recognize the truth.

E.   I FEEL LIKE[1]

Hoshíi desu.	I'd like to have it. I feel like having it. I want to have it.
Ikitaku arimasén.	I don't feel like going there. I don't want to go.
Ano hón ga hoshíi.	I want that book.
Aisukuríimu ga hoshíi desu.	I feel like having some ice cream.
Aisukuríimu ga tabetái desu.	I feel like eating some ice cream.
Kono éiga wa mitái desu ka?	Would you like to see this movie?

F.   AT THE HOME OF

The choice of the particle *de* or *ni* depends on the verb that follows it.

... otaku de ⎱ **... otaku ni** ⎰	at the home of (someone else)
uchi de ⎱ **uchi ni** ⎰	at my home

---

[1] See Lesson 29 for "I want to."

Senséi no otaku ni imáshita.[1]	We were at the home of our teacher.
Yamada-san no otaku de aimashóo.[2]	I'll see you at the Yamadas' house.
Genkín wa uchi ni arimasén.	There is no cash at home.
Uchi de páatii o shimáshita.	We had a party at my home.

QUIZ 29

1. *Íkura ka no okane.*	a. To the end.
2. *Ichido*	b. I need that.
3. *Owari máde.*	c. Please come sometime.
4. *Irimásu.*	d. Some money.
5. *Ítsu ka kité kudasái.*	e. Once.

ANSWERS

1–d; 2–e; 3–a; 4–b; 5–c.

REVIEW QUIZ 4

1. *Kono machi no namae wa* _____ (what) *desu ka?*
    a. *dáre*
    b. *nán*
    c. *dóko*

2. *Áno katá wa* _____ (who) *desu ka?*
    a. *dónata*

[1] Notice that *ni* is used here because it appears in conjunction with a form of the verb *imásu*.
[2] Notice that *de* is used here because it appears in conjunction with a form of the verb *áu*.

b. *dónna*
c. *dótchi*

3. _____ (When) *kimásu ka?*
   a. *Íkutsu*
   b. *Ítsu*
   c. *Íkura*

4. _____ (Why) *sonna koto o iú n desu ka?*
   a. *Dónna*
   b. *Dóo*
   c. *Dóoshite*

5. *Dái* _____ (twelfth) *kai.*
   a. *juuní*
   b. *níjuu*
   c. *nijuuní*

6. *Kono booshi wa* _____ (two thousand) *en shi-máshita.*
   a. *niman*
   b. *nihyaku*
   c. *nisen*

7. *Ni-choome* _____ (seventeen) *bánchi ni súnde imásu.*
   a. *shichijuu*
   b. *juushichi*
   c. *juuhachi*

8. _____ (Noon) *desu.*
   a. *Hirú*
   b. *Yóru*
   c. *Ása*

9. _____ (Six) *ji ni aimashóo.*
    a. *Sán*
    b. *Kú*
    c. *Rokú*

10. *Sore o suru* _____ (time) *désu.*
    a. *hito*
    b. *jikan*
    c. *tokoro*

11. *Kyóo wa* _____ (Wednesday) *desu.*
    a. *Kayóobi*
    b. *Suiyóobi*
    c. *Getsuyóobi*

12. *Raishuu no* _____ (Tuesday) *ni demásu.*
    a. *Kayóobi*
    b. *Mokuyóobi*
    c. *Nichiyóobi*

13. *Kyóo wa* _____ (June) *no tsuitachí desu.*
    a. *Rokugatsu*
    b. *Shichigatsu*
    c. *Hachigatsu*

14. *Kore wa* _____ (doesn't need).
    a. *ikimasén.*
    b. *irimasén.*
    c. *arimasén.*

15. *Kono kotobá wa Nihongo de* _____ (how)
    kakimásu ka?
    a. *dóre*
    b. *dóo*
    c. *dáre*

16. *Watakushi wa Shigatsu* _____ (eleventh) *ni umaremáshita.*
    a. *júuyokka*
    b. *níjuuninichi*
    c. *juuichinichí*

17. _____ (How many) *nokótte imásu ka?*
    a. *Íkutsu*
    b. *Kokónotsu*
    c. *Mittsú*

18. _____ (Intend to go) *désu.*
    a. *Iku hazu*
    b. *Iku tsumori*
    c. *Iku jikan*

19. *Ashita* _____ (I must go).
    a. *ikanákereba narimasén.*
    b. *ikanákute mo íi desu.*
    c. *itté mo íi desu.*

20. *Yamada-san wa sono kotó o* _____ (is supposed to know).
    a. *shitte imásen deshita.*
    b. *shitte iru hazu désu.*
    c. *shiritái deshoo.*

ANSWERS
1–b; 2–a; 3–b; 4–c; 5–a; 6–c; 7–b; 8–a; 9–c; 10–b; 11–b; 12–a; 13–a; 14–b; 15–b; 16–c; 17–a; 18–b; 19–a; 20–b.

LESSON 34

DÁI SÁNJUU YÓNKA

A. ON THE ROAD

Chótto ukagaimásu ga, kono machi no namae wa nán deshoo ka?	Excuse me, but what is the name of this town?
Tookyoo máde dono kurai arimásu ka?	How far is it to [as far as] Tokyo?
Koko kara Tookyoo máde nán kiro arimásu ka?	How many kilometers from here to Tokyo?
Koko kara júkkiro desu.	It's ten kilometers from here.
Koko kara níjukkiro desu.	That's twenty kilometers from here.
Koko kara Tookyoo máde dóo ikimásu ka?	How do I get to Tokyo from here?
Kono michi o ikimásu.	Follow this road.
Kono banchi e dóo ikú no ka oshiete kudasái.	Can you tell me how I can get to this address?
Koko e dóo ikú no ka oshiete kudasái.	Can you tell me how I can get to this place?
Kono toori no namae wa nán to iimásu ka?	What is the name of this street?
. . . wa dóko desu ka?	Where is . . . ?
Ginza Dóori wa dóko desu ka?[1]	Where is Ginza Doori?

[1] *dóko desu ka?* is the same as *dóko ni arimásu ka?*

Koko kara toói desu ka?	Is it far from here?
Koko kara chikái desu ka?	Is it near here?
Migi e toorí mittsu mukoo désu.	It's the third block to the right.
Kono michi o ikimásu.	Go this way.
Massúgu ikimásu.	Go straight ahead.
Kádo made itte hidari e magarimásu.	Go to the corner and turn left.
Migi ni magarimásu.	Turn right.
Garéeji wa dóko ni arimásu ka?	Where is the garage?
Keisatsusho wa dóko desu ka?	Where is the police station?
Shiyákusho wa dóko desu ka?	Where is City Hall?

B. Bus, Train, Subway, Taxi

Kono básu wa dóko kara kimásu ka?	Where does this bus come from?
Shinjuku kara kimásu.	It comes from Shinjuku.
Basutei wa dóko desu ka?	Where is the bus stop?
Chuushingai ni iku basu wa dore desu ka?	Which bus goes to the center of town?
Dóno eki de orimásu ka?	What station do I get off at?
Dóko de orimásu ka?	Where do I get off?
Chikatetsu no éki wa dóko desu ka?	Where's the subway station?

Densha no éki wa dóko ni arimásu ka?	Where is the train station?
Tookyoo yuki no densha ní wa dóko kara norimásu ka?	Where do I get the train for Tokyo?
Niban sen désu.	On track two.
Densha wa íma demáshita.	The train just left.
Tsugí no densha wa nánji ni demásu ka?	What time does the next train leave?
Kyooto yuki no oofukukíppu o kudasái.	May I have a round-trip ticket for Kyoto?
Íkura desu ka?	How much is that?
Nisen gohyaku gojúu en desu.	Two thousand five hundred and fifty yen.
Jikan wa dono kurai kakarimásu ka?	How long does it take to get there?
Kujíkan to chótto desu.	A little over nine hours.

C. WRITING AND MAILING LETTERS AND FAXES

Tegami o kakitái n desu ga . . .	I'd like to write a letter, but (would you mind if I did?)
Enpitsu o mótte imásu ka?	Do you have a pencil?
Pén o mótte imásu ka?	Do you have a pen?
Waapuro o mótte imásu ka?	Do you have a word processor?

Fuutoo o mótte imásu ka?	Do you have an envelope?
Kitté o mótte imásu ka?	Do you have a postage stamp?
Kitté wa dóko de kaemásu ka?	Where can I buy a postage stamp?
Kookuubin no kitté o mótte imásu ka?	Do you have an airmail stamp?
Yuubínkyoku wa dóko desu ka?	Where is the post office?
Kono tegami o da-shitái n desu ga . . .	I'd like to mail this letter.
Kitté wa nánmai irimásu ka?	How many stamps do I need on this letter?
Pósuto wa dóko ni arimásu ka?	Where is the mailbox?
Kádo ni arimásu.	At the corner.
Fakkuso o okuritái n desu ga . . . Dóko de okuremásu ka?	I'd like to send a fax. Where can I send it?
Kono jimúsho de okuremásu.	You can send it in (from) this office.
Soko e tsukú no ni dono kurai kakarimásu ka?	How long will it take to get there?

D. TELEPHONING

Koko ni denwa ga arimásu ka?	Is there a phone here?
Dóko de denwa ga kakeraremásu ka?	Where can I phone?
Denwa wa dóko ni arimásu ka?	Where is the telephone?

Denwa no bókkusu wa dóko ni arimásu ka?	Where is the phone booth?
Tabakoya ni arimásu.	In the cigar store [tobacco shop].
Denwa o kashite kudasái.	May I use your phone? [Please lend me your phone.]
Dóozo otsukai kudasái.	Go ahead! [Please use (it).]
Chookyori dénwa o onegai shimásu.	May I have long distance, please?
Tookyoo é no tsuuwa wa íkura desu ka?	How much is a call to Tokyo?
Goo róku kyuu réi no ichi íchi ichi ní ban o onegai shimásu.	5690-1112, please.
Chótto omachi kudasái.	One moment, please.
Ohanashichuu désu.	The line's busy.
Móshi moshi, chigau bangóo ni kakari-máshita.	[Hello, hello,] Operator, you gave me the wrong number.
Ohenji ga gozai-masén.	There is no answer (*extra polite*).
Yamada-san o onegai shimásu.	May I speak to Mr. Yamada, please?
Watakushi désu.	Speaking.
Kochira wa Táitasu desu.	This is Titus speaking. [This side (it) is Titus.]

E. WORD STUDY

anaúnsaa	announcer
antena	antenna
daiyaru	dial
nyúusu	news
purojúusaa	producer
purogúramu	program
rájio	radio
sáikuru	cycle
suítchi	switch
térebi	television

LESSON 35

DÁI SÁNJUU GÓKA

A. WHAT'S YOUR NAME?

Onamae wa nán to osshaimásu ka?	What is your name?
Yamada Yoshio to mooshimásu.[1]	My name is Yoshio Yamada.
Anó hito no namae wa nán to iimásu ka?	What is his name?
Anó hito no namae wa Tanaka Makoto désu.	His name is Makoto Tanaka.
Anó hito no namae wa nán to iimásu ka?	What is her name?

---

[1] *moosu* = call, say (*humble verb*).

Anó hito wa Sátoo Míchiko to iimásu.	Her name is Michiko Sato.
Anó hitótachi no namae wa nán to iimásu ka?	What are their names?
Ano otoko no hito no namae wa Shimada Yukio de, ano onna no hito no namae wa Takáhashi Nóriko desu.	His name is Yukio Shimada and hers is Noriko Takahashi.
Anó hito no namae wa nán to iimásu ka?	What's his first name?
Anó hito no namae wa Nobuo desu.	His first name is Nobuo.
Anó hito no myóoji wa nán to iimásu ka?	What is his last name?
Anó hito no myóoji wa Yasuda to iimasu.	His last name is Yasuda.

B. WHERE ARE YOU FROM? HOW OLD ARE YOU?

Okuni wa dóchira desu ka?	Where are you from?
Tookyoo désu.	I'm from Tokyo.
Anáta wa dóko de umaremáshita ka?	Where were you born?
Nágoya de umaremáshita.	I was born in Nagoya.
Otoshi wa íkutsu desu ka?	How old are you?

Hátachi[1] desu.	I'm twenty.
Kúgatsu de níjuu ichí ni narimásu.	I'll be twenty-one in September.
Watakushi wa sén kyúuhyaku nanajúu nen no Hachigatsu juukú nichi ni umaremáshita.	I was born August 19, 1970.
Anáta no otanjóobi wa ítsu desu ka?	When is your birthday?
Watakushi no tanjóobi wa nishúukan saki no Ichigatsu níjuu sánnichi desu.	My birthday is in two weeks—January twenty-third.
Otoko no kyóodai wa nánnin arimásu ka?	How many brothers do you have?
Áni ga hitóri to otootó ga hitóri imásu.	I have one older brother and one younger brother.
Áni wa níjuu gó sai desu.	My older brother is twenty-five.
Sono áni wa daigaku ni itte imásu.	He attends the university.
Otootó wa juushichí desu.	My younger brother is seventeen.
Otootó wa kootoogákkoo no sannénsei desu.	He's in the third year of senior high school.
Onéesan ya imooto san wa nánnin desu ka?	How many older and younger sisters do you have?
Imootó ga hitóri áru daké desu.	I have just one younger sister.

[1] *hátachi* = twenty years old.

Imootó wa júugo désu.	She's fifteen.
Imootó wa chuugákkoo no sannénseí desu.	She is in the third year of junior high school.

C. Professions

Donna o shigoto o shiteirasshaimásu ka?	What do you do?
Otóosan no oshígoto wa nán desu ka?	What does your father do?
Okáasan no oshígoto wa nán desu ka?	What does your mother do?
Chichí wa bengóshi desu.	He's [Father is] a lawyer.
Chichí wa kenchikuka désu.	He's an architect.
Kyóoshi desu.	He's a teacher.
Daigaku kyóoju desu.	He's a university professor.
Okáasan no oshígoto wa nán desu ka?	What does your mother do?
Isha désu.	She's a doctor.
Kaisháin desu.	She's a company employee.
Orimonogáisha o yatte imásu.	She's in the textile business.
Hyakushóo desu.	She's a farmer.
Koomúin desu.	She's a government employee.
Jidoosha kóojoo de hataraite imásu.	He works in an automobile factory.

D. FAMILY MATTERS

Koko ni goshinseki ga oari desu ka?	Do you have any relatives here?
Gokázoku wa minna koko ni súnde irasshaimásu ka?	Does your whole family live here?
Sofúbo no hoka wa kázoku wa minna koko ni súnde imásu.	All my family except my grandparents.
Sofúbo wa Nágoya ni súnde imasu.	They live in Nagoya.
Anáta wa Taketomi-san no goshinseki désu ka?	Are you related to Mr. Taketomi?
Watakushi no oji désu.	He's my uncle.
Anó hito wa watakushi no itóko desu.	He's my cousin.
Anáta wa Sákata-san no goshinseki désu ka?	Are you related to Ms. Sakata?
Watakushi no oba désu.	She's my aunt.
Watakushi no itóko desu.	She's my cousin.

REVIEW QUIZ 5

1. _____ (This) *machi no namae wa nán to iimásu ka?*
    a. *Koko*
    b. *Kore*
    c. *Kono*

2. *Koko kara Tookyoo máde* _____ (how) *iki-másu ka?*
   a. *dóko*
   b. *dóo*
   c. *dóre*

3. *Kono toori no namae wa* _____ (what) *to iimásu ka?*
   a. *dóre*
   b. *náze*
   c. *nán*

4. *Ginza Dóori wa* _____ (where) *desu ka?*
   a. *dóko*
   b. *nán*
   c. *dóre*

5. _____ (Post Office) *wa dóko desu ka?*
   a. *Yuubínkyoku*
   b. *Shiyákusho*
   c. *Basutei*

6. *Kádo made itte* _____ (left) *e magarimásu.*
   a. *hidari*
   b. *migi*
   c. *higashi*

7. _____ (How much) *desu ka?*
   a. *Íkutsu*
   b. *Íkura*
   c. *Ítsu*

8. *Tegami o* _____ (would like to write) *n desu ga.*
   a. *dashitái*
   b. *kakitái*
   c. *mitái*

9. _____ (Postage stamp) *wa dóko de kaemásu ka?*
    a. *kitté*
    b. *zasshi*
    c. *shinbun*

10. _____ (Corner) *ni arimásu.*
    a. *Kádo*
    b. *Tonari*
    c. *Asoko*

11. _____ (Here) *ni denwa ga arimásu ka?*
    a. *Koko*
    b. *Soko*
    c. *Asoko*

12. _____ (Wrong) *bangóo ni kakarimáshita.*
    a. *Chigau*
    b. *Hoshíi*
    c. *Byooin no*

13. *Anó hito no* _____ (first name) *wa nán to iimásu ka?*
    a. *namae*
    b. *myóoji*
    c. *jimúsho*

14. *Anáta wa dóko de* _____ (was born) *ka?*
    a. *kaimáshita*
    b. *umaremáshita*
    c. *aimáshita*

15. *Otootó wa* _____ (seventeen) *desu.*
    a. *juushichí*

b. *juuichí*
c. *juuhachí*

16. *Chichí wa* _____ (lawyer) *desu.*
    a. *hyakushóo*
    b. *bengóshi*
    c. *isha*

17. _____ (Government employee) *desu.*
    a. *Koomúin*
    b. *Kyóoshi*
    c. *Kaisháin*

18. *Anáta wa Taketomi-san no* _____ (relative)
    desu ka?
    a. *goshinseki*
    b. *tomodachi*
    c. *bengóshi*

19. _____ (Birthday) *wa ítsu desu ka?*
    a. *Goryokoo*
    b. *Tanjóobi*
    c. *Gokekkon*

20. *Koko kara* _____ (far) *desu ka?*
    a. *tooí*
    b. *chikái*
    c. *nán kiro*

21. *Niban* _____ (track) *désu.*
    a. *sen*
    b. *mé*
    c. *réssha*

22. _____ (Next) *densha wa nánji ni demásu ka?*
    a. *Tsugí no*

    b. *Ása no*
    c. *Gógo no*

23. _____ (Envelope) *o mótte imásu ka?*
    a. *Fuutoo*
    b. *Enpitsu*
    c. *Kitté*

24. _____ (Line's busy) *désu.*
    a. *Ohanashichuu*
    b. *Chigau bangóo*
    c. *Táshika*

25. *Sofúbo* _____ (except) *kázoku wa minna koko ni súnde imasu.*
    a. *no hoka*
    b. *to issho ni*
    c. *to*

ANSWERS
1–c; 2–b; 3–c; 4–a; 5–a; 6–a; 7–b; 8–b; 9–a; 10–a; 11–a; 12–a; 13–a; 14–b; 15–a; 16–b; 17–a; 18–a; 19–b; 20–a; 21–a; 22–a; 23–a; 24–a; 25–a.

LESSON 36

DÁI SÁNJUU RÓKKA

A. *KAIMONO* SHOPPING

Study the notes at the end of this section for greater comprehension.

1. **Íkura desu ka?**
   How much is it?

2. **Sén en desu.**
   One thousand yen.

3. **Chótto takasugimásu ga, hoka ni arimasén ka?**
   It's [a little] too expensive. Don't you have anything else?

4. **Onaji shúrui no desu ka?**
   Of the same kind?

5. **Onaji shúrui no ka nitá no ga hoshíi n desu ga.**
   I want the same kind or something similar.

6. **Koo yuú no ga gozaimásu.**
   We have this (sort).

7. **Móo hoka ní wa arimasén ka?**
   Don't you have anything else (to show me)?

8. **Mótto oyasúi no desu ka?**
   Less expensive [one]? [Cheaper one?]

9. **Móshi áttara.**
   If possible. [If there is.]

10. **Kore wa ikága desu ka?**
    Would you like this? [How about this one?]

11. **Sore wa nedan ni yorimásu ne.**
    That depends on the price. [(I think it is all right) depending on the price.]

12. **Kore wa hassen en désu.**
    This is eight thousand yen.

13. **Kore wa dóo desu ka? Máe no yori yasúi n desu ka, takái n desu ka?**
How about this? Is it cheaper or more expensive (than the former one)?

14. **Mótto takái desu.**
More expensive.

15. **Hoka ni arimasén ka née?**
Don't you have anything else?

16. **Íma wa gozaimasén ga, atarashíi kata nó ga chikajika kúru hazu désu ga ...**
Not at the moment, but I'm expecting some new styles soon. [... new style ones are supposed to come soon.]

17. **Itsu goro désu ka?**
When? [About when?]

18. **Moo jikí da to omoimásu ga. Konshuu matsu góro otachiyori kudasai máse.**
Any day now. Drop in toward the end of the week. [I think it'll be very soon ...]

19. **Ja soo shimásu. Tokoró de kore wa íkura desu ka?**
I'll do that. By the way, how much is this?

20. **Issoku sanbyakú en desu.**
Three hundred yen a pair.

21. **Ichi dáasu kudasái.**
Let me have a dozen. [Give me a dozen, please.]

22. **Omochi ni nanimásu ka?**
Will you take (them with you)?

23. **Iie, haitatsu shite kudasái.**
No. Please deliver them.

24. **Gojúusho wa onaji désu ne?**
At the same address? [The address is the same, isn't it?]

25. **Onaji désu.**
It's still the same.

26. **Maido arígatoo gozaimásu.**
Thank you very much. [Thank you (for your patronage) each time (you come).]

27. **Sayonara.**
Good-bye.

28. **Sayonara.**
Good-bye.

NOTE

Title: *Kaimono* = Shopping

4. *Shúrui no:* same as *shúrui no monó* = one(s) of the same kind. See also #13 for similar construction.

5. *Nitá no ga* = one (that) resembles (it).

6. *Gozaimásu:* an extra-polite form of *arimásu* which would be used by the shopkeeper to the customer.

8. *Oyasúi:* an extra-polite form of *yasúi* or *yasúi desu* containing the "honorific" prefix o-.

Nearly all adjectives can take this prefix "honoring" the person to whom or about whom you are speaking. However, an adjective that itself begins with *o* cannot add the honorific prefix *o*. For instance, *omoshirói* [It is interesting] cannot become *oomoshirói*.

10. *Ikága* is extra-polite for *dóo.*
11. *Ni yorimásu* = depending on.
13. *Máe no:* same as *máe no monó* = one(s) of the previous time.
16. *Chikajika* = very recently.

Kúru hazu désu ga: When the particle *ga* is used to terminate a clause, it signifies "but" or "and," but does not have quite the same force. It serves to make the sentence less sharp or less pointed, and is commonly used in extra-polite speech.

Otachiyori kudasái (respect): same as *tachiyotte kudasái.*

Note the construction: *O* plus the pre-*masu* form plus *kudasái.*

For example: *okaki kudasái* = *káite kudasái; otabe kudasái* = *tábete kudasái.*

19. *Ja:* same as *dé wa* = well, then.
Tokoró de = by the way.
20. *Soku* = a counter for socks, stockings, shoes.
22. *Omochi ni narimásu ka* (respect): same as *mochimásu ka* or *mótte ikimásu ka.* Notice the construction: *o* plus the pre-*masu* form plus *ni narimásu.* This method for the construction of the respect form of a verb can be used for almost any plain verb (i.e., a verb which is not already respect). Further examples: *okaki ni narimásu* = *kakimásu; otabe ni narimásu* = *tabemásu; okai ni narimáshita* = *kaimáshita.*

24. *Gojúusho* (respect): same as *júusho*. *Goojúusho* and all other respect words of expressions introduced here cannot be used for things or actions pertaining to the speaker or persons identified with the speaker.
26. *Maido arígatoo gozaimásu:* The usual expression used by shopkeepers.

QUIZ 30

1. _____ (How much) *desu ka?*
   a. *Íkura*
   b. *Ikága*
   c. *Íkutsu*

2. *Onaji* _____ (kind) *no desu ka?*
   a. *shúrui*
   b. *nedan*
   c. *tokoro*

3. *Onaji shúrui no* _____ (or) *nitá no ga hoshíi n desu ga . . .*
   a. *ga*
   b. *ka*
   c. *to*

4. _____ (This type) *ga gozaimásu ga . . .*
   a. *Dóo yuú no*
   b. *Soo yuú no*
   c. *Koo yuú no*

5. _____ (Less) *oyasúi no desu ka?*
   a. *Sukóshi*
   b. *Mótto*
   c. *Taihen*

6. _____ (That) *wa nedan ni yorimásu ne.*
   a. *Sore*
   b. *Kore*
   c. *Dóre*

7. *Íma wa gozaimasén* _____ (but) *atarashíi kata nó ga chikajika kúru hazu désu ga . . .*
   a. *kara*
   b. *ga*
   c. *noni*

8. _____ (Around when) *désu ka?*
   a. *Ítsu*
   b. *Nanji gurai*
   c. *Itsu goro*

9. _____ (One dozen) *kudasái.*
   a. *Ichí mai*
   b. *Ichi dáasu*
   c. *Issatsu*

10. _____ (Deliver) *shite kudasái.*
    a. *Haitatsu*
    b. *Benkyoo*
    c. *Kekkon*

ANSWERS
1–a; 2–a; 3–b; 4–c; 5–b; 6–a; 7–b; 8–c; 9–b; 10–a.

B. WORD STUDY

baketsu	bucket
booru	bowl
fóoku	fork
furaipan	frying pan

gásu	gas
míkisaa	mixer
nafukin	napkin
náifu	knife
supúun	spoon
tóosutaa	toaster

LESSON 37

DÁI SÁNJUU NANÁ KA

A. *ASAGÓHAN* **BREAKFAST**

Study the notes at the end of this section for greater comprehension.

1. Mr. Y:[1] **Onaka ga suitádaroo.**
   Mr. Y: You must be hungry.

2. Mrs. Y: **Ée, náni ka itadakitái wa.**
   Mrs. Y: Yes, (I) would like to have something.

3. Mr. Y: **Kono hóteru ni wa íi resutoran ga áru to yuú kara sokó e itte miyóo.**
   Mr. Y: They say there is a good restaurant in this hotel. Let's go there.

4. Mrs. Y: **Sore ga íi wa. Soo shimashóo.**
   Mrs. Y: That's a good idea. Let's do that.

5. Mr. Y: **Chótto sumimasén!**
   Mr. Y: Hello! [Excuse me.]

---

[1] *Mr. Y* stands for "Mr. Yamada," *Mrs. Y* for "Mrs. Yamada," *W* for "Waiter."

6. W: **Oyobi de gozaimásu ka?**
   W: Yes? [(You) called, (sir)?]

7. Mr. Y: **Asagóhan o tabetái n desu ga ...**
   Mr. Y: We'd like some breakfast.

8. Mrs. Y: **Náni ga itadakemásu no?**
   Mrs. Y: What can we have?

9. W: **Onomímono wa koohíi koocha hotto chokoréeto. Nán ni itashimashóo ka?**
   W: Coffee, black tea, or hot chocolate. What would you like to have? [What shall I make it to be?]

10. Mrs. Y: **Hoka no móno wa?**
    Mrs. Y: What else?

11. W: **Roorú pan ni tóosuto, sore kara hotto kéeki mo dekimásu.**
    W: Rolls, toast, and hotcakes, too.

12. Mrs. Y: **Bátaa wa tsukánai n desu ka?**
    Mrs. Y: No butter?

13. W: **Mochíron tsukimásu. Hoka ni jámu mo otsuke shimásu.**
    W: Of course, butter and jelly. [Of course, (we) will serve (it). (We) will serve jelly also.]

14. Mrs. Y: **Déwa watakushi wa koohíi to tóosuto daké ni shimásu.**
    Mrs. Y: I'd like to have some coffee and toast.

15. Mr. Y: **Kochira mo sore to onaji ni shite sonó hoka ni hanjuku támago o tsukéte kudasái.**
Mr. Y: The same for me, and a soft-boiled egg as well.

16. W: **Kashikomarimáshita. Hoka ni náni ka?**
W: Certainly, sir. Would you like anything else?

17. Mr. Y: **Íya, sore de takusan.**
Mr. Y: No, that'll be all.

18. Mrs. Y: **Nápukin o mótte kite kudasaimásu ka?**
Mrs. Y: May I have a napkin, please?

19. Mr. Y: **Sore kara fooku mo. Koko ní wa fóoku ga nái yoo da kara.**
Mr. Y: Would you also get a fork, please? I don't have one. [(It) seems (it) is not here.]

20. Mrs. Y: **Osatoo mo onegai shimásu.**
Mrs. Y: And some sugar, too, please.

21. W: **Omatase itashimáshita.**
W: Here you are, madam. [Sorry to have kept you waiting.]

22. Mrs. Y: **Kono koohíi wa sukkári tsumetaku nátte iru wa. Atsúi no to torikaete kudasaimásu ka?**
Mrs. Y: My coffee is cold. Please bring me another cup.

23. W: **Kashikomarimáshita.**
W: Gladly.

24. Mr. Y: **Denpyoo o motté kite kudasái.**
    Mr. Y: May I have the check?

25. W: **Omatase itashimáshita.**
    W: Here you are, sir. [Sorry to have kept you waiting.]

26. Mr. Y: **Ja kore de tótte kudasái. Otsuri wa íi desu.**
    Mr. Y: Here, keep the change.

27. W: **Maido arígatoo gozaimásu.**
    W: Thank you very much, sir.

28. Mr. Y: **Ja sayonara.**
    Mr. Y: Good-bye.

NOTE

Title: *Asagóhan* = Breakfast
1. The conversation here is first carried on between husband and wife; later it is continued between the couple and the waiter. Notice how freely the plain forms instead of the usual *-másu* or *-désu* forms of verbs and adjectives are used in such a conversation.
   Onaka ga suitádaroo (from *onaka ga suku* = get hungry [The stomach gets empty]. *-daróo* [must be, probably]) is the plain form of *-deshóo. -daróo* at the end of a sentence is used exclusively by men in casual conversation.
2. *Itadakitai* (extra polite, humble)[1] (from *itadaku*) = want to eat, drink, receive.

[1] *Humble,* as opposed to *respect,* is a word form that demotes the status of the speaker. Usually it is the speaker who humbles him- or herself.

Wa: a particle used exclusively by women in casual conversation. It appears at the end of a sentence and adds a feminine touch.

8. *No:* another particle used almost exclusively by women which takes the place of *no desu* or *n desu* at the end of a sentence. With a rising intonation, it is, like the particle *ka,* a spoken question mark.

12. *Tsukánai* (from *tsúku*) = does not go with; is not served with.

13. *Otsuke shimásu: otsuke* comes from *tsukéru* = serve something with. It is a transitive verb to be paired with *tsúku* (see #12, above). The construction employed here, that is, *o* plus the pre-*masu* form plus *suru* is the one used in extra-polite (humble) speech when the speaker discusses doing something for the person with whom or about whom s(he) is talking.

14. *Ni shimásu* = one makes (his/her choice or decision) to be; one decides on (taking).

15. *Kochira* = this side, this way; sometimes used in place of *watakushi* [I]. Similarly, *sochira* or *sochira sama* can be used for ''you,'' ''he,'' ''she,'' or ''they.''

18. *-kudasaimásu ka:* one type of a request form. It is softer than *-kudasái.*

20. *Onegai shimásu:* an idiom used when the speaker requests someone to do something.

22. *Tsumetaku nátte iru* = is cold, is chilled [is in the state of having become cold].

26. *Ja:* a variant of *dé wa* = Well, then, if that is the case, when used at the beginning of a sentence. *Kore de tótte kudasái* = Using this (money), please take (what I owe you). *Otsuri wa íi desu* = Keep the change. [As for the change (it) will be all right (for you to keep it).]

B. A Sample Menu

KONDATE	MENU
Suimono	Clear Soup
sáyori	snipe fish
wárabi	brackens
namayuba	fresh bean curds
Sasimí	Sashimi
maguro	tuna
Sunómono	Salad
sázae	turbo
údo	udo (Japanese asparagus)
karashisúmiso	dressed with vinegar, mustard, and bean paste
Yasai Nimono	Cooked Vegetables
kuwai	arrowhead bulbs
sayaéndoo	snow peas
takenoko	bamboo shoots
údo	udo
Yakimono	Fish
kói-teriyaki	broiled carp
tsukeawase	served with fancy relish
Kóbachi	Small Bowl
tsukushi-	omelet
tamagó-toji	with horsetails
Góhan	Rice
satoimo-	rice cooked with
góhan	taros
Mishoshíru	Soybean Paste Soup
tóofu	tofu
négi	green onions
Tsukemono	Pickles
takúan	pickled white radish
narazuke	pickles seasoned with sake
kabura	turnips

REVIEW QUIZ 6

1. *Onaka ga* _____ (must be hungry).
   a. *tsúitadaroo.*
   b. *suitádaroo.*
   c. *káitadaroo.*

2. _____ (Something) *itadakitái wa.*
   a. *Nani mo*
   b. *Náni ka*
   c. *Nán de mo*

3. *Kono hóteru ni wa íi résutoran ga* _____
   (there is).
   a. *arimásu.*
   b. *imásu.*
   c. *shimásu.*

4. *Kono koohíi wa* _____ (cold) *nátte iru wa.*
   a. *wáruku*
   b. *sámuku*
   c. *tsumetaku*

5. *Kochira mo sore to* _____ (the same) *ni shite
   kudasái.*
   a. *nita*
   b. *onaji*
   c. *chigau*

6. _____ (Sugar) *o motté kite kudasaimásu ka?*
   a. *Osatoo*
   b. *Ocha*
   c. *Tamágo*

7. *Sore kara fóoku* _____ (also).
   a. *moo.*

    b. *to.*
    c. *mo.*

8. _____ (Check) *o motté kite kudasái.*
    a. *Denpyoo*
    b. *Kippu*
    c. *Tanjóobi*

9. *Fóoku ga* _____ (missing) *yoo da.*
    a. *nái*
    b. *inai*
    c. *ikanai*

10. _____ (Change) *wa íi desu.*
    a. *Denpyoo*
    b. *Okane*
    c. *Otsuri*

ANSWERS
1–b; 2–b; 3–a; 4–c; 5–b; 6–a; 7–c; 8–a; 9–a; 10–c.

LESSON 38

DÁI SÁNJUU HACHI KA

A. IN, ON, UNDER

    1. *Ni, De, E, No* In, Into

Sore wa jibikí ni arimásu.	That's in the dictionary.
Pokétto ni iremáshita.	He put it in his pocket.
Anó hito no heyá ni arimásu.	You'll find it in his room.

Hikidashi ni irete kudasái.	Put it into the drawer, please.
Mé ni náni ka hairimáshita.	I have something in my eye. [Something got into my eyes.]
Tookyoo de kaimáshita.	I bought it in Tokyo.
Tookyoo no hakubútsukan de mimáhista.	I saw it in the museum in Tokyo.

2. *No naka ni* (. . . *de,* . . . *e,* . . . *no,* . . . *o*) Inside

Sono kaban no náka o míte kudasái.	Please look in that briefcase. [Please look in the within of that briefcase.]
Gakkoo no náka no shokudoo de góhan o tabemáshita.	We ate [had our meal] in the dining room of [in the within of] the school.
Yamada-san to issho ni tatémono no náka e hairimáshita.	Together with Mr. Yamada, we entered the inside of the building.
Kusuriya wa sono tatémono no náka ni arimásu.	The drugstore is in [inside] that building.

3. *No ue ni* (. . . *de,* . . . *no,* . . . *e*) On

Kono tegami o, sonó hito no tsukue no ué ni oite kudasái.	Please put this letter on his desk.
Oka no ué de asonde imásu.	They are playing on the hill.

Fuutoo no ué ni káite kudasái.	Please write it on the envelope.

4. *No shita ni (. . . de, . . . no, . . . e)* Under

Isu no shitá ni arimásu.	It's under the chair.
Sono hón wa hoka no hón no shitá ni arimásu.	You'll find the book under the others.
Béddo no shitá ni okimáshita.	She put it under the bed.
Hashi no shitá de hiroimáshita.	I picked it up under the bridge.

5. *Náka* Place inside

Náka wa samúi desu.	It is cold inside.
Náka o mínaide kudasái.	Please do not look inside.

6. *Ue* Top, Surface

Ue ni oite kudasái.	Put it on top.
Ue o míte kudasai.	Look on the top.

7. *Shita* Bottom, Place under, Place below

Sore o shitá ni oite kudasái.	Please put that underneath.
Kono shitá o mité kudasái.	Please look under here.

B. IF, WHEN

1. *Moshi*[1] *. . . -ba; -nara* If

---

[1] *Moshi* is optional.

Notice that the -(*r*)*eba* ending form of a verb, the *kereba*- ending form of an *i*- adjective, and the *nara* form of a copula express the idea "if (something) happens," or "if (something) is the case."[1]

These forms are called the "provisional" and are used *only* for a present or future hypothetical condition.

móshi dekíreba	if I can
móshi juubún okane ga áreba	if I have enough money
Soko e ikéba minná ni aemásu.	If you go there, you can meet everybody.
Sámukereba súgu kaerimásu.	If it is cold, I will come back right away.
Yásukereba kau tsumori désu.	If it is inexpensive, I intend to buy it.
Ténisu ga joozú nara íi n desu ga . . .	I hope she is good at tennis. [If she is good at tennis, it is good . . .]
Sashimí nara nán demo kékkoo desu.	If it is raw fish, anything is fine.

2. -*Tara* If, When

Notice that the -*tara* form is made by adding -*ra* to the -*ta* form. It is used to express a condition of the past, present, or future. The -*tara* form is called the "conditional."

---

[1] Use -*eba* with consonant verbs; use -*reba* with vowel verbs. For further discussion of the formation of -*ba* form, see Section 36 of the Summary of Japanese Grammar.

Ashita áme ga futtára ikimasén.	If it rains tomorrow, I won't go.
Ashita átsukattara ikimasén.	If it's hot tomorrow, I won't go.
Okane ga nákattara kaemasén.	If you don't have the money, you can't buy it.
Anmari takái to ittára yásuku shimáshita.	When I said it was too expensive, he lowered the price [he made it cheap].
Tabetákattara tábete mo íi desu.	If you want to eat it, you can [eat it].
Tákakattara honmono désu.	If it is expensive, it is [a] genuine [thing].
Sono kusuri o nóndara súgu yóku narimáshita.	When I took [drank] that medicine, I got well right away.

3. *To* If, When, Whenever

Notice that *to* is used only when what follows it is a natural consequence to what is stated in the clause that precedes it. *To* is always preceded by the present form of a verb, an adjective, or the copula; it cannot be used when the terminal clause ends in *-te kudasái.*

Kono michi o mas- súgu iku to bijútsu- kan no máe ni demásu.	If you follow [go] this road straight ahead, you will come to the front of the Fine Arts Museum.
Básu de iku to gojí- kan kakarimásu.	If you go by bus, it takes five hours.

Wakaránai kotó ga áru to Yamada-san ni kikimásu.	When there are things that I don't understand, I ask Mr. Yamada.
Áme ga fúru to kúru hitó ga sukunáku narimásu.	When it rains, fewer persons come [persons who come get fewer].
Máinichi káku to joozú ni narimásu.	When you write it every day, you become more skillful [in it].

C. WITHOUT

1. *Nashi ni* Without

okane náshi ni	without money
nani mo náshi ni	without anything
machigái náshi ni	without fail
kónnan náshi ni	without difficulty
Kónnan náshi ni dekimásu.	You can do it without any difficulty.

2. *-Nai de* Without

Asagóhan o tabénai de dekakemáshita.	I went out without having breakfast.
Benkyoo shinái de shikén o ukemáshita.	Without studying, I took a test.

QUIZ 31

1. *Sore o shita ni oite kudasái.*

a. It's in the dictionary.

2. *Pokétto ni ire-*
   máshita.
3. *Sore wa jibikí ni*
   arimásu.
4. *Fuutoo no ué ni*
   káite kudasái.
5. *Oka no ué de*
   asonde imásu.
6. *Ue o míte kudasái.*

7. *yásukereba*

8. *móshi juubún*
   okane ga áreba
9. *anmari takái to*
   ittára
10. *machigái nashi ni*
11. *kónnan náshi ni*

12. *okane náshi ni*

13. *sámukereba*
14. *Ue ni oite kudasái*
15. *Sono hón wa hoka*
    no hón no shitá ni
    arimásu.

b. Please put that un-
   derneath.
c. He put it in his
   pocket.
d. They are playing
   on the hill.
e. Write it on the en-
   velope, please.
f. You will find the
   book under the
   others.
g. Put it on top,
   please.
h. Look on the top,
   please.
i. if it is cold

j. if it is inexpensive
k. if I have enough
   money
l. when I said it was
   too expensive
m. without money
m. without fail
o. without difficulty

ANSWERS

1–b; 2–c; 3–a; 4–e; 5–d; 6–h; 7–j; 8–k; 9–l; 10–n;
11–o; 12–m; 13–i; 14–g; 15–f.

REVIEW QUIZ 7

1. _____ (That one) *ga hoshíi desu.*
   a. *Asoko*

    b. *Are*
    c. *Anna*

2. _____ (This) *wa ikága desu ka?*
    a. *Kore*
    b. *Kono*
    c. *Koko*

3. *Nihongo de* _____ (how) *iimásu ka?*
    a. *dóre*
    b. *dónna*
    c. *dóo*

4. *Soko e itta* _____ (never).
    a. *tsumori désu.*
    b. *kotó ga arimasén.*
    c. *hazu désu.*

5. _____ (Nothing) *kaimasén deshita.*
    a. *Nán de mo*
    b. *Náni ka*
    c. *Nani mo*

6. *Kono hon wa* _____ (her) *desu.*
    a. *dóno hito no*
    b. *sono otoko no hitó no*
    c. *anó hito no*

7. *Watashi no* _____ (aunt) *désu.*
    a. *oba*
    b. *oji*
    c. *itóko*

8. _____ (One week) *kakarimásu.*
    a. *Ikkágetsu*
    b. *Isshúukan*
    c. *Ichínen*

9. _____ (Next) *basu de ikimashóo.*
   a. *Ashita no*
   b. *Tsugí no*
   c. *Asátte no*

10. *Dóomo* _____ (thanks).
    a. *wakarimasén.*
    b. *arígatoo gozaimásu.*
    c. *dekimasén.*

11. *Ni san* _____ (days) *shitára denwa o kákete kudasái.*
    a. *jíkan*
    b. *nichi*
    c. *nen*

12. *Kono káta o* _____ (know) *ka?*
    a. *gozónji desu*
    b. *sagashite imásu*
    c. *goshookai itashimásu*

13. *Iie, soo* _____ (don't think).
    a. *ikimasén.*
    b. *omoimasén.*
    c. *kimasén.*

14. *Kyóoto de* _____ (bought).
    a. *tsukurimáshita.*
    b. *kikimáshita.*
    c. *kaimáshita.*

15. *Sono tegami wa* _____ (wrote) *ka?*
    a. *mimáshita*

   b. *kakimáshita*
   c. *uketorimáshita*

16. *Watakushi wa* _____ (morning) *wa koohíi o nomimásu.*
   a. *hirú*
   b. *yóru*
   c. *ása*

17. *Éki de tomodachi ni* _____ (met).
   a. *hanashimáshita.*
   b. *aimáshita.*
   c. *kikimáshita.*

18. *Anáta no denwa bángoo o* _____ (give me).
   a. *shitte imásu.*
   b. *kudasái.*
   c. *agemashóo.*

19. *Sore wa taihen* _____ (good) *desu.*
   a. *kékkoo*
   b. *omoshirói*
   c. *yasúi*

20. _____ (Soon) *kimásu.*
   a. *Súgu*
   b. *Ashita*
   c. *Áto de*

ANSWERS
1–b; 2–a; 3–c; 4–b; 5–c; 6–c; 7–a; 8–b; 9–b; 10–b;
11–b; 12–a; 13–b; 14–c; 15–b; 16–c; 17–b; 18–b;
19–a; 20–a.

D. *Shakuya Sagashi* HOUSE HUNTING

Study the notes at the end of this section for greater comprehension.

1. **Kashiya ga áru soo desu ga.**
   I hear you have a house to rent.

2. **Dóchira deshoo ka? Futatsu áru n desu ga.**
   Which one? We have two.

3. **Shinbun no kookoku o míte shittá no desu ga.**
   It's the one advertised in the paper.

4. **Hái, wakarimáshita.**
   Oh, that one.

5. **Dónna ie ka sukóshi setsumei shite moraemásen ka?**
   Can you describe them?

6. **Ookíi hoo wa go-eru-dii-kée desu.**
   The larger of the two is 5LDK.

7. **Chiisái hoo wa dóo desu ka?**
   How about the smaller one?

8. **Yon-eru-dii-kée desu.**
   (It) is 4LDK.

9. **Ookíi hoo wa gáreeji ga tsúite imásu ka?**
   Does the larger house have a garage?

10. **Hái, tsúite imasu.**
    Yes, it does.

11. **Niwa ga arimásu ka?**
Is there a garden there?

12. **Hái, gozaimásu. Nihonshiki no rippa na niwa désu.**
Yes, there is. It's a fine, Japanese-style garden.

13. **Chiisái hoo wa?**
How about the smaller house?

14. **Niwa to iu hodo no niwa wa gozaimasén ga miharashi no íi takadai ni gozaimásu.**
There isn't any garden to speak of, but the house is situated on top of a hill and has a nice view. [(It)'s not much of a garden that there is . . .]

15. **Shízuka na tokoro désu ka?**
Is it in a quiet neighborhood?

16. **Hái, oodóori kara hanárete imásu kara taihen shízuka desu.**
Yes, it is away from big streets and it's very quiet there.

17. **Yáchin wa dono kurai désu ka?**
What's the rent?

18. **Ookíi hoo wa tsuki nijuuman en désu.**
The rent for the larger house is two hundred thousand yen per month.

19. **Chiisái hoo wa?**
And the smaller house?

20. **Tsuki juugoman en désu.**
One hundred and fifty thousand yen per month.

21 **Kágu zoosaku wa dóo nan desu ka?**
    What about furniture and other equipment?

22. **Mina tsúite orimásu. Tatami mo harikáeta bákari desu.**
    (It)'s well furnished. The floor mats have been completely repaired.

23. **Reizóoko nádo wa nái deshoo ne?**
    I suppose a refrigerator is not included?

24. **Iie, saishinshiki no reizóoko ga tsúite orimásu.**
    There is a late-model refrigerator. [There is a refrigerator of the latest style.]

25. **Ichínen no keiyaku de karitái to omótte irú n desu ga, sore de íi desu ka?**
    I would like to get a lease for a year. Do you think that's possible [agreeable]?

26. **Sono ten wa yánushi to gosoodan itadakitái to omoimásu.**
    You'd have to see the owner for that.

27. **Shikíkin wa irú n desu ka?**
    Do I have to pay key money? [Is key money necessary?]

28. **Hái, sankagetsúbun itadaku kóto ni nátte orimásu.**
    Yes, we ask three months' rent (for it).

29. **Hoka ní wa?**
    Nothing else?

30. **Hoshóonin ga irimásu.**
You have to have references.

31. **Tsuide ni okiki shimásu ga denwa wa tsúite imásu ka?**
Is there a telephone already installed?

32. **Ainiku tsúite orimasén.**
No, there isn't. [Sorry, but it isn't installed.]

33. **Áa sóo desu ka.**
I see.

34. **Chikatetsu ya JR no éki ni mo chikákute taihen bénri na tokoro désu.**
The house is located not too far from the subway and the JR-line station. So it's quite convenient.

35. **Áa sóo desu ka. Soko kara Marunóuchi made wa dono kurai kakarimásu ka?**
I see. How much time does it take from there to Marunouchi?

36. **Yáku nijuppun gúrai desu.**
I would say about twenty minutes.

37. **Básu mo chikáku o tóotte imásu ka?**
Is there any bus line running nearby?

38. **Hái, Tookyoo-eki yuki ga kádo hitótsu saki o tóotte imásu.**
Yes, there is one a block away. The bus goes to Tokyo Station.

39. **Sono uchí wa íma itte miraremásu ka?**
May we see the house now?

40. **Sumimasén ga gozen-chuu shíka ome ni kakerarénai n desu ga.**
I'm sorry, but it is open for inspection only in the morning.

41. **Áa sóo desu ka. Sore ja ashita no ása kimásu. Iroiro oséwasama deshita.**
Very well. I'll come tomorrow morning. Thanks a lot.

42. **Dóo itashimáshite. Kochira kóso shitsúrei itashimáshita.**
Not at all. Glad to be able to help you.

NOTE

Title: *Shakuya Ságashi* = Searching (for) a House to Rent.
  1. *Áru soo desu* = I understood that there is.
  2. *Dóchira* = which (of the two).
  3. *Kookoku* = advertisement.
  5. *Setsumei shite moraemasén ka* = Can't I have you explain the details for me?
  6. *Go-eru-dii-kée* = 5LDK (5 rooms, L = living room, DK = dining kitchen).
  9. *Tsuite imásu* = are attached; are equipped.
 14. *Niwa to iu hodo no niwa* = a garden (worthy of) calling it a garden; (there isn't any) garden to speak of.
     Miharashi = view.
     Takadai = top of a hill (within a city area).
 16. *Hanárete imásu* = is away from.
 17. *Yáchin* = house rent.

18. *Tsuki* = per month.
21. *Kagu zoosaku* = furniture and other equipment(s).
22. *Tatami* = Japanese-style floor mat.
    Harikáeta bákari desu = We have just replaced the mat covers with new ones (the *-ta* form of a verb plus *bákari desu* = just finished doing . . .).
23. *Reizóoko nádo* = a refrigerator and things like that.
24. *Iie* = no. Notice that this is used where "yes" would be used in English, for the thought is, "No, what you have mentioned is not correct." *Saishinshiki no reizóoko* = latest-model refrigerator.
    Orimásu: a synonym for *imásu,* but more formal.
25. *Keiyaku* = contract; lease.
26. *Yánushi* = landlord.
    Gosoodan itadakitái = I would like to have you consult.
27. *Shikíkin* = key money, security.
28. *Sankagetsúbun* = the equivalent of three months' (rent). (*-bun* = the portion for.)
    Kotó ni nátte orimásu = It is arranged that, it is fixed that (we receive).
30. *Hoshóonin* = reference (i.e., one who guarantees).
34. *Chikatetsu* = subway.
35. *Marunóuchi* = the heart of the business section in Tokyo.
38. *Tookyoo-eki yuki* = bound for Tokyo: *yuki* = bound for, when used after a place-name.
39. *Miraremásu* = can see. The same form—made by adding *-(r)areru* to the base—is used for both the passive voice and respect expressions.

40. *Ome ni kakerarénai* = can't show (you); *kakerarénai:* a negative form of *kakeraréru,* which is a potential form made from *kakéru* by adding *-rareru* to the base.

41. *Oséwasama deshita* = thanks: a common way of expressing thanks for services rendered.

QUIZ 32

1. _____ (Quiet) *na tokoro désu ka?*
   a. *Rippa*
   b. *Shízuka*
   c. *Bénri*

2. *Oodóori kara* _____ (away from) *imasu.*
   a. *hanárete*
   b. *hanáshite*
   c. *tooi*

3. _____ (Rent) *wa dono kurai désu ka?*
   a. *Yáchin*
   b. *Nedan*
   c. *Shikíkin*

4. *Sankagetsúbun* _____ (receive) *kóto ni nátte orimásu.*
   a. *haráu*
   b. *itadaku*
   c. *tazunéru*

5. _____ (Furniture) *wa tsúite imásu ka?*
   a. *Tatami*
   b. *Reizóoko*
   c. *Kágu zoosaku*

6. *Yáku* _____ (twenty minutes) *gúrai desu.*
   a. *nijuppun*
   b. *juunifun*
   c. *nijuufun*

7. _____ (Garden) *ga arimásu ka?*
   a. *Heyá*
   b. *Niwa*
   c. *Takadai*

8. *Gozenchuu* _____ (only) *ome ni kakerare-masén.*
   a. *démo*
   b. *hoka*
   c. *shíka*

9. _____ (Tomorrow) *no ása kimásu.*
   a. *Kinoo*
   b. *Ashita*
   c. *Asátte*

10. *Iroiro* _____ (thanks for your service) *deshita.*
    a. *omachidoosama*
    b. *ohanashichuu*
    c. *oséwasama*

ANSWERS
1–b; 2–a; 3–a; 4–b; 5–c; 6–a; 7–b; 8–c; 9–b; 10–c.

LESSON 39

DÁI SÁNJUU KYÚU KA

A. *Kuru*   To Come

Kimásu.	I (you, he, she, we, they) come.
Kité kudasái.	Please come!
Koko e kité kudasái.	Come here, please.
Watakushi to issho ni kité kudasái.	Come with me, please.
Mata kité kudasái.	Come again, please.
Uchi máde kité kudasái.	Come to the house, please.
Ítsu ka yóru kité kudasái.	Come some night, please.
Kónaide kudasái.	Please don't come.
Dóko kara kimásu ka?	Where are you coming from?
Tookyoo kara kimásu.	I am coming from Tokyo.
Gekijoo kara kimásu.	I am coming from the theater.
Súgu kimásu.	I am coming right away.

-ta bákari desu = to have just completed an action.

Amerika kara kitá bákari desu.	I have just come from the United States.
Sono tegami wa íma kitá bákari desu.	That letter has just arrived.

-te kuru = to have just started to, to have started and continued to the present doing.

Áme ga futté kimá-shita.	The rain has started to fall.
Nihongo ga wakátte kimáshita.	I have started to understand Japanese. [Japanese has begun to be clear to me.]
Nihongo o rokkágetsu benkyoo shite ki-máshita.	I have been studying Japanese for six months.
Nihongo no hón bákari yónde ki-máshita.	I have been reading nothing but books in Japanese.

B. *Iu (yuu)* To Say

Iimásu.   I (you, he, she, we, they) say

to iu = to say that . . .

Ikanai to iimáshita.	I said that I wouldn't go. [(I) said, "(I) will not go."]
Ikanái ka to ii-máshita.	I said, "Aren't you going?" He said, "Aren't you going?"

tó ka iu = to say something to the effect that, to say something like.

Ikanái ka tó ka ii-máshita.	He said something like, "Aren't you going?" (but I am not exactly sure what he said).

Hitóri de ittá to ka iimáshita.	He said something to the effect that he went alone.
Iinikúi desu.	It's hard to say.
Itte kudasái.	Say (it)! Tell (it), please.
Moo ichido itte kudasái.	Say it again, please.
Nihongo de itte kudasái.	Say it in Japanese, please.
Yukkúri itte kudasái.	Say it slowly, please.
Iwanáide kudasái.	Don't say that, please.
Sonó hito ni itte kudasái.	Tell (it) to him, please.

yoo ni iu = to tell someone to.

Kúru yoo ni itte kudasái.	Tell him to come, please.
Kónai yoo ni itte kudasái.	Please tell him not to come.
Kau yóo ni itte kudasái.	Please tell him not to buy (it).
Kawanai yóo ni itte kudasái.	Please tell him not to buy (it).
Sonó hito ni iwanáide kudasái.	Don't tell it to him, please.
Sonó hito ni nani mo iwanáide kudasái.	Don't tell him anything, please.
Dare ni mo iwanáide kudasái.	Please don't tell that to anybody.
Nán to iimáshita ka?	What did you say?
Nán to osshaimáshita ka?	What did you say (*respect*)?
Nani mo iimasén deshita.	She hasn't said anything.

QUIZ 33

1. *Gekijoo kara kimasu.*	a. Come with me, please.
2. *Hitóri de ittá to ka iimáshita.*	b. Where are you coming from?
3. *Súgu kimasu.*	c. Come some night, please.
4. *Dóko kara kimásu ka?*	d. I'm coming right away.
5. *Itte kudasái.*	e. I'm coming from the theater.
6. *Nihongo de itte kudasái.*	f. Say it in Japanese, please.
7. *Áme ga futté kimáshita.*	g. I have just come from the United States.
8. *Ítsu ka yóru kité kudasái.*	h. The rain has started to fall.
9. *Watakushi to issho ni kité kudasái.*	i. He said something to the effect that he went alone.
10. *Amerika kara kita bákari desu.*	j. Tell me, please.

ANSWERS
1–e; 2–i; 3–d; 4–b; 5–j; 6–f; 7–h; 8–c; 9–a; 10–g.

C. *Suru* To Do

Shimásu.
I (you, he, she, we, they) do.

Shite imásu.
I'm doing it.

Náni o shite imásu ka?
What are you doing?

Dóo shimásu ka?	How do you do that?
Náni o shite imáshita ka?	What have you been doing?
Shináide kudasái.	Please don't do it!
Moo shináide kudasái.	Please don't do it anymore.
Shinákereba narimasén.	You must do it.
Shité wa ikemasén.	You mustn't do it.
Moo shité wa ikemasén.	You mustn't do it anymore.
Shite shimaimáshita.	It's done. [(I)'ve finished doing (it).]
Nani mo shite imasén.	I'm not doing anything.
Nani mo shináide kudasái.	Don't do anything, please.
Moo ichido shite kudasái.	Please do it once more.
Háyaku shite kudasái.	Do it quickly, please!
Chúui shite kudasái.	Pay attention, please!
Benkyoo shite kudasái.	Please study it.
Íma shita bákari desu.	I've just done it now.
Moo oai shimáshita.	I've already met her (*respect*).
Dóo shimashóo ka?	What's to be done? What shall we do? What can be done? [How shall we do?]
Dáre ga shimáshita ka?	Who did that?
Dóo shitára íi ka wakarimasén.	I don't know what to do.
Óokiku shimáshita.	We enlarged (it).

Iku kotó ni shimá-
shita.

We've decided to go.
[(We)'ve acted on
(our) going.]

QUIZ 34

1. *Dóo shimásu ka?*
2. *Shinái de kudasái.*

3. *Shite shimaimásh-*
   ita.
4. *Dóo shimashóo*
   ka?
5. *Chúui shite kuda-*
   sái.
6. *Óokiku shimáshita.*
7. *Moo ichido shite*
   kudasái.
8. *Dáre ga shimásh-*
   ita ka?
9. *Íma shita bákari*
   desu.
10. *Iku kóto ni shi-*
    máshita.
11. *Shinákereba ike-*
    masén.
12. *Shité wa ikemasén.*

13. *Náni o shite imásu*
    ka?
14. *Háyaku shite kuda-*
    sái.
15. *Náni o shite*
    imáshita ka?

a. You mustn't do it.
b. Do it quickly,
   please.
c. What are you do-
   ing?
d. How do you do
   that?

e. Please don't do it.

f. It's done.
g. You must do it.

h. What's to be done?

i. What have you
   been doing?
j. Do it once more,
   please.
k. Pay attention,
   please.
l. We've decided to
   go.
m. I've just done it
   now.
n. We made it large.

o. Who did that?

ANSWERS
1–d; 2–e; 3–f; 4–h; 5–k; 6–n; 7–j; 8–o; 9–m; 10–l;
11–g; 12–a; 13–c; 14–b; 15–i.

REVIEW QUIZ 8

1. *Súgu* _____ (I'm coming).
   a. *kité imasu.*
   b. *kimásu.*
   c. *kimáshita.*

2. _____ (Hard to say) *desu.*
   a. *Inikúi*
   b. *Ikinikúi*
   c. *Iinikúi*

3. *Náni o* _____ (do) *imásu ka?*
   a. *shitte*
   b. *shite*
   c. *shiite*

4. *Dóo* _____ (do) *íi ka wakarimasén.*
   a. *ittára*
   b. *mítara*
   c. *shitára*

5. *Anó hito wa rippa na uchí o* _____ (have).
   a. *tsukútte imasu.*
   b. *mótte imasu.*
   c. *sagashite imásu.*

6. _____ (Don't take) *kudasái.*
   a. *Toránaide*
   b. *Mínaide*
   c. *Nománaide*

7. *Súgu* _____ (stop) *kudasái.*
   a. *tomatte*
   b. *tátte*
   c. *tábete*

8. *Ashita wa íi otenki ni náreba ii to* _____ (think).
   a. *iimásu.*
   b. *omoimásu.*
   c. *kakimáshita.*

9. *Watakushi wa* _____ (did not see).
   a. *ma ni aimasén deshita.*
   b. *mairimasén deshita.*
   c. *mimasén deshita.*

10. *Moo ichido* _____ (see) *kudasái.*
    a. *míte*
    b. *nite*
    c. *shite*

11. *Anó hito no banchi wa* _____ (do not know).
    a. *arimasén.*
    b. *shirimasén.*
    c. *chigaimásu.*

12. *Sono kóto wa máe kara yóku* _____ (know).
    a. *shite imásu.*
    b. *shitte orimásu.*
    c. *benkyoo shite orimásu.*

13. *Íma denwa de* _____ (is talking).
    a. *kotáete imasu.*
    b. *kiite imásu.*
    c. *hanáshite imasu.*

14. *Íma súgu iku* _____ (can).
   a. *tsumori désu.*
   b. *kotó ga dekimásu.*
   c. *hazu désu.*

15. *Anó hito wa watakushi no iu kotó ga yóku* _____ (understands).
   a. *dekimásu.*
   b. *wakarimásu.*
   c. *kikoemásu.*

16. *Booshi o* _____ (please buy).
   a. *tótte kudasái.*
   b. *katte kudasái.*
   c. *mótte kudasái.*

17. *Kono machí ni* _____ (person I know) *wa dare mo orimasén.*
   a. *yónde iru hitó*
   b. *shite iru hitó*
   c. *shitte iru hitó*

18. *Moo sukóshi* _____ (want) *desu.*
   a. *hóshikatta*
   b. *hóshiku nái*
   c. *hoshíi*

19. *Íkutsu* _____ (left) *imásu ka?*
   a. *nokótte*
   b. *katte*
   c. *mótte*

20. *Ítsu* _____ (must you go) *ka?*
   a. *ikanákute mo íi desu*
   b. *ikanákereba narimasén*
   c. *itté wa ikemasén*

ANSWERS
1–b; 2–c; 3–b; 4–c; 5–b; 6–a; 7–a; 8–b; 9–c; 10–a;
11–b; 12–b; 13–c; 14–b; 15–b; 16–b; 17–c; 18–c;
19–a; 20–b.

D. I'M A STRANGER HERE

Gomen kudasái.
Hello. [Pardon.]

Áa Súmisu-san desu ka. Omachi shite orimáshita.
Oh, Ms. Smith. I've been waiting for you.

Kyóo wa dóo mo oisogashíi tokoró o arígatoo goza-imásu.
I certainly appreciate your taking time out for me.
[Thank you (for taking the time for me) when you are
so busy.]

Dóo itashimáshite. Oyasui goyóo desu. Dé wa súgu dekakemashóo.
Don't mention it. It is an easy task. Shall we get
going?

Watakushi wa máda migi mo hidari mo wakari-masén kara yoroshiku onegai itashimásu.
I'm a total stranger here. [(I) can't even tell right from
left, and would appreciate (your) taking me around.]

Hái, kashikomarimáshita. Yuubínkyoku ni goyóo ga áru to osshaimáshita ne.
Surely. You said you wanted to go to the post office,
didn't you?

É, sóo na n desu.
Yes, that's right.

Dó wa kono michi o ikimashóo.
Then let's take this street.

Kono michi no namae wa nán to yuú n desu ka?
What's the name of this street?

Shoowa Dóori to iimásu. Ómo na misé wa taitei koko ni arimásu.
It's Showa Street. Most of the important stores are here.

Nakanaka nigíyaka na tokoro désu ne.
It's quite busy here, isn't it?

E, ítsu mo kóo desu.
Yes, it is always crowded here, day and night.

Áa, ano ookíi tatémono wa nán desu ka?
Oh, yes. What's that big building over there?

Áa, aré desu ka?
You mean that one?

Ée.
Yes (that one).

Are wa depáato desu.
Oh, a department store.

Hoo, asoko ní wa Amerika no shokuryóohin nado mo arimásu ka?
[Oh, I see.] Do they sell any American food?

Íkura ka arimásu.
Not much but some.

Sore kara íma no depáato no tonari no tatémono wa nán desu ka?
What's that building next to the department store? [And then . . .]

Shiyákusho desu. Súgu ushiro ni keisatsushó ga arimásu.
That is City Hall. The police station is right back of it.

Hoo, kore wa zúibun ookíi kusuriya désu ne.
Isn't that a big drugstore! [Oh I see . . .]

Ée, kore wa Amerikan Fáamashii to itte Nippon no kusuri mo gaikoku no kusuri mo utte imásu.
Yes, this is called (the) American Pharmacy and carries both Japanese and foreign drugs.

Sóo desu ka? Kono machí ni wa íi byooin ga arimásu ka?
Is that right? Is there a good hospital in this city?

Hái, íkutsu mo arimásu ga, ma, Daigaku Byóoin ga ichiban íi deshoo.
Yes, there are quite a few of them, but—well—perhaps the best is the University Hospital.

Aa sóo desu ka.
Oh, I see.

Daigaku Byóoin ni wa Eigo no yóku dekíru isha ga takusan imásu.
There are many doctors there who speak English.

Sóo desu ka? Dóko ni áru n desu ka?
Is that right? Where is it?

Daigaku no kóonai desu ga, koko o hashítte iru básu de iku to nijuppun gúrai desu.

It's on the university campus. If you take the bus from here, you can get there in twenty minutes.

Mmm? Kore wa rippa na hóteru desu ne.

Hmm? This is a fine hotel, isn't it?

Sóo desu née. Gaikokújin wa taitei koko ni toma-rimásu.

Yes. Foreigners usually stay here.

Haa? Sore kara éki wa dóko desu ka?

I see. Then where is the railroad station?

Tsugí no kádo o migi ni magatte kádo hitótsu saki désu.

You turn right at the next corner. It's one block from there.

Áa densha no jikokuhyoo ga hoshíi n desu ga ...

[Oh, (I remember).] I wanted to get a timetable.

E! Sore nára éki made ikanákute mo té ni hairi-másu. Sono kádo no hón'ya de utte imásu.

[Yes,] if that's the case, you don't have to go to the station. You can buy [get hold of] (one) at the book-store on the corner.

Densha no jikokuhyoo wa kaú n desu ka?

So you have to pay for it, do you?

Ée, sóo na n desu. Kono kuni dé wa jikokuhyoo wa kawanákereba narimasén.

That's right. In this country you have to buy train timetables.

Sóo desu ka. Sore wa shirimasén deshita.
Oh, I see. I didn't know that.

Yuubínkyoku wa súgu soko désu ga, jikokuhyoo o kaú no wa íma ni shimásu ka, soretómo áto ni shimásu ka?
The post office is right there, but do you want to buy the timetable now or [otherwise] later?

Sóo desu née. Áto ni shimásu. Saki ni kakitome o dáshite shimaitái desu kara.
Let me see. I'll buy it later. I would like to send registered mail first.

Áa sóo desu ka. Sore ja súgu ikimashóo.
Oh, I see. Then let's go right away.

Onegai itashimásu.
That'll be fine.

Kore ga yuubínkyoku desu.
This is the post office.

Zúibun kónde imásu ne.
It's quite crowded, isn't it?

Kakitome no madóguchi wa hidari no hóo desu.
The registered mail window [window for registered mail] is to the left.

Áa wakarimáshita. Asoko désu ne.
Oh, yes. I see it. That's it, isn't it?

Sóo desu. Watakushi wa koko no bénchi de omachi shimásu.
Right. I'll be waiting for you at the bench here.

Sóo desu ka. Dé wa onegai itashimásu.
Fine! I would appreciate that.

Goyukkúri dóozo.
Don't hurry.

QUIZ 35

1. _____ (Don't mention it.)
    a. *Gomen kudasái.*
    b. *Dóo itashimáshite.*
    c. *Kashiko-
       marimáshita.*

2. _____ (The post office) *ni ikimashóo.*
    a. *Yuubínkyoku*
    b. *Shiyákusho*
    c. *Jimúsho*

3. *Migi mo hidari mo* _____ (can't tell).
    a. *miemasén.*
    b. *wakarimasén.*
    c. *kakimasén.*

4. *Kono machí ni wa* _____ (hospital) *ga arimásu ka?*
    a. *byooin*
    b. *byooki*
    c. *biyóoin*

5. *Kono* _____ (street) *no namae wa nán to iimásu ka?*
    a. *machí*
    b. *michi*
    c. *uchi*

6. *Ano ookíi* _____ (building) *wa nán desu ka?*
   a. *tabemóno*
   b. *uchi*
   c. *tatémono*

7. *Depáata no* _____ (next) *ni Shiyákusho ga arimásu.*
   a. *tonari*
   b. *ushiro*
   c. *máe*

8. *Gaikokújin wa taitei kono hóteru ni* _____ (stay).
   a. *sumimásu.*
   b. *yasumimásu.*
   c. *tomarimásu.*

9. _____ (Registered mail) *o dáshite shimaitai desu.*
   a. *Denwa*
   b. *Densha*
   c. *Kakitome*

10. _____ (The station) *wa dóko desu ka?*
    a. *Éki*
    b. *Densha*
    c. *Shiyákusho*

ANSWERS
1–b; 2–a; 3–b; 4–a; 5–b; 6–c; 7–a; 8–c; 9–c; 10–a.

LESSON 40

DÁI YONJÚKKA

A. THE MOST COMMON VERB FORMS

1. Plain Forms

	I EAT (VOWEL VERB)	I FINISH (CONSONANT VERB)	I COME (IRREGULAR VERBS)	I DO
PRESENT AFFIRMATIVE (DICT. FORM)	*tabéru*	*owaru*	*kúru*	*suru*
-ta FORM (PAST)	*tábeta*	*owatta*	*kitá*	*shita*
-te FORM TENTATIVE	*tabeyóo*	*owaróo*	*koyóo*	*shiyóo*

Verbs ending in *-eru* or *-iru,* with some exceptions, take all the forms listed above for *tabéru.* For example:

haréru	the sky clears
atsuméru	gather (something)
hajimeru	start (something)
ochíru	fall

All other verbs, except *kúru* [come] and *suru* [do], which are irregular, are declined like *owaru.* For construction of the *-ta* forms, see Lesson 12 and Section 17 of the Summary of Japanese Grammar. For example:

| *agaru* | rise |
| *arau* | wash |

atsumáru   gather
hakáru   measure

2. Polite Forms

tabemásu   I eat, I'll eat
tabemáshita   I ate
Tabemashóo.   I think I'll eat.

owarimásu   I finish, I'll finish
owarimáshita   I finished
owarimashóo   I think I will finish . . .

kimásu   I come
kimáshita   I came
Kimashóo.   I think I'll come.

shimásu   I do, I'll do
shimáshita   I did
shimashóo   I think I'll do

3. Future

tabemásu	*owarimásu*	*kimásu*	*shimásu*
tabemashóo	*owari-*	*kimashóo*	*shimashóo*
	mashóo		
tabéru	*owarú*	*kúru deshoo*	*surú deshoo*
deshóo	*deshoo*		

Notice that the forms used to express the future vary. If the event under discussion is definite, you use *-masu,* the same form used for the present. If it is not definite, you use *-mashoo* or *-(r)u deshoo.* Use *-mashoo* when whether or not the event will take place depends on the speaker. Usually, the event will take place for the sake of the non-speaker. Use -(r)u de-shoo when it does not depend on you. Compare these forms:

Tabemásu.	I shall eat it. I will eat it. I eat it. [Eating takes place definitely, in the present or the future.]
Tabemashóo.	I think I'll eat it. Let's eat it. [(It)'s not definite but (I) think (I)'ll eat; (the choice) is up to me (us).]
Tabéru deshoo.	I think he will eat it. [(It)'s not definite, but he will probably eat it; it's not up to me.]
Denwa o kakemashóo.	Let's phone.
Kawáku deshoo.	It'll dry, I think.
Júppun de kawaki-másu.	It will dry in ten minutes (definitely).
Koko ni oitára nakunaru deshóo.	If you leave it here, it will get lost (I think).
Súgu naóru deshoo.	He'll get well soon.
Tanaka-san ni tano-mimashóo.	Let's ask Ms. Tanaka to do it.
Yamada-san ga tetsudáu deshoo.	Mr. Yamada will probably help you.

Sonna ni hataraitára   If you work so hard,
   tsukaréru deshoo.   you will probably
                              get tired.

Tsuzukemashóo.   Let's continue it.

4. Past

tabe-	*owari-*	*ki-*	*shimá-*
máshita	*máshita*	*máshita*	*shita*
(from	(from	(from	(from
tabéru)	*owaru*)	*kúru*)	*suru*)

The *-máshita* form expresses an action or state that is already completed, and in most cases is equivalent to the past and present perfect tenses in English. For example:

Tsutsumimáshita.	I wrapped it up.
Ugokashimáshita.	I moved it.
Ugokimáshita.	It moved.
Urimáshita.	I sold it.
Utaimáshita.	I sang it.
Wakemáshita.	I divided it.
Waraimáshita.	I laughed.
Warimáshita.	I broke it.
Watashimáshita.	I handed it.
Yaburimáshita.	I tore it.

5. I Used to . . .

Tábeta monó deshita. *Tábeta monó desu.* }	I used to eat.
Owatta monó deshita. *Owatta monó desu.* }	I used to finish.
Kitá monó deshita. *Kitá monó desu.* }	I used to come.

Shita monó deshita. ⎫
  Shita mono désu. ⎰   I used to do.

Use the *-ta* form plus *monó deshita* (or *desu*) when referring to an action or state that used to take place but no longer does. For example:

Bikkúri shita monó deshita.	I used to be surprised.
Té de hakonda monó deshita.	I used to carry it by hand.
Maitoshi hikkóshita monó deshita.	I used to move every year.
Ichínen ni nijippóndo mo futótta monó deshita.	I used to gain as much [weight] as twenty pounds every year.

6. I Have . . .
(EXPERIENCE)

Tábeta kotó ga arimásu.	I have eaten it.
Yónda kotó ga arimásu.	I have read it.
Kitá koto ga arimásu.	I have come.
Shita kotó ga arimásu.	I have done (it).

Most of the ideas expressed in English by the present perfect (''have'' plus the past participle) are expressed in Japanese by the use of the *-máshita* form. However, when you mean that you have had the experience of doing something one or more times in the past, you use the *-ta* form plus *koto ga arimásu*, as seen above. Other examples:

Eigo ni yakúshita kotó ga arimásu.	I [have] once translated it into English.
Eigo ni yakushimá-shita.	I [have] translated it into English.

Tabako wa máe ni yameta kotó ga arimásu.	I have once before stopped [discontinued] smoking.
Hyaku póndo made yaseta kotó ga arimásu.	Once my weight was down to one hundred pounds. [I have once lost my weight down to one hundred pounds.]
Sono kotó ni tsúite shirábeta kotó ga arimásu.	I have [once] made an investigation concerning that matter.

7. I Had . . .

Káite arimáshita.	I had written it. [(It) had been written.]
Yónde arimáshita.	I had read it. [(It) had been read.]
Kité imáshita.	I had come.
Shite arimáshita.	I had done it. [(It) had been done.]

In most cases the ideas expressed in English by the past perfect ("had" plus the past participle) can be expressed in Japanese by *-te arimáshita* for transitive verbs and *-ta imáshita* for intransitive verbs. Note that in the case of transitive verbs, however, the object of the verb in Japanese becomes the subject in English. For example:

Kudámono wa katte arimáshita.	I had purchased the fruit (when he arrived). [The fruit had been purchased . . .]

Haná wa móo chitte imáshita.	The flowers had already fallen off (the trees when we went there).
Purogúramu wa móo hajimatte imáshita.	The program had already started (when we arrived there).
Zaseki wa tótte arimáshita.	She had already taken the seats (for us when we arrived).

8. Commands and Requests

Each verb has a form called the "plain imperative," which is very brusque and is used almost exclusively in conversations between men. This form should not be used in a normal, quiet situation. To form the plain imperative, add *-ro* to the base for vowel verbs and *-e* to the base for consonant verbs.

Tabéro!	Eat!
Déte ike!	Leave!
Damáre!	Shut up!
Kói![1]	Come!
Háyaku shiro![2]	Do it quickly!

Another command expression is the pre-*masu* form plus *nasái.* An adult will usually use this form when ordering a child to do something.

Soko e ikinasái.	Go there.
Heyá o katazukenasái.	Tidy up the room.
Sugu nenasái.	Go to bed right away.

---

[1] Irregular: from *kúru.*
[2] Irregular: from *suru.*

Notice that an ordinary polite request ends in *-te ku-dasái* for the affirmative. An adult will usually use this form when ordering a child to do something.

Yománaide kudasái.	Please don't read.
Tabénaide kudasái.	Please don't eat.

To form an even more polite expression of request, prefix the pre-*masu* form of the verb with *o-* and add *kudasái* or *ni nátte kudasái* for the affirmative. Form the negative as in the paragraph above.

Otori kudasái. ⎫ *Otori ni nátte kudasái.* ⎬	Take it, please (*respect*).
Otori ni naránaide kudasái.	Please do not take it (*respect*).
Tetsudátte kudasái.	Please help me! [Give a hand, please.]
Moo sukóshi motté kite kudasái.	Bring me some more, please.
Watakushi no tokoro e motté kite kudasái.	Bring it to me. [Bring it to my place, please.]
Tomatte kudasái!	Stop, please!
Súgu tomatte kudasái!	Stop right here, please!
Sonó hito o tomete kudasái!	Stop him, please!
Koshikákete kudasái. ⎫ *Okoshikake kudasái.* ⎬	Sit down./Have a seat, please.
Shínjite kudasái.	Please believe me!
Kiite kudasái.	Please listen.
Watakushi no iu kóto o kiite kudasái.	Listen to me. [Listen to what I say, please.]

Kore o kiite kudasái.	Listen to this, please.
Chúui shite kiite kudasái.	Listen carefully, please.
Anó hito no iu kóto o kiite kudasái.	Listen to him, please.
Anó hito no iu kóto o kikanáide kudasái.	Please don't listen to him.
Háitte kudasái.	Please come in! Please enter!
Ohairi kudasái.	Come in. Enter, please.
Sonó hito no tokoró e okutte kudasái.	Send it to him, please.
Watakushi no tokoró e okutte kudasái.	Send them (it) to me, please.
Sonó hito no tokoro e íkuraka okutte kudasái.	Send him some, please.
Watakushi no tokoró e íkuraka okutte kudasái.	Send me some, please.
Taméshite kudasái.	Please try. [Please check!]
Tamesánaide kudasái.	Please don't try!
Tábete mite kudasái.	Please try eating it.
Yónde mite kudasái.	Please try reading it.
Kao o aratte kudasái.	Please wash yourself [wash your face]!
Tátte kudasái.	Please stand up! Please get up!
Otachi kudasái.	Please stand up. Kindly rise.
Yónde kudasái.	Please read that!
Watakushi o soko e tsurete itte kudasái.	Please take me there!
Moo hitótsu otori kudasái.	Please take another one. [Please take one more.]

Densha de itte kudasái.	Please take the train. [Please go by train.]
Densha de oide kudasái.	Please take the train. [Please go by train.]
Tákushii de itte kudasái.	Take a taxi, please.
Míte kudasái.	Please look!
Goran ni nátte kudasái.	Please look!
Moo ichido míte kudasái.	Please look again!
Koko o míte kudasái.	Please look here!
Watakushi o míte kudasái.	Please look at me!
Kore o míte kudasái.	Please look at this!
Mínaide kudasái.	Please don't look.
Goran ni naránaide kudasái.	Please don't look.
Káeshite kudasái.	Please return it to me.
Okaeshi ni nátte kudasái.	Please return it to me.
Soko o agatte kudasái.	Go up there, please.
Mísete kudasái.	Please show me!
Misénaide kudasái.	Please don't show it!
Wasurenáide kudasái.	Please don't forget.
Déte itte kudasái.	Please leave!
Súgu déte itte kudasái.	Please leave quickly! Please go right away!
Déte ikanáide kudasái.	Please don't leave!
Kore o asoko e motté itte kudasái.	Carry this over there, please.
Tótte kudasái.	Take it, please.
Otori kudasái.	Please take it.
Toránaide kudasái.	Please don't take it.
Otori ni naránaide kudasái.	Please don't take it (*respect*).
Uchi e káette kudasái.	Please go home!
Háyaku uchi e káette kudasái.	Please go home early!

Moo ichido itte kudasái.	Please say it again.
Moo ichido osshátte kudasái.	Please say it again (*respect*).
Ite kudasái.	Please stay.
Koko ni ite kudasái.	Please stay here.
Shízuka ni shite kudasai.	Please be quiet.
Ugokánaide kudasái.	Please be still. Please don't move.
Tsúite kite kudasái.	Please follow. Please follow me.
Anó hito ni tsúite itte kudasái.	Please follow him.
Sawaranáide kudasái.	Please don't touch!
Koohíi o tsuide kudasái.	Please pour me some coffee.

B. *KYUUYUU TO NO SAIKAI*
   MEETING AN OLD FRIEND

Study the notes at the end of this section for greater comprehension.

1. Y: **Zúibun hisashiburi désu ne? Ogénki desu ka?**
   Y: Well! (Long time no see!) How are you?

2. S: **Okage sama de. Otaku wa?**
   S: Fine, thanks. (And) you and your family?

3. Y: **Arígatoo. Minna génki desu. Nagái goryokoo de otsukare deshóo.**
   Y: Thanks, we're all well. (You're) not too tired from your trip?

4. S: **Íya. Betsu ni.**
   S: Not at all.

5. Y: **A! Kánai o goshookai shimashóo.**
   Y: [Oh, yes.] I'd like you to meet my wife.

6. S: **Dóozo.**
   S: I'd be very happy to.

7. Y: **Kochira wa Sátoo-san.**
   Y: This is (my friend) Sato.

8. S: **Hajimemáshite. Dóozo yoroshiku.**
   S: I am very happy to know you.

9. Mrs. Y: **Kochira kóso.**
   Mrs. Y: Glad to know you.

10. S: **Yaa. Hisashiburi de yúkai desu ne.**
    S: Yes, indeed. It's really good to see you again.

11. Y: **Yáa. Mattaku dookan désu. Tokoróde Satoo-san anáta wa chittó mo kawarimasén ne.**
    Y: Yes, indeed. By the way, you haven't changed a bit.

12. S: **Iyaa. Sono ten ja anáta mo sukóshi mo kawatte imasén yo.**
    S: Neither have you. [No, in that respect you haven't changed a bit.]

13. Mrs. Y: **Ókusama wa Amerika no go-seikatsu o otanoshimi désu ka?**
    Mrs. Y: How does your wife like the United States?

14. S: **Ée. Hijoo ni tanoshínde orimásu.**
    S: [Yes.] She likes it a lot.

15. Mrs. Y: **Achira wa Tookyoo tó wa daibu chigaú no deshóo ne?**
    Mrs. Y: It must be very different from Tokyo.

16. S: **Táshika ni chigau tokoró wa arimásu ne.**
    S: There certainly are lots of very curious things in the United States!

17. Mrs. Y: **Tatóeba dóo iu tokoró nan desu no?**
    Mrs. Y: For example?

18. S: **Tatóeba desu ne, soo, kusuriya de shokuji o surú nado to itté mo chótto gosoozoo ni narénai deshoo?**
    S: For example [so, (here is a good one)], it certainly wouldn't occur to you to have a meal in a pharmacy.

19. Y: **Joodán deshoo.**
    Y: You're joking!

20. S: **Íya. Majime na hanashí desu yo.**
    S: Not at all. I'm very serious.

21. Mrs. Y: **Máa! Kusuriya de oshukuji o na-sáru!**
    Mrs. Y: (Imagine) eating [having a meal] in a pharmacy!

22. S: **Sóo na n desu yo. Bifuteki dátte áru n desu yo, ókusan.**
    S: Yes, you can even have a steak.

23. Y: **Kusuriya ni?**
    Y: In a pharmacy?

24. S: **Sóo na n desu. Dezáato ni wa oishii aisukuríimu ga arimásu shi ne.**
    S: Yes, in a pharmacy—with excellent ice cream for dessert.

25. Mrs. Y: **Démo kusuri no niói ga oki ni narimasén?**
    Mrs. Y: But the smell of the pharmacy—doesn't that bother you?

26. S: **Niói nanka shimasén yo.**
    S: There isn't any smell.

27. Y: **Hee? Kusuri o utte ité mo desu ka?**
    Y: Really? Even when they sell drugs?

28. S: **Ée. Sore ga shinái n desu yo. Amerika no Doraggu Sutóa wa.**
    S: No [yes, (what you said is right)] there isn't any in American "drugstores."

29. Y: **Hoo ... á, wakátta. Iwáyuru Nihón de yuu kusuriya to chigaú n desu ne.**
    Y: [Hmm . . .] Oh! That's the trick! It's a different place from the kind of place we call pharmacy in Japan, isn't it?

30. Y: **Dákara yakkyoku ja nái to iu wáke na n desu ne.**
    Y: Therefore it's no longer a pharmacy.

31. S: **E. Doraggu sutóa de wa omócha tó ka, kitte tó ka, tabako tó ka okáshi no yóo na**

monó made mo utterú n desu.
S: You also find many other things in a drug-store: toys, stamps, cigarettes, candy . . .

32. Y: **Hoo . . . ! Kawatte irú n desu ne?**
Y: Hmm! That's really very funny.

33. S: **Máda sono ué ni hón mo áru, bunbóogu mo áru, daidokoro yóohin mo áru, keshóohin mo áru, máa, náni mo ká mo áru to itta katachi désu yo.**
S: . . . books, stationery, cooking utensils, cosmetics, and what have you.

34. Y: **Hmm! Ma, yorozuya to iu wáke desu ne.**
Y: Hmm? [So to speak] it's a general store, then?

35. S: **Ée, démo kusuri wa chan to utterú n desu yo.**
S: Yes, but it's (still) a pharmacy!

NOTE

Title: *Kyuuyuu tó no Saikai* = Meeting an Old Friend
1. *Hisashiburi désu* = It has been a long time since (I saw you last).
2. *Otaku wa* = your family, you.
3. *Goryokoo de* = on account of a long trip.
Otsukare deshóo = You must be tired.
4. *Íya* (same as *iie*) = no.
Betsu ni = (not) especially.
7. *Sátoo-san:* Note the use of *san* in spite of Sato's being Yamada's old friend. Adding a *san* is a common practice regardless of the extent

of the friendship. The first name is not usually mentioned in a situation like this.

11. *Mattaku dookan désu* = I'm in complete agreement with you. [The] same here.
    Tokoróde = by the way.
    Satoo-san: Notice the use of the surname of the person with whom you are speaking.
    Kawarimasén = (you) don't change.

12. *Kawatte imasén* = You haven't changed. [You are not in the state of having changed.]

13. *Tanoshímu* = enjoy; *otanoshimi désu:* o plus the pre-*masu* form plus *désu,* a respect expression.

17. *Tatóeba* = for instance.

18. *Desu ne* = a meaningless expression similar to the American phrase "you know."
    Gosoozoo ni narénai = You cannot imagine (*respect*); *naréru* = potential form derived from the consonant verb *náru.*

22. *Dátte* (same as *dé mo*) = even (used in everyday speech).

24. *Shi:* adds the feeling of "and it's in addition to what I've said."

25. *Oki ni narimasén* (when spoken with a rising intonation) = Doesn't it bother you? (a respect form of *ki ni náru* [something bothers]).

26. *Nánka* = and things like that (used in everyday speech); *nánka* is usually mutually exclusive with the particles *ga, wa,* and *o.*

27. *Utte ité mo desu ka* = Is it so even when they are selling medicines?

28. Notice the inverted word order used in informal conversation.

29. *Wakátta* = I've got it. [(It) has become clear.]

30. *Yakkyoku* = pharmacy.

31. ... *tó ka* ... *tó ka* ... *tó ka* (comparable to ...

ya , .. ya ... ya) = and ... and ... and (with the implication that the listing is incomplete).
32. *Kawatte iru* = is different.
33. *Sono ué ni* = on top of that.
Náni mo ká mo = and what have you; everything.
34. *To iu wáke desu* = it amounts to saying; it means. *Yorozuya* = ten-thousand-variety shop; general store.

QUIZ 36

1. _____ (Long time no see) *désu ne.*
   a. *Omoshirói*
   b. *Atatakái*
   c. *Hisashiburi*

2. _____ (Fine, thanks) *sama de.*
   a. *Oki no doku*
   b. *Okage*
   c. *Omachidoo*

3. *Nagái goryokoo de* _____ (tired) *deshoo.*
   a. *omoshírokatta*
   b. *otanoshimi*
   c. *otsukare*

4. _____ (Wife) *o goshookai shimashóo.*
   a. *Kánai*
   b. *Kodomo*
   c. *Tomodachi*

5. *Hisashiburi de* _____ (pleasure) *desu ne.*
   a. *arigatái*
   b. *yúkai*
   c. *saiwai*

6. _____ (Not at all) *kawarimasén ne.*
   a. *Anmari*
   b. *Sukóshi shika*
   c. *Chittó mo*

7. _____ (Serious) *na hanashí desu.*
   a. *Majime*
   b. *Kantan*
   c. *Hén*

8. _____ (Delicious) *aisukuríimu ga arimásu.*
   a. *Oishii*
   b. *Takái*
   c. *Yasúi*

9. _____ (Bother) *ni narimasén ka?*
   a. *Oki*
   b. *Okaki*
   c. *Oyomi*

10. _____ (On top of that) *hón mo bunbóogu mo arimásu.*
    a. *Sono kawari ni*
    b. *Sono ué ni*
    c. *Sono misé ni*

ANSWERS
1–c; 2–b; 3–c; 4–a; 5–b; 6–c; 7–a; 8–a; 9–a; 10–b.

C. THE MOST COMMON VERBS AND VERB PHRASES

1. *Miru*   To see

PLAIN	POLITE[1]	
míru	*mimásu*	I see
míta	*mimáshita*	I saw
míte	*míte*	I see (saw) and . . .
miyóo	*mimashóo*	let's see
mínai	*mimasén*	I don't see
Mimashóo.		Let's see. Let's take a look.
Mimasén.		I don't see.
Nán de mo mimásu.		I see everything.

Notice that *míru* means "to see" only in the sense of perceiving by the eye. Study the following:

Níkko o míta kotó ga arimásu ka?	Have you ever seen the Nikko (Shrine)?
Yamada-san ni átta[2] kotó ga arimásu ka?	Have you ever seen Mr. Yamada?
Íma atta bákari desu.	I've just seen him.
Watakushi wa éiga o mimasén.	I don't go to the movies. [I don't see movies.]
Anata no iu kotó ga wakarimasen.[3]	I don't see what you mean.
Dónata ni oai ni narimásu ka?	Whom do you see?

---

[1] In the verb forms that follow, the plain form will be given in the first column, the polite form in the second column.

[2] *au* = see (meet).

[3] *wakáru* = see (understand).

Íma átte itadakemásu ka?	Can you see me now (*humble*)? [Can (I) have (you) see me now?]
Ítsu ka yóru asobi ni kité kudasái.[1]	Please come to see us some night.

2. *Shitte iru* To know
    Shiru To learn, To get to know

shitte iru	*shitte imásu*	I know
shitte ita	*shitte imáshita*	I knew
shitté ite	*shitté ite*	I know (knew) and . . .
shiranai	*shirimasén*	I don't know
shiru	*shirimásu*	I learn
shitta	*shirimáshita*	I learned
shitte	*shitte*	I learn (learned) and . . .
shiróo	*shirimashóo*	Let's learn
shiranai	*shirimasén*	I don't know

Shitte imásu.	I know it. [I'm in the state of having learned it.]
Shirimasén.	I don't know. [I haven't learned.]
Yóku shitte imásu.	I know it well.
Nani mo shirimasén.	He doesn't know anything.
Sono kóto ni tsúite wa nani mo shirimasén.	I don't know anything about it.

---

[1] *asobi ni kúru* = come to see (visit).

Koko ni iru kóto o shitte imásu.	I know that he is here. [I know the fact that he is here.]
Sore o shitte imásu ka?	Do you know that?
Dóko ni irú ka shitte imásu ka?	Do you know where she is?
Sono kóto ni tsúite wa kore íjoo shirimasén.	She doesn't know any more [than this] about it.
Sono kóto ni tsúite wa anáta ga shitte iru yóo ni wa shirimasén.	She doesn't know any more about it than you do [know].
Sono kóto wa shinbun de shirimáshita.	I learned (of) it through the newspaper.

3. *Mótsu* To hold

mótsu	*mochimásu*	I hold
mótta	*mochimáshita*	I held
mótte	*mótte*	I hold (held) and ...
motóo	*mochimashóo*	I think I'll hold, let's hold
motánai	*mochimasén*	I don't hold

Kore o chótto mótte kudasái.	Hold this for me a moment, please.
Té ni booshi o mótte imásu.	He's holding a hat in his hand.
Íma wa mótte imasu.	I have it now.
Shikkári mótte kudasái.	Hold firm, please.

Notice that the ideas expressed by the English word "have" and "possess" are expressed in Japanese by using the *-te* form of the verb *mótsu* [to hold] plus *imásu*. See also Lesson 14. Compare the following:

Okane wa íkura mótte imásu ka?	How much money do you have?
Nisen en mótte imasu.	I have two thousand yen.
Sore wa omosugimásu kara hitóri de mótsu koto wa dekimasén.	It's too heavy [and] so I can't hold it alone.

Notice also that the ideas expressed in English by "take (to)," "bring," and "carry around," are expressed in Japanese by using the *-te* form of the verb *mótsu* together with the verb *iku* [go], *kúru* [come], *arúku* [walk]. Compare the following:

Kása o mótte itte kudasái.	Please take your umbrella (with you).
Kása o motté kite kudasái.	Please bring over (your) umbrella.
Anó hito wa ítsu mo kása o mótte arukimásu.	He always carries his umbrella around.

4. *Dekiru*   To be able

dekíru	*dekimásu*	I can
dékita	*dekimáshita*	I could
dékite	*dékite*	I can (could) and ...
dekínai	*dekimasén*	I can't

Suru kotó ga dekimásu.	I can do it.
Kúru koto ga dekimásu ka?	Can you come?

Sono shitsumon ní wa kotaéru kotó gu deki masén.	I can't answer the question.
Soko e iku kotó ga de-kimasén.	I can't go there.
Ítsu déru koto ga deki-másu ka?	When can we leave?
Tetsudátte kudasáru koto ga dekimásu ka?	Can you help me?

The idea "to be able to (do something)" or "can (do something)" can be expressed in several ways. The most common is by the use of a dictionary form plus *kotó ga dekíru,* demonstrated above. Another way is to use a derived potential verb as follows:

a. For consonant verbs:

Drop the final *-u* of the dictionary form and add *-eru.* The resulting form is a vowel verb which means "capable of doing something."

CONSONANT VERB		DERIVED POTENTIAL VERB	
iku	go	*ikeru*	can go
kau	buy	*kaeru*	can buy
hanásu	speak	*hanaséru*	can speak

Ashita ikemásu ka?	Can you go tomorrow?
Shirokiya de kaemásu ka?	Can you buy it at Shirokiya's (department store)?

b. For vowel verbs:

Drop the final *-eru* or *-iru,* and add *-rareru* in its place.

VOWEL VERB	DERIVED POTENTIAL VERB	
táberu	*taberaréru*	can eat
míru	*miraréru*	can see
okíru	*okiraréru*	can get up

Kore wa náma de tab-eraremásu ka?

Can we eat this raw?

Nára e iku to furúi tatémono ga takusan miraremásu.

If you go to the city of Nara, you can see many ancient buildings.

c. For the irregular verbs:

IRREGULAR VERB	DERIVED POTENTIAL VERB	
kúru	*koraréru*	can come
suru	*dekíru*	can do

Koko e súgu koraremásu ka?

Can you come here right away?

Kónnan náshi ni dekimásu.

You can do it without any difficulty.

5. *Wakaru* To understand

wakáru	*wakarimásu*	I understand
wakátta	*wakarimáshita*	I understood
wakátte	*wakátte*	I understand (understood) and . . .
wakaránai	*wakarimasén*	I don't understand

Anó hito wa kore ga wakarimasén.

He doesn't understand this.

Yóku wakarimásu.	I understand very well.
Watakushi no iu kotó ga wakarimásu ka?	Do you understand me [what (I) say]?
Watakushi no iu kotó ga wakarimasén ka?	Don't you understand me?
Wakarimásu ka?	Do you understand?
Nihongo ga wakarimásu ka?	Do you understand Japanese?
Eigo ga wakarimásu ka?	Do you understand English?
Anó hito ga anáta ni itte iru kóto ga minna wakarimásu ka?	Do you understand everything he's saying to you?
Wakarimasén.	I don't understand.
Wakarimáshita ka?	Did you understand?
Watakushi no iu kotó ga wakátte moraemasén.	I can't make myself understood. [(I) can't have what (I) say understood.]
Anó hito wa shóobai no koto wa sukóshi mo wakarimasén.	He doesn't understand [not a bit] about business.
Zenzen wakarimasén. *Kaimoku wakarimasén.* *Sukóshi mo wakarimasén.*	I don't understand it at all. I don't understand anything about it. It's a mystery to me. I'm completely in the dark.

6. *Oku* To put, To place

oku	*okimásu*	I put
oita	*okimáshita*	I put (*past*)
oite	*oite*	I put and . . .
okóo	*okimashóo*	I think I'll put, let's put
okanai	*okimasén*	I don't put

Soko ni oite kudasái.	Put it there, please.
Dóko ni okimáshita ka?	Where did you put it?
Anó hito wa jibun de monó o oita tokoró o súgu wasuremásu.	He never knows where he puts (his) things. [He forgets right away the place where he has put (his) things himself.]

You use *oku* when you are talking about "putting" or "placing" a thing someplace. To express the thought of "putting on" wearing apparel, you may use several different words. For example:

kabúru	to put on one's head; to put a thing over one's head
Booshi o kabútte kudasái.	Put your hat on, please.
kiru	to wear on the body
Nihon no kimono o kimáshita.	She wore a Japanese kimono.
haku	to wear on the foot or leg
Kurói kutsú o haite ikimáshita.	He was wearing black shoes (when) he went.

When *oku* follows another verb using the *-te* form, it implies that the action of the verb preceding *oku* takes place in anticipation of some future situation. For example:

Sono kóto wa Yamada-san ni denwa de shirasete okimáshita.[1]	I [have] notified Mr. Yamada in advance over the telephone.

[1] The statement implies, "I have the intention of explaining it in detail when I see him, but for now . . ."

Konshuu wa Doyóobi ni kaimono ga dekí-nai node Suiyóobi ni kaimono o shite oki-máshita.		Since I can't do any shopping on Satur-day, I did the shop-ping on Wednesday.

7. *Kúru* To come

kúru	*kimasu*	I come
kita	*kimáshita*	I came
kite	*kite*	I come and . . .
koyóo	*kimashóo*	I think I'll come, let's come
kónai	*kimasén*	I don't come

Hitóri de kimáshita.	I came alone. I came by myself.
Hitóri de kúru deshoo.	I think she is coming alone.
Moo kité imasu.	He is already here. [He is in the state of hav-ing come already.]
Sánji made ni kóna-kattara saki ni iki-mashóo.	If he doesn't come by three, let's go ahead of him.

8. *Mátsu* To wait

mátsu	*machimásu*	I wait
mátta	*machimáshita*	I waited
mátte	*mátte*	I wait (waited) and . . .
matóo	*machimashóo*	I think I'll wait, let's wait

matánai	*machimasén*	I don't wait

Koko de mátte kudasái.	Wait here, please.
Watakushi o mátte kudasái.	Wait for me, please.
Sukóshi mátte kudasái.	Wait a little, please.
Chótto mátte kudasái.	Wait a minute, please.
Matánaide kudasái.	Don't wait, please.
Sonó hito o mátte imasu.	I'm waiting for her.
Hoka no hitótachi o mátte irú no desu.	She is waiting for the others.
Dáre o mátte irú no desu ka?	Whom are you waiting for?
Náze mátte irú no desu ka?	Why are you waiting?
Matásete[1] sumimasén deshita. } *Omachidoo sama déshita.*	I'm sorry I kept you waiting. [I caused you to wait; I'm sorry.]

9. *Kiku* To ask

Asoko de kiite kudasái.	Ask over there, please.
Asoko de sonó hito no kotó o kiite kudasái.	Ask about him over there, please.
Náni o kiite irú no desu ka?	What's she asking?
Michi ga wakaránaku náttara hito ni kiite kudasái.	Please ask your way if you get lost.
Sonó hito ni jikan o kiite kudasái.	Ask him the time, please.

[1] *matsu* plus *-aseru* (causative ending) = *mataséru:* cause someone to wait, make (have, let) someone wait.

Kiité kite kudasái.	Please go and ask him. [Please ask and come back (to this place).]
Dáre ka watakushi no kotó o kiitára súgu káette kúru to itte kudasái.	If someone asks for me [please tell him that], I'll be back in a moment.
Dóko ni áru ka kikimáshita.	She asked where it is.
Denwa o kákete kiite kudasái.	Call her on the phone [and ask], please.

10. *-tai* To want to (do something)

Ikitai.	*Ikitái desu.*	I want to go.
Ikitákatta.	*Ikitákatta desu.*	I wanted to go.
Ikitákute ...	*Ikitákute ...*	I want (wanted) to go and ...
Ikitái daroo.	*Ikitái deshoo.*	I suppose he wants to go.
Ikitaku nái.	*Ikitaku nái desu.*	I don't want to go.
Kaitái desu.		I want to buy it.
Nani mo kaitáku arimasén.		I don't want to buy anything.
Dekíru no desu ga shitaku nái no desu.		He can do it, but he doesn't want to.
Kaeritái no desu ka?		Does she want to return?

Watakushítachi to issho ni ikitái[1] desu ka?	Do you want to come with us?

Notice that the expression *-tái desu* is used when you want to do something. When you want to have or get something you use *hoshíi desu*. For example:

Hoshíi desu.	I want it.
Hóshiku nái desu. } *Hóshiku arimasén.*	I don't want it.
Nani mo hóshiku ari-masén.	I don't want anything.
Sukóshi hoshíi desu.	I want some.
Náni ga hoshíi desu ka?	What do you want?

For *-tái desu* and *hoshíi desu,* see Lesson 29 and Lesson 33, also.

11. *-(a)nakereba narimasén* To have to

PLAIN PRESENT NEGATIVE	→	-BA FORM	→	HAVE TO
ikanai	don't go	*ikanáke-reba*		*ikanákereba narimasén*
tabénai	don't eat	*tabénake-reba*		*tabénakereba narimasén*
kónai	don't come	*kónake-reba*		*kónakereba narimasén*
shinai	don't do	*shináke-reba*		*shinákereba narimasén*

---

[1] Notice the use of *iku* (going away from where we are now).

See Lesson 27 and Lesson 33, and Section 28 of the
Summary of Japanese Grammar also.

Ikanákereba nari-masén.	I must go.
Kónakereba narimasén.	He should (has to) come.
Koko ni inákereba na-rimasén.	She should (has to) be here.
Sonó hitotachi wa soko ni inákereba nari-masén.	They have to be there.
Sóko e ikanákereba narimasén ka?	Do you have to go there?
Watakushi wa náni o shinákereba naránai no desu ka?	What do I have to do?
Íkura okaeshi shi-nákereba naránai no desu ka?	How much do I owe you?
Nani mo harawánakute íi desu.	You don't owe me anything. [You need not pay anything.]
Kyóo wa kónakute mo íi desu.	You don't have to come today.

Notice that the idea of "don't have to" or "need not"
is expressed by a sequence quite different from that
for "have to" or "need to":

PLAIN PRESENT NEGATIVE	→	-TE FORM	→	DON'T HAVE TO
ikanai don't go		*ikanákute*		*ikanákute mo*[1] *íi desu*

[1] The use of *mo* is optional.

tabénai	don't eat	*tabénakute*	*tabénakute mo íi desu*
kónai	don't come	*kónakute*	*kónakute mo íi desu*
shinai	don't do	*shinákute*	*shinákute mo íi desu.*

12. *Sukí desu* To love, To like (something)

Anáta wa anó hito ga sukí desu ka?	Do you like him (her)?
Sore wa sukí ja arimasén.	I don't like it.
Moo hitótsu no hóo ga sukí desu.	I like the other better.
-kotó ga sukí desu	to love, to like to do (something)
Sanpo suru kotó ga sukí desu.	I love to [take a] walk.
Gaikokugo o naráu kotó ga sukí desu.	I like to learn foreign languages.
Kuruma de ryokoo suru kotó ga sukí desu.	I like to travel by car.

For *súki desu,* see also Lesson 31.

13. *-(r)aréru*

a. For the Passive (to be, to get plus a past participle)

b. For the Potential (to be able to)

c. Respect

CONSONANT VERB		→	PASSIVE, POLITE (RESPECT)
káku	write		*kakaréru*
yómu	read		*yomaréru*

VOWEL VERB

tomeru	stop	tomerareru
okíru	get up	okiraréru

IRREGULAR VERB

kúru	come	koraréru
suru	do	sareru

For potential verbs, see Lesson 40.

a. Passive

Keikan ni tomerare-máshita.	I was stopped by a policeman.
Watakushi wa Yamuda-san ni Tanaka-san to machigaerar-emáshita.	I was mistaken by Mr. Yamada for Ms. Tanaka.
Iriguchi de namae o kikaremáshita.	I was asked my name at the entrance. [At the entrance, I was asked to state my name.]
Áme ni furaremáshita.	We were caught in the rain. [We underwent the falling of the rain.]
Tomodachi ni ko-raremáshita.	We were visited by a friend (when we didn't want anyone to come).

Notice that the agent of the action is designated by the particle *-ni,* and the person who is affected by the action of the verb is marked with *wa* or *ga.*

b. Potential

Anó hito wa górufu ga sukí de yamerare-masén.	He likes golf and can't stop (playing) it.
Okane ga nái node tsuzukeraremasén.	As I do not have (enough) money, I can't continue it.
Kippu no nái hitó wa toosemasén.	We can't admit [pass] persons who have no tickets.
Toshókan ga shimátte iru node shiraberare-masén.	The library is closed, so I can't check it.
Kore wa anmari hídoku kowáreta node móo naosemasén.	This has been damaged so badly that we can't repair it any longer.

c. Respect

Note that all of the following sentences are spoken very politely.

Senséi wa ítsu káette koraremásu ka?	When is the teacher coming back?
Yamada sensei[1] wa Kyóoto ni ryokoo saremáshita.	Mr. Yamada, the teacher, traveled to Kyoto.
Yóshino-san wa sakunen nakuna-raremáshita.	Mr. Yoshino died last year.
Tanaka-san wa sono tanomí o kotowarare máshita.	Mr. Tanaka refused that request.

[1] *sensei:* teacher, sir [one who was born earlier]. *Yamada-sensei:* Mr. Yamada (said with great respect).

Sátoo-san wa súgu Shígeta-san ni denwa o kakeraremáshita.		Mr. Sato phoned Ms. Shigeta right away.

14. -(s)aseru To make (have, let, allow, force) one to (do something)—Causative

CONSONANT VERB		→	CAUSATIVE
iku	go		*ikaseru*
tobu	fly		*tobaseru*
VOWEL VERB			
tabéru	eat		*tabesaséru*
oshieru	teach		*oshiesaseru*
IRREGULAR VERB			
kúru	come		*kosaséru*
suru	do		*saseru*

Kodomo ni erabase-máshita.	I had the child choose them.
Musumé ni nímotsu o hakobasemáshita.	I had my daughter carry the baggage.
Kyóo wa sánji ni uchi e kaerásete kudasái.	Please let me go home at three o'clock.
Sono tegami o watakushi ni yomásete kudasái.	Please let me read that letter.
Kono kusuri o yojikan óki ni nomásete kudasái.	Please have him take this medicine every four hours.

QUIZ 37

1. *Mísete kudasái.*	a. Please look at this.
2. *Ohairi kudasái.*	b. Please look here.
3. *Wasurenáide kuda-sái.*	c. Please take the train.

4. *Moo ichido itte kudasái.*
d. Please take another one.

5. *Mátte kudasái.*
e. Please take it.

6. *Otori kudasái.*
f. Please wait.

7. *Densha de itte kudasái.*
g. Please don't forget.

8. *Moo hitótsu otori kudasái.*
h. Say it again, please.

9. *Koko o míte kudasái.*
i. Come in, please.

10. *Kore o míte kudasái.*
j. Show me, please.

ANSWERS
1–j; 2–i; 3–g; 4–h; 5–f; 6–e; 7–c; 8–d; 9–b; 10–a.

D. PUBLIC NOTICES AND SIGNS

Kooji	Public Notice	公示
Dánshi	Gentlemen	男子
Fujin	Ladies	婦人
Danshi(yoo) tearaijo	Men's Room	男子(用)手洗所
Fujin (yoo) tearaijo	Ladies' Room	婦人(用)手洗所
Benjó, Tearaijo	W.C.	便所、手洗所
Kin'en, Tabako goenryo kudasái	No Smoking	禁煙 煙草ご遠慮下さい。
Eigyoochuu	Open	営業中
(Hónjitsu) heiten	Closed (Today)	(本日)閉店
(Hónjitsu) kyuuggoo	Closed (Today)	(本日)休業
Iriguchi	Entrance	入口
Déguchi	Exit	出口

Hijónguchi	Emergency Exit	非常口
Erebéetaa	Elevator	エレベーター
Ikkai	The First Floor	一階
Osu	Push	押す
Mawasu	Turn	廻す
Béru o narash-ite kudasái	Please Ring	ベルを鳴らして下さい。
Tachiiri kinshi	Keep Out!	立入禁止
Tsuukoo kinshi	No Thorough-fare!	通行禁止
Ohairi kudasái	Come In	お入り下さい。
Nókku muyoo *Nókku o shináide ohairi kudasái*	Enter Without Knocking	ノック無用 ノックをしないでお入り下さい。
Nókku o shite kudasái	Knock	ノックをして下さい。
Nókku o shité kara ohairi kudasái	Knock Before Entering	ノックをしてからお入り下さい。
Kaisoo ni tsuki kyuugyoo	Closed for Repairs	改装につき休業
Shinsoo kaiten	Under New Management	新装開店
Nyuujoo okoto-wari	No Admittance	入場お断り
Kínjitsu kaiten	Will Open Shortly	近日開店
Shuuya éigyoo	Open All Night	終夜営業
Tsúba o haká naide ku-dasái	No Spitting	つばを吐かないで下さい。
Tsúba o háku bekárazu		つばを吐くべからず

Hakimono o nugútte kudasái	Wipe Your Shoes	履物を拭って下さい。
Inú o kusari kara hanasánaide kudasái	Leash Your Dog	犬をくさりから放さないで下さい。
Hokóosha okotowari	Pedestrians Keep Out	歩行者お断り
Kujoo soodanjo } *Kujoo shoríbu*	Complaint Department	苦情相談所 苦情処理部
Madóguchi de omooshikomi kudasái	Apply at the Window	窓口でお申し込み下さい。
Ryoogaejo	Money Exchanged	両替所
Urimono	For Sale	売物
Chintai itashimásu } *Chingashi itashimásu*	For Rent	賃貸いたします。
Kashi apáato kágu náshi	Unfurnished Apartment for Rent	貸アパート家具なし
Kashi apaato kágu tsuki	Furnished Apartment for Rent	貸アパート家具付
Waribiki hánbai } *Tokka hánbai*	Reduction	割引販売 特価販売
Uridashi	Sale	売り出し
Keitaihin azukarijo	Check Room, Cloakroom	携帯品預り所
Dookyúu shitsu	Billiard Room	撞球室

Yoomúinshitsu	Janitor's Room	用務員室
Ukai	Detour	迂回
Koojichuu	Under Construction	工事中
Káabu kiken	Dangerous Curve	カーブ危険
Chuusha kinshi	No Parking	駐車禁止
Ippoo kootsuu	One Way Street	一方交通
Sénro o yoko-giránaide kudasái *Sénro no oodan kinshi*	Don't Cross the Tracks	線路を横切らないで下さい。 線路の横断禁止
Fumikiri	Railroad Crossing	踏切
Tetsudoo	Railroad	鉄道
Gáado	Underpass/Overpass	ガード
Tomare	Stop!	止まれ！
Chúui	Caution!	注意！
Oodanhódoo	Pedestrian Crossing	横断歩道
Koosáten	Crossroads	交差点
Básu teiryuu-joo	Bus Stop	バス停留所
Harigami kin-shi	Post No Bills	貼紙禁止
Jisoku sanjuk-kiro íka	Max. Speed 30 K.P.H.	時速30キロ以下
Jokoo	Go Slow	徐行
Gakkoo kúiki jokoo	School—Go Slow	学校区域徐行
Kiken, Abunái	Danger!	危険！危い！
Penki nuri-tate	Fresh Paint	ペンキ塗りたて

Mádo kara kao ya té o dasánaide kudasái	Don't Lean Out of the Window!	窓から顔や手を出さないで下さい。
Keihóoki	Alarm Signal	警報機
Kooatsusen chúui	High Voltage	高圧線注意
Chikatetsu iriguchi	Subway Entrance	地下鉄入口
Keitaihin ichiji azukarijo	Baggage Room, Check Room	携帯品一時預り所
Machiáishitsu	Waiting Room	待合室
Ittoo	First Class	一等
Nitoo	Second Class	二等
Santoo	Third Class	三等
Toochaku	Arrival	到着
Hassha	Departure (Trains, Buses)	発車
Purattohóomu, Hóomu	Platform	プラットホーム、ホーム
Annaijo	Information	案内所
Kippu úriba	Box Office	切符売場
Yuubínkyoku	Post Office	郵便局
Posuto	Mailbox	ポスト
Nyuujooken úriba *Kippu úriba*	Ticket Office	入場券売場 切符売場
Kasaihoochíki	Fire Alarm Box	火災報知機
Kooritsu toshókan	Public Library	公立図書館
Keisatsusho	Police Station	警察署
Gasorin sutándo	Gas Station	ガソリンスタンド
Shóten	Bookstore	書店
Shiyákusho	City Hall	市役所

Rihátsuten	Barber Shop	理髪店
Biyóoin	Beauty Shop	美容院
Íshi	Physician	医師
Íin	Physician's Office	医院
Shiká	Dentistry	歯科
Kutsu shúuri	Shoe Repairing	靴修理
Máchinee *Chuukankóogyoo* }	Matinee	マチネー
Yakan kóogyoo hachíji sanjúppun kaien	Evening Performance at 8:30	夜間興業 8時30分開演
Seisoo chakuyoo	Formal Dress	正装着用
Heifuku chakuyoo	Informal Dress	平服着用
Renzoku kóogyoo	Continuous Performance	連続興業
Bangumi henkoo	Change of Program	番組変更
Kissáten	Coffee Shop	喫茶店

FINAL REVIEW QUIZ

1. _____ (Fine) *desu ka?*
   a. *Íkura*
   b. *Ogénki*
   c. *Ítsu*

2. *Yukkúri* _____ (speak) *kudasái.*
   a. *hanáshite*
   b. *káite*
   c. *tábete*

3. *Tabako ga* _____ (have) *ka?*
   a. *hoshíi desu*
   b. *kaitái desu*
   c. *arimásu*

4. *Ményuu o* _____ (show me) *kudasái.*
   a. *mísete*
   b. *tótte*
   c. *motté kite*

5. *Koohíi o íppai* _____ (give me).
   a. *nomimáshita.*
   b. *kudasái.*
   c. *agemáshita.*

6. _____ (Breakfast) *wa hachíji ni tabemáshita.*
   a. *Yuuhan*
   b. *Asagóhan*
   c. *Hirugóhan*

7. *Supúun o* _____ (bring).
   a. *mótte itte kudasái.*
   b. *motté kite kudasái.*
   c. *mótte kudasái.*

8. _____ (Station) *wa dóko ni arimásu ka?*
   a. *Denwa*
   b. *Éki*
   c. *Yuubínkyoku*

9. _____ (Which way) *desu ka?*
   a. *Sochira*
   b. *Kochira*
   c. *Dóchira*

10. *Taihen* _____ (near) *desu.*
    a. *tooí*

b. *chikái*
c. *ookíi*

11. *Okane o* _____ (does he have) *ka?*
    a. *hoshíi desu*
    b. *uketorimáshita*
    c. *mótte imasu*

12. *Watakushi no tegami ga* _____ (are there) *ka?*
    a. *arimasén*
    b. *arimásu*
    c. *arimáshita*

13. _____ (Do you understand) *ka?*
    a. *Shitte imásu*
    b. *Wakarimásu*
    c. *Kiite imásu*

14. *Hajímete* _____ (glad to know you).
    a. *ome ni kakarimásu.*
    b. *ryokoo shimáshita.*
    c. *sore o kikimáshita.*

15. *Sukóshi hoshíi desu ka* _____ (want a lot) *desu ka?*
    a. *sukoshi mo hóshiku nái*
    b. *takusan hoshíi*
    c. *anmari hóshiku nái*

16. *Yamada-san ni* _____ (must see).
    a. *hanasánakereba narimasén.*
    b. *awánakereba narimasén.*
    c. *kikanákereba narimasén.*

17. *Sore wa Nihongo de dóo* _____ (does one say)
   ka?
   - a. *kikimásu*
   - b. *iimásu*
   - c. *kakimásu*

18. *Denwa wa san réi rokú no* _____ (3307) *ban
   desu.*
   - a. *sánjuu san shichi*
   - b. *san sán rei naná*
   - c. *sansen sanhyaku shichí*

19. _____ (What time) *desu ka?*
   - a. *Nan'yóobi*
   - b. *Nánnichi*
   - c. *Nánji*

20. _____ (Tomorrow morning) *kité kudasái.*
   - a. *Ashita no yóru*
   - b. *Ashita no ása*
   - c. *Ashita no gógo*

21. *Ittá keredomo* _____ (couldn't meet).
   - a. *átta kotó ga arimasén deshita.*
   - b. *áu kotó ga dekimasén deshita.*
   - c. *au tsumori ja arimasén deshita.*

22. _____ (I want to go) *desu.*
   - a. *Ikitái*
   - b. *Hoshíi*
   - c. *Iku kóto ga sukí*

23. *Tanaka-san wa íma Tookyoo ni inai* _____ (I
   hear).
   - a. *sóo desu.*

    b. *to omoim ásu.*
    c. *no deshóv.*

24. _____ (Check) *o motté kite kudasái.*
    a. *Otsuri*
    b. *Ocha*
    c. *Denpyoo*

25. *Kyóoto e* _____ (I have been to).
    a. *iku kotó ga dekimasén.*
    b. *itta kotó ga arimásu.*
    c. *iku kotó ga sukí desu.*

ANSWERS
1–b; 2–a; 3–c; 4–a; 5–b; 6–b; 7–b; 8–b; 9–c; 10–b;
11–c; 12–b; 13–b; 14–a; 15–b; 16–b; 17–b; 18–b;
19–c; 20–b; 21–b; 22–a; 23–a; 24–c; 25–b.

SUMMARY OF JAPANESE GRAMMAR

All accent marks are omitted for this grammar summary.

1. THE ALPHABET AND ROMANIZATION

The sounds of Japanese have been transcribed into the Roman alphabet, and all letters of the English language except "l," "q," and "x" are employed. Generally speaking, the *r*-sound is close to "l." Note that *c* is used only in the combination *ch*.

There are two major systems of Romanization: the Hepburn System and the Japanese National System. The Hepburn System has a longer history and wider acceptance than the Japanese National System. The National System is more logical and reflects the phonological structure of the language better.

A slightly modified form of the Hepburn System is used here to present Japanese words and sentences. The system has been modified as follows:

a. So-called "long vowels" are written as double vowels instead of with a macron (¯) over the vowel symbol (i.e., *Tookyoo* instead of *Tōkyō; kuuki* instead of *kūki*).

b. The syllabic *n* is written as an *n* at all times instead of as an *m* when it precedes *p, b,* or *m.*

The following table illustrates the various ways in which consonants and vowels are combined in the Hepburn System to produce the sounds of Japanese.

Chart I aligns *vertically* the five vowel sounds, and shows *horizontally* the basic (mostly voiceless) consonants with which they can be used to create the basic syllables of Japanese. Chart II shows the sounds (the voiced counterparts) into which these consonants can change. The same relationship that exists between Charts I and II exists also between Charts III and IV.

A blank occurring in the charts (at the junction of a vertical and horizontal column) denotes that that combination of consonant and vowel is *never* used.

TABLE I
SYLLABLES OF THE MODIFIED HEPBURN SYSTEM IN MODERN JAPANESE[1,2]

		0	1	2	3	4	5	6	7	8	9	10
CHART I — V	1	a	ka	sa	ta	na	ha[3] (fa)	ma	ya	ra	wa	n
O	2	i	ki	shi	chi (ti)	ni	hi (fi)	mi		ri		
W E	3	u	ku	su	tsu (tu)	nu	hu	mu	yu	ru		
L	4	e	ke	se	te (tse)	ne	he (fe)	me		re		
S	5	o	ko	so	to	no	ho (fo)	mo	yo	ro		

[1] The *o* in column 9 and the *o* in column 0 are pronounced the same, but are represented by different *hiragana;* see The Writing System. The *o* in column 9 is used only for the particle *o*.

[2] The syllables in parentheses appear in borrowed words.

[3] Notice that in vertical column 5, the *h* of Chart I is converted to either *b* or *p* in Chart II.

		0	1	2	3	4	5	6	7	8	9	10
CHART	1		ga	za	da		ba	pa				(va)
II	2		gi	ji	(di)		bi	pi				(vi)
	3		gu	zu	(du)		bu	pu				(vu)
	4		ge	ze	de		be	pe				(ve)
	5		go	zo	do		bo	po				(vo)

CHART	1	kya	sha	cha	nya	hya	mya		rya		
III	3	kyu	shu	chu	nyu	hyu	myu		ryu		
	5	kyo	sho	cho	nyo	hyo	myo		ryo		
			(she)	(che)							

CHART	1	gya	ja			bya	pya				
IV	3	gyu	ju			byu	pyu				
	5	gyo	jo			byo	pyo				

CHART		-kk-	-ss-	-tt-		-pp-				
V			-ssh-	-tch-						
				-tts-						
		-(gg)-	-(zz)-	-(dd)-						
				-(dj)-						

The differences between the Hepburn and National Systems are limited to the syllables listed below:

HEPBURN SYSTEM	JAPANESE NATIONAL SYSTEM	HEPBURN SYSTEM	JAPANESE NATIONAL SYSTEM
shi	*si*	*chu*	*tyu*
chi	*ti*	*cho*	*tyo*
tsu	*tu*	*ja*	*zya*
fu	*hu*	*ju*	*zyu*
ji	*zi*	*jo*	*zyo*
sha	*sya*		
shu	*syu*		
sho	*syo*		
cha	*tya*		

TABLE II
SYLLABLES OF THE NATIONAL SYSTEM IN MODERN JAPANESE

Syllables in italics are spelled differently in the Hepburn system. See the list of syllables on page 000 for a comparison.

			0	1	2	3	4	5	6	7	8	9	10
CHART	V	1	a	ka	sa	ta	na	ha	ma	ya	ra	wa	n
I	O	2	i	ki	*si*	*ti*	ni	hi	mi		ri		
	W E	3	u	ku	su	*tu*	nu	*hu*	mu	yu	ru		
	L	4	e	ke	se	te	ne	he	me		re		
	S	5	o	ko	so	to	no	ho	mo	yo	ro		

CHART													
II	1	ga	za	da		ba	pa					va	
	2	gi	*zi*	*zi*		bi	pi					vi	
	3	gu	zu	zu		bu	pu					vu	
	4	ge	ze	de		be	pe					ve	
	5	go	zo	do		bo	po					vo	

CHART												
III	1	kya	*sya*	*tya*	nya	hya	mya		rya			
	3	kyu	*syu*	*tyu*	nyu	hyu	myu		ryu			
	5	kyo	*syo*	*tyo*	nyo	hyo	myo		ryo			

CHART											
IV	1	gya	*zya*			bya	pya				
	3	gyu	*zyu*			byu	pyu				
	5	gyo	*zyo*			byo	pyo				

CHART									
V	-kk-	-ss-	-tt-		-pp-				

2. SIMPLE VOWELS

a like the "a" in "father," but short and crisp.
i like the "e" in "keep," but short and crisp.
u like the "u" in "put," but without rounding the lips.
e like the "ay" in "may," but without the final *y* sound.

o like the "o" in "go," but without the final *u* sound.

Remember that *i* and *u* differ from the other vowels in that they tend to become "voiceless" or whispered (1) when they are surrounded by voiceless consonants *ch, f, h, k, p, s, sh, t, ts,* or (2) when they are preceded by a voiceless consonant and followed by a silence or pause (as at the end of a sentence). This is especially true when the syllable is not accented. In the following examples, the vowel with a circle underneath is a devoiced vowel:

arimasu̥	there is
ki̥tte	postage stamp

3. VOWEL CLUSTERS

a. **Double Vowels**

All simple vowels can appear in double[1] or "long" vowels. A double vowel is always pronounced twice as long as a simple vowel:

aa pronounced twice as long as a single *a: haato* [heart]

ii pronounced twice as long as a single *i: riiru* [reel]

uu pronounced twice as long as a single *u: suugaku* [math]

ee pronounced twice as long as a single *e: teeburu* [table]

oo pronounced twice as long as a single *o: Tookyoo* [Tokyo]

---

[1] Double vowels can be indicated by writing the single vowel with a "macron" over it: e.g., *ā* (for *aa*).

b. **Other Vowel Clusters**

All simple vowels can also appear in combination with one or more other simple vowels to form a "vowel cluster." In such combinations, each of the vowels has equal weight and is pronounced so that it retains the sound it has as a simple vowel. Vowel clusters should *not* be pronounced like diphthongs, which combine two vowels to make a new sound. For example:

au *a* and *u* are both pronounced and given equal clarity and length.

ai *a* and *i* are both pronounced and given equal clarity and length.

4.   CONSONANTS AND SEMI-VOWELS

a. The letters *b, d, j, k, m, p, s, ts, v,* and *y* in Japanese sound almost like the same letters in English. Pronounce the other sounds as follows:

ch as in "cheese."

f by forcing the air out from between the lips.

g at the beginning of a word, somewhat like the "g" in the English word "go"; in the middle of a word, it resembles the "ng" in "singer."

h like the "h" in "high," when it precedes *a, e, o;* like the "h" in "hue," when it comes before *i* or *y.*

n as in "name" (but with the tip of the tongue touching the back of the teeth) when it precedes *a, e, o, u;* as in "onion" when it precedes *i* or *y.*

r by placing the tip of the tongue near the back of the upper teeth and quickly bringing it down; it sometimes sounds like the "r" in a British version of "very" ("veddy").

sh somewhat like the English "sh" in "sheep."

t as in the English "to," but with the tip of the tongue touching the back of the upper teeth.

w like the "w" in "want," but without rounding or protruding the lips; occurs only before *a*.

z at the beginning of a word, like the *ds* in "beds"; in the middle of a word, like the *z* in "zero" (but some Japanese speakers do not make this distinction; they use the two sounds interchangeably).

b. When a word begins with *ch, h, k, s, t,* or *ts,* and it joins with another word (which then *precedes* it) to make a new compound word, the initial letter or letters may undergo a change:

 ch may become *j,* as it does in the change from *chie* [wisdom] to *warujie* [guile, wiles].

 f and *h* may become *p* or *b,* as *h* does in the change from *hanashi* [story] to *mukashibanashi* [a story of the past].

 k may become *g,* as it does in the change from *ken* (a counter for houses) to *sangen* [three houses].

 s may become *z,* as it does in the change from *sen* [one thousand] to *sanzen* [three thousand].

 sh may become *j,* as it does in the change from *shika* [deer] to *ojika* [male deer].

 t may become *d,* as it does in the change from *to* [door, windows] to *amado* [storm window, Japanese rain-window].

 ts may become *z,* as it does in the change from *tsuki* [month] to *tsukizuki* [monthly].

5. DOUBLE CONSONANTS

When a double *p, t, k,* or *s* (*d, z,* or *g* in borrowed words) appears in a word, then the initial consonant of the cluster has one syllable length. This same lengthening takes place when *tch, tts,* or *ssh* (*dj* in borrowed words) appears in a word:

kippu	ticket
mattaku	indeed
nikki	diary
itchi	agreement

6. THE SYLLABIC *N*

The syllabic *n* differs from the ordinary *n* in several ways:

a. It always forms a full syllable by itself (that is, it is always held as long as one full syllable). It *never* joins with a vowel or another consonant to form a syllable. If a vowel follows the syllabic *n,* there is always a syllable boundary between the *n* and the vowel. For example, the word *gen'in* [cause] has four syllables—*ge-n-i-n*—since each of the syllabic *n*'s has the value of a full syllable.

b. The syllabic *n* seldom appears at the beginning of a word.

c. Its sound changes, depending on what follows it:

   (1) Before *n, ch, t,* and *d,* it is pronounced like the English ''n'' in ''pen,'' but the sound is held longer.

konna	this sort of
hanchoo	group leader
chanto	properly
kondo	this time

(2) Before *m, p,* or *b,* it is pronounced like the English "m" but the sound is held longer.

SPELLING	PRONUNCIATION	MEANING
sanmai	*sammai*	three sheets
shinpai	*shimpai*	worry, anxiety
kanban	*kamban*	signboard

(3) Before a vowel or a semi-vowel (*w, y*), the syllabic *n* is pronounced somewhat like the English "ng" in "singer," but without finishing the *g* sound, and the preceding vowel is often somewhat nasalized. Notice that an apostrophe is used when a vowel or *y* follows the syllabic *n.*

gen'an	original plan
tan'i	unit
hon'ya	bookstore
shinwa	mythology

(4) When the syllabic *n* precedes *k, g,* or *s,* or when it appears at the end of a word (that is, when it is followed by a pause), it is pronounced as in paragraph 3, above.

sonkei	respect
sangen	three houses
son	loss
kansei	completion

7. CONTRACTIONS

a. The particle *de* [at, by means of] sometimes combines with the particle *wa* [as for] thus: *de* plus *wa = ja.*

Nihon ja yasui desu.	It is cheap in Japan (but not here).

b. The *-te* form of the copula *de* (from *desu*) also can combine with the particle *wa* thus: *de* plus *wa = ja.*

Nihonjin ja arimasen.	She is not a Japanese.

c. The *-te* form of a verb sometimes combines with the particle *wa* thus: *-te* plus *wa = cha,* or *-de* plus *wa = ja.*

Itcha ikemasen.	You mustn't go.
Yonja ikemasen.	You mustn't read it.

8. ACCENT

Word accent in Japanese is indicated by lowering the pitch of the voice *after* the accented syllable.

Some words have, some do not have, an accent in Japanese. Accentless words are spoken with the voice pitch held even on all syllables of the word except the first; here the pitch is slightly lower. This is true regardless of the length of the word.

Certain words lose their accent when they are placed next to an accented word. Hence the accents are sometimes marked and sometimes not marked within the same sentence.

The inclusion or omission of accent is further determined by various subsidiary rules, not all of which are thoroughly understood at the present time. The student can learn much about the refinements of accentuation through listening to native Japanese speakers.

Note that all accents are omitted in this Summary of Grammar.

9. INTONATION

a. **In a Declarative Sentence:**
   There is a marked drop in the pitch of the voice on the last-voiced syllable.

b. **In a Direct Question:**
   There may be a rising intonation on the last-voiced syllable. This rise in pitch is optional when the sentence ends with the question-particle *ka* or contains a question phrase such as *doko e* [where to]. When neither a question particle nor question word is used, the rising intonation is used.

c. **Suspension:**
   The last-voiced syllable is spoken in approximately the same level tone as what precedes it.

10. NOUNS

a. Most nouns in a sentence are accompanied by one or two noun-particles[1] (i.e., *wa, ga, o, mo, no, ni, de, kara*) or by some form of the copula *desu* [it is]. Nouns are not declined.

[1] See the material on page 313 for particles used with nouns.

| *Nihon ni wa yama ga takusan arimasu.* | There are many mountains in Japan. |
| *Fujisan wa takai yama desu.* | Fuji is a high mountain. |

a. There are certain nouns, usually having to do with time, degree, or quantity, which may or may not appear with a particle. Such nouns may have the functions not only of nouns but also of adverbs, and may be used to modify predicates or entire clauses.

| *Kinoo ikimashita.* | I went there yesterday. |
| *Kinoo wa ikimasen deshita.* | I didn't go there yesterday. |

Here is a list of some more of these nouns:

maiasa	every morning
mainichi	every day
ima	present time, now
moto	former time, previously
sukoshi	a small amount, a little, some
takusan	a large amount, a great deal, plentifully, in a large quantity
hotondo	nearly all, almost completely
mada	as yet, still
zenzen	whole, completely (used with a negative predicate)
nakanaka	quite, considerably

c. Some nouns frequently take on a special function: i.e., they are used to relate or tie one part of a sentence to another, assuming a role comparable in the English language to that of a preposition, adverb, or conjunction. When so used, these nouns are always modified by a clause. They are sometimes classified as particles rather than as nouns. The list that follows contains some of the most widely used functional nouns:

NOUN	NOUN MEANING	FUNCTIONAL WORD MEANING
aida	duration, space; interval	during; as long as; while
ato	site; place behind; time following; condition following	after, subsequent to (usually preceded by the *-ta* form of a verb and followed by *de*)
baai	occasion; situation	in the event that, in case; when; should (something) happen
dake	height; extent	as much as
hazu	notch (of an arrow)	it (something) is "in the cards," it is expected that, it is supposed that (when followed by *desu*); it is not reasonable to expect that, it is hardly possible that (when followed by *wa* or *ga arimasen*)
hodo	approximate degree	to the extent of; not as ... as ... (usually followed by a negative predicate):
A wa B hodo yoku arimasen.		A is not as good as B.

Sono sake wa nomeba nomu hodo motto nomitaku narimasu.

The more you drink that sake, the more you want to drink; the more . . . the more . . . (when preceded by a single verb in the present tense or a verb in the provisional form together with the same verb in the present)

hoo side, direction, alternative direction

the use of this word denotes that a comparison is being made:

Kono hoo ga yasui desu.

This is cheaper.

Kusuri o nonda hoo ga ii desu.

It would be better (for you) to take some medicine.

ijoo (wa) the above-mentioned

now that, since, inasmuch as, because of

kagiri limits, bounds; maximum degree

as far as, so long as, as much as, provided that

kekka result, outcome, consequence

with the result that, as a result of, because of

kiri limit

nothing happened after

Nippon e itta kiri tayori ga arimasen.

There is no news from him since he went to Japan.

koto fact; thing (abstract)

the act of doing . . . ; the act of having done . . . (makes a noun equivalent out of inflected words; used in many idiomatic expressions):

Hanasu koto wa dekimasen.		Talking is not permitted [possible]. I can't talk.
Hanashita koto wa arimasen.		I've never talked (with him). [The experience of having talked with him does not exist.]
mae	the front; prior time, former time	before, prior to [usually followed by *ni*]
mama	will (wish)	as it is (without doing anything further, without taking additional action); as it stands; exactly as; according to
mono	thing (tangible); person	the thing which; the one who; it's because (when it is used at the end of a sentence, usually in talk by a woman—a use similar to *kara* or *node*); that's the thing to do, you should, it is expected that (when preceded by a verb in the present form and followed by *desu*); used to do (when preceded by the *-ta* form of a verb and followed by *desu*)
nochi	the time after	after (used either with or without *ni* following it); subsequent to having done . . . (when it is preceded by the *-ta* form of a verb)

tabi	occasion, time	every time that
tame	sake	for the sake of; for the purpose of; because of
toki	time	(at the time) when
tokoro	place	just when, in the act of (when followed by *ni* or *de*); even if, no matter who, no matter what (when followed by *de*); to be on the point of (when preceded by the present form of a verb and followed by *desu*); to have just finished doing ... (when preceded by the *-ta* form of a verb and followed by *desu*)
toori	the way, avenue	exactly as
tsu-mori	idea in mind	intend to, plan to (when preceded by the present tense of a verb and followed by *desu*); (*my*) notion [recollection] about it is that (something) was the case (when preceded by the *-ta* form of a verb and followed by *desu*)
uchi	the inside [the within]	while, during the time when

ue	top, surface, place over	on top of doing, having done (something), upon doing . . . , besides (doing) . . . ; upon finishing, after (doing something), (when followed by *de*)
wake	reason, meaning, logic	that's the background of it, that's the story of it, that's what it is (when followed by *desu*); it is hardly believable that (something) should happen (or should have happened) (when followed by *ga arimasen*).

d. Some nouns are converted into verbs when they are used with *suru*. The resultant combination means "do the action of (something)." For instance:

shookai	introduction
shookai suru	to introduce
ryokoo	travel
ryokoo suru	to travel

e. The pre-*masu* form can function as a noun:

yomu	to read
yomi	reading; pronunciation
tsuru	to fish
tsuri	fishing

f. The stem of an adjective (i.e., the plain-present

affirmative minus the final *i*) can function as a noun:

akai red   *aka* the color red

The stem of an adjective can also function as a noun by adding *sa* or *mi:*

akai red	*akasa* redness
fukai deep	{*fukasa* depth (as a measure)
	{*fukami* depth (of thought)

g. Particles[1] used with nouns:

Following is a list of special particles used with nouns, and many of their functions:

ga marks an emphatic grammatical subject (see *mo,* below).

wa marks a sentence-topic that may either be the subject or object of the sentence, or a modifier. Some of the modifiers in b. above can be used with *wa,* also.

no links a noun to another noun. It is most frequently used for the possessive (''of '').

ni links a noun or noun equivalent (such as the pre-*masu* form of a verb) to a verb, adjective, or copula.

o marks the thing acted on (see *mo,* below).

[1] Note that Japanese has many of these so-called ''particles,'' which show the grammatical relationship of one word to another within a sentence; see also Lesson 11. Mastery of these particles is a key to rapid learning of Japanese. See Particles Used with Verbs, Section 18 of the Summary of Japanese Grammar.

mo can be used instead of *ga* or *o* (see above) but carries the additional meaning of "that thing also."

e links a noun to a verb and marks the direction toward which an action is performed.

to does one of two things: (i) it links nouns together in a complete list (see *ya,* page 314) or (ii) it marks the partner with whom the action is being performed.

ya links nouns together in an incomplete list (see *to,* page 314).

yori marks a noun or noun-equivalent as the standard against which a comparison is made.

kara marks a starting point in time or space.

made marks the ending point in time or space.

de marks the means, way, or manner in which an action is performed.

bakari has one of two functions: (i) it can be used in place of (or sometimes together with) *ga* or *o* to carry the additional meaning of "nothing else," or (ii) if it follows a number, it signifies that the number is only approximate.

dake can be used in place of or together with *ga* or *o* to carry the additional meaning of "that was the limit."

hodo can be used (i) to mark a thing against which a comparison is made and which is about the same in degree or extent as the thing compared, or (ii) to mark a number that is only approximate.

kurai (or *gurai*) marks the approximate quantity, quality, or degree, and can often be used interchangeably with *hodo* (see above).

ka shows that (i) a statement is a question, or (ii) it has the meaning of "either . . . or."

11. COUNTERS

"Counters" form a subclass of nouns often used adverbially to mean "to the extent of." There are several types:

a. **Unit Counters**

(1) "Unit" counters name specifically what is being counted. The following unit counters are used with primary numbers: *ichi, ni, san* [one, two, three], etc.—and are suffixed to these numbers. Where an exception to the general rule occurs, it is shown.

COUNTER	MEANING	EXCEPTIONS
-jikan	hours	*yojikan* = four hours
-ji	o'clock	*yoji* = four o'clock
-fun (or *-pun*)	minutes	See also Section 4b of the grammar summary for change of sound.
-byoo	seconds	
-nichi	days	See also Lesson 25 for variations.
-shuukan	weeks	
-kagetsu	months	
-gatsu	name of the month	
-nen	years	*yonen* = four years

-en	yen (Japanese currency)
-sento	cent (U.S. currency)
-doru	dollar (U.S. currency)
-shiringu	shillings (British currency)
-pondo	pounds (unit of weight or of British currency)
-meetoru	meters
-kiro	kilometers, kilograms
-kiroguramu	kilograms
-kiromeetoru	kilometers
-mairu	miles
-inchi	inches
-do	times
-peeji	pages; page number
-gyoo	lines; line number
-wari	one-tenth
-paasento	percent
-kai	story (of a building)

(2) The following unit counters are used with secondary numbers (*hito-, futa-, mi-,* etc.). They are usually used to count amounts less than four.

-ban	nights
-heya	room
-ma	room

b. Class Counters

(1) "Class counters" are used in a general rather than specific sense. The following class counters are used with primary numerals (*ichi, ni, san . . .*):

COUNTER	MEANING	EXCEPTIONS
-hiki (or *-biki*, or *-piki*)	animals, fish, insects	*ippiki, sanbiki, roppiki, jip-piki*
-too	large animals (such as horses, cows)	
-wa (or *-ba*, or *-pa*)	birds	*sanba, roppa, jippa*
-satsu	bound volumes (of books and maga-zines)	
-mai	flat, thin things (such as sheets, news-papers, hand-kerchiefs)	
-hon (or *-pon*, or *-bon*)	thin, long things (such as pencils, tubes, sticks, matches, cig-arettes)	*ippon, sanbon, roppon, jip-pon*
-ken (or *-gen*)	houses	*sangen*
-tsuu	documents, letters, tele-grams	

-dai	vehicles (such as cars, wagons), machines (such as typewriters, sewing machines)	
-ki	planes and other aircraft	
-chaku	suits of clothes	
-soku (or *-zoku*)	pairs of things worn on the feet or legs (such as shoes, socks, stockings)	*sanzoku*
-ko	lumps (such as apples, stones, candy)	
-hai (or *-pai* or *-bai*)	something in containers (such as water, coffee)	

(2) The following class counters are used with secondary numerals (*hito-*, *futa-*, *mi-*, etc.):

-fukuro	bagful (of)
-hako	boxful (of)
-kumi	set, group, couple (of people)
-soroi	set, group
-iro	kind, variety
-kire	slices
-tsumami	pinch

12. PRONOUNS

All of the Japanese words that correspond to English pronouns are nouns. They take the same particles as other nouns and are modified by the same type of words, phrases, and clauses that are used to modify other nouns. Note that in Japanese there are more varieties of words that correspond to personal pronouns than there are in English.

A list of Japanese equivalents of personal pronouns and instructions for using them follows:

a. **I, We**

SINGULAR	PLURAL	MEANING AND USAGE
watakushi	*watakushitachi*	I, we (formal)
watashi	*watashitachi*	I, we (slightly less formal than *watakushi* and used most widely)
boku	*bokutachi*	I, we (used by males only: informal)
ore	*oretachi*	I, we (used by males, but not in refined speech)

b. **You**

Avoid using any definite word for "you" as long as the sentence meaning is clear without it. If you cannot avoid using such a word, use the name (usually the surname) of the person you are addressing and add -*san* with the appropriate particle. If you are speaking to a small child, use the child's given name with -*kun* (for male) or -*chan* (for female). If you are speaking to a teacher, a doctor, etc., use *sensei*[1] either preceded by or without the surname of the person you are addressing. If you must employ the pronoun instead of the name, use *anata* [you (sing.)], *anatagata* [you (pl.)], *minasan* [you (pl.)], or *minasama* [you (pl., very formal)]. Many of the sentence examples in this course contain *anata* or *anatagata,* but it is well to remember that these should be replaced in actual conversation by the name of the person to whom you are speaking, whenever possible.

c. **He, She, They**

SINGULAR	PLURAL	MEANING AND USAGE
ano kata	*ano katagata*	he, she, they (*respect*)
ano hito	*ano hitotachi*	he, she, they (*respect*)
ano otoko no kata	*ano otoko no katagata*	he, they (respect: used only when it is necessary to indicate specifically "he [that man]" or "they [those men]")
ano otoko no hito	*ano otoko no hitotachi*	he, they (neutral: same as above)

ano onna no kata	*ano onna no katagata*	she, they (polite: used only when there is need to indicate specifically "she" or "they" [those women])
ano onna no hito	*ano onna no hitotachi*	she, they (neutral: same as above)
kare	*karera*	he, they (most often used in translations from English or in sample sentences in texts; also used widely by post–World War II generations but not yet widely accepted as good usage
kanojo	*kanojora*	she, they (same as above)

d. **Possessives**

There are no possessive pronouns as such in Japanese. To form the possessive, combine a noun (used for the person referred to) with *no* [things of], as in the following examples:

watakushi no	my, mine
anato no (or the name of the person) plus *no*	your, yours
ano hito no	his, hers
watakushitachi no	our, ours
anatagata no ⎫ *minasan no* ⎭	your, yours (*pl.*)
ano hitotachi no	their, theirs

13. PRENOUNS

"Prenouns"—words such as *kono* [this] or *konna* [this sort of] precede a noun and modify its meaning. No particle is used to separate the prenoun and noun. Prenouns do not change their forms.

kono	this
sono	that
ano	that over there
dono	which?
konna	this sort of
sonna	that sort of
anna	that sort of
donna	what sort of?

14. *Ko-So-A-Do* WORDS

Some Japanese nouns and prenouns come in sets of four words that are usually pronounced alike, except for the first syllable. These sets of words are called "ko-so-a-do words" because the first syllable is always one of the following four: *ko-*, *so-*, *a-*, or *do-*. Note that the word in such a group that begins with *do* is always a question word.

a. *Ko-so-a-do* Nouns[1]

kore	this one
sore	that one
are	that one over there
dore	which one?
koko	this place
soko	that place
asoko[2]	that place over there
doko	which place? where?
kochira, kotchi	this way, this one (of two)
sochira, sotchi	that way, that one (of two)
achira, atchi	that way, that one (of two)
dochira, dotchi	which way, which (of two)?

b. *Ko-so-a-do* Prenouns

kono	this
sono	that
ano	that over there
dono	which?
konna	this sort of
sonna	that sort of (for something not far removed in feeling or time)
anna	that sort of (for something more remote in feeling or time)
donna	what sort of?

15. ADJECTIVES

a. *I-* Adjectives

I- adjectives can end in *-ai, ii, ui,* or *-oi,* but never in *-ei.*

---

[1] See Lesson 17.
[2] An irregular form.

akai	(is) red
utsukushii	(is) beautiful
samui	(is) cold
kuroi	(is) black

I- adjectives are conjugated as follows:

(1) **Plain Forms**

PRESENT	*takai*	it is high
PAST	*takakatta*	it was high
TENTATIVE PRESENT	*takai daroo*	it is probably high
TENTATIVE PAST	*takakatta daroo*	it was probably high

(2) **Polite Forms**

PRESENT	*takai desu*	it is high
PAST	*takakatta desu*	it was high
TENTATIVE PRESENT	*takai deshoo*	it is probably high
TENTATIVE PAST	*takakatta de-shoo*	it was probably high

(3) **Other Forms**

-TE FORM	*takakute*	it is (was) high, and . . .
-KU FORM	*takaku*	it is (was) high, and . . . highly
-BA FORM	*takakereba*	if it is high
-TARA FORM	*takakattara*	if (when) it is (was) high

b. **Na- Adjectives**

(1) **Plain Forms**

PRESENT	*shizuka da*	it is quiet
PAST	*shizuka datta*	it was quiet
TENTATIVE PRESENT	*shizuka daroo*	it is probably quiet
TENTATIVE PAST	*shizuka datta daroo*	it was probably quiet

(2) **Polite Forms**

PRESENT	*shizuka desu*	it is quiet
PAST	*shizuka deshita*	it was quiet
TENTATIVE PRESENT	*shizuka deshoo*	it is probably quiet
TENTATIVE PAST	*shizuka datta deshoo*	it was probably quiet

(3) **Other Forms**

-TE FORMS	*shizuka de*	it is (was) quiet and . . .
-NI FORMS	*shizuka ni*	quietly
-TARA FORMS	*shizuka dattara*	if (when) it is (was) quiet and . . .

16. COMPARISONS

There are several ways to show comparison:

a. Use *no hoo* [the side of] to show what is being compared:

Kyooto no hoo ga suki desu.   I like Kyoto better.

Tookyoo no hoo ga samui desu.	Tokyo is colder [in climate]
Kuruma de iku hoo ga ii desu.	It is better to go by car.

Notice that when a verb comes before *hoo, no* is omitted.

b. Use *yori* [than] to mark the standard against which a comparison is made:

Kyooto yori samui desu.	It is colder than Kyoto.
Kore wa sore yori takai desu.	This is more expensive than that.

c. Use both *no hoo* and *yori* in the same sentence to show that a comparison is being made:

Tookyoo no hoo ga Kyooto yori samui desu.	Tokyo is colder than Kyoto.
Yomu hoo ga hanasu yori muzukashii desu.	Reading is more difficult than speaking.

d. Use *zutto* [by far the more] either with or without *no hoo* or *yori:*

Sono densha no hoo ga kono densha yori zutto hayai desu. *Sono densha ga zutto hayai desu.*	That train is much faster (than this train).
Kore wa zutto yasashii desu.	This is much easier.

e. Use *motto* [still more] either with or without *no hoo* or *yori:*

Sore wa motto takai desu. *Sore wa kore yori motto takai desu.*	That is still more expensive (than this one).
Motto yukkuri hanashite kudasai.	Please speak more slowly.

f. Use *ichiban* [number one, most of all] or *mottomo* [the most] when comparing more than two things. (*Mottomo* is more formal than *ichiban*.)

Ano hito ga ichiban takai desu. *Ano hito ga mottomo takai desu.*	He is the tallest.
Ichiban ii no o kudasai.	Give me the best kind, please.

g. Use *dochira* or *dotchi* [which of the two], or *dore* [which of more than two] when asking a question involving a comparison:

Nagoya to Kyooto de wa dochira ga chikai desu ka?	Which is nearer— Nagoya or Kyoto?
Nagoya to Kyooto to Hiroshima de wa dore ga ichiban tooi desu ka?	Which is the farthest— Nagoya, Kyoto, or Hiroshima?

h. Use *hodo* (to show approximate degree) and a negative predicate when making a comparison between two things that are not quite alike:

Nagoya wa Oosaka hodo tooku arimasen.	Nagoya is not as far as Osaka.

Tanaka-san wa Yamada-san hodo kanemochi ja arimasen.	Ms. Tanaka is not as rich as Mr. Yamada

i. Use *hodo* also to describe situations resulting in extreme, intense, or severe effects:

Kimochi ga waruku naru hodo takusan tabemashita.	I ate so much that I began to feel sick.
Onaka ga itaku naru hodo waraimashita.	I laughed so much that I began to get a stomachache.

j. Use *no yoo ni* [in the likeness of, in the manner of] or *kurai* (or *gurai*) [more or less] when making a comparison between two things or situations that are pretty much alike:

Yamada-san wa Eigo ga Amerikajin no yoo ni yoku dekimasu.	Mr. Yamada knows English as well as a native American.
Yamada-san wa Eigo ga Amerikajin gurai dekimasu.	Mr. Yamada knows English as well as [just like] a native American.

17. THE CLASSES AND FORMS OF VERBS

a. **Verb Classes**

There are three classes of verbs in Japanese:

Class I—Consonant Verbs: includes all verbs except those in Class II and Class III.

Class II—Vowel Verbs: includes the majority of verbs that, in their plain present form, terminate in *-eru* or *-iru*.

Class III—Irregular Verbs: *kuru* [come] and *suru* [do].

The base of a *consonant* verb is that part left over after the final *-u* has been dropped from the plain present affirmative form (= dictionary form). The base always ends in a consonant except where there is another vowel before the final *-u*.

The base of a *vowel* verb is that part remaining after the final *-ru* has been dropped from the plain present form. It always ends in either *-e* or *-i*.

b. *-Masu* Forms

-Masu forms (= polite present affirmative forms) are formed in the following ways:

Consonant verbs: Drop the final *u* of the dictionary form, and add *imasu*.

Vowel verbs: Drop the final *ru* of the dictionary form, and add *masu*.

DICTIONARY FORM → -MASU FORM

consonant verb

kaku	*kakimasu*	write
yomu	*yomimasu*	read
vowel verb		
taberu	*tabemasu*	eat
miru	*mimasu*	see

-Masu forms of some respect verbs are formed irregularly:

DICTIONARY FORM	→	-MASU FORM	
irassharu		*irasshaimasu*	go, come, be
ossharu		*osshaimasu*	say
kudasaru		*kudasaimasu*	give
nasaru		*nasaimasu*	do

These respect verbs are consonant verbs. Notice that in their *-masu* forms, *r* is dropped. For example, the *-masu* form of *irassharu* is *irasshaimasu*, not *irassharimasu*.

c. **The Tenses**

In Japanese, a verb form referred to as a "tense" actually describes the *mood* of the action or state.

(1) The present tense (or *-u*-ending form) expresses an *incomplete* action or state and may have several English translations:

Hanashimasu.	I speak. I do speak. I will speak.
Tabemasu.	I eat. I do eat. I will eat.

(2) The past tense (or *-ta* form) expresses a *completed* action or state. It, too, can have several English translations:

Hanashimashita.	I spoke. I have spoken.
Tabemashita.	I ate. I have eaten.

The plain form of the past tense is formed from the plain present as follows:

> (a) For consonant verbs:
> > (i) When the final syllable in the plain present is *-u, -tsu,* or *-ru,* drop it and add *-tta:*

PRESENT	PAST	
Kau.	*Katta.*	I bought.
Tatsu.	*Tatta.*	I stood up.
Toru.	*Totta.*	I took it.

     (ii) When the final syllable in the plain present is *-mu, 'nu,* or *-bu,* drop it and add *-nda:*

Nomu.	*Nonda.*	I drank it.
Shinu.	*Shinda.*	He died.
Yobu.	*Yonda.*	I called.

    (iii) When the final syllable is *-ku* or *-gu,* drop it and add *-ita* in place of *-ku* and *-ida* in place of *-gu:*

Kaku	*Kaita*	I wrote.
Isogu	*Isoida*	I hurried.

    (iv) When the final syllable is *-su,* drop it and add *-shita:*

Hanasu.	*Hanashita.*	I spoke.
Kasu.	*Kashita.*	I lent it.

  (b) For vowel verbs:
     Drop the final syllable *-ru* and add *-ta:*

Taberu.	*Tabeta.*	I ate.
Miru.	*Mita.*	I saw it.

  (c) For irregular verbs:

Kuru.	*Kita.*	I came.
Suru.	*Shita.*	I did.

The polite form of the past tense is formed from the polite present (the *-masu* form) by replacing the final syllable *-su* with *-shita*.

POLITE PRESENT	POLITE PAST	
Ikimasu.	*Ikimashita.*	I went.
Tabemasu.	*Tabemashita.*	I ate.
Mimasu.	*Mimashita.*	I saw it.

(3) The tentative (polite: *-mashoo;* plain: *-oo* or *-yoo*) expresses an action or state that is not certain, definite, or completed. It can have several English translations:

Yomimashoo.	I think I will read. Let's read.
Yomimashoo ka?	Shall we read?

The plain tentative is formed from the plain present as follows:

(a) For consonant verbs:
Drop the final *-u* and add *-oo*.

PRESENT	TENTATIVE	
Hanasu.	*Hanasoo.*	I think I'll speak. Let's talk.
Yomu.	*Yomoo.*	I think I'll read. Let's read.

(b) For vowel verbs:
Drop the final *-ru* and add *-yoo*.

Taberu.	*Tabeyoo.*	I think I'll eat. Let's eat.
Miru.	*Miyoo.*	I think I'll see it. Let's see it.

The polite tentative is formed from the polite present by dropping the final *-su* and adding *-shoo.*

POLITE PRESENT	POLITE TENTATIVE	
Hanashimasu.	*Hanashimashoo.*	I think I'll talk. Let's talk.
Tabemasu.	*Tabemashoo.*	I think I'll eat. Let's eat.

a. *-Te* forms

(1) The *-te* form is formed exactly like the plain past affirmative (see section 17-C-2, above) except that the final vowel is *-e.* A *-te* form actually has no tense; the "tense" feeling is determined by the "tense-mood," that is, the ending (*-u, -ta, -yoo*), of the terminal verb.

Kusuriya e itte kusuri o kaimashita.	I went to a drugstore and bought some medicine.

Normally, when there is more than one verb in a sentence, the *-te* form is used for all but the last verb. The pre-*masu* form is sometimes used instead of the *-te* form, but this is considered "bookish."

Kusuriya e itte kusuri o katte uchi e kaette sore o nonde sugu nemashita.	I went to the drugstore and bought some medicine and returned home and took it and went to bed right away.

(2) The *-te* form is also used:

   (a) Adverbially: To modify a verb or adjective.

Isoide ikimashita.	He went hurriedly.
Naite hanashimashita.	He spoke in tears.
Yorokonde shigoto o hikiukemashita.	She took on the job gladly.

   (b) With *kudasai:* to form a request.

Kesa no shinbun o katte kudasai.	Please buy me this morning's paper.

   (c) With *imasu:* to form the progressive.

Hanashite imasu.	I am speaking.
Tabete imasu.	I am eating.

   (d) To form the "stative," which expresses the state resulting from a completed action, (i) add *arimasu* to the *-te* form, or (ii) add *imasu* to the *-te* form. The latter kind is identical with the progressive in form, but not in function. Usually, *arimasu* is used after the *-te* form of a transitive verb, and *imasu* after the *-te* form of an intransitive verb.

Te de kaite arimasu.	It's handwritten. [It is in the state of his having written it by hand.]
Moo kekkon shite imasu.	She is married already. [She is in the state of her being married since she got married.]

PLAIN PRESENT AFFIRMATIVE (DICTIONARY FORM)

CLASS I VERBS (CONSONANT VERBS)	CLASS II VERBS (VOWEL VERBS)	CLASS III VERBS (IRREGULAR VERBS)
hanasu	*taberu*	*suru*
speak	eat	do
will speak	will eat	will do

PLAIN PAST AFFIRMATIVE

hanashita	*tabeta*	*shita*
spoke	ate	did
have spoken	have eaten	has done

POLITE PRESENT AFFIRMATIVE (-*MASU* FORM)

hanashimasu	*tabemasu*	*shimasu*
speak	eat	do
will speak	will eat	will do

POLITE PAST AFFIRMATIVE

hanashimashita	*tabemashita*	*shimashita*
spoke	ate	did
have spoken	have eaten	have done

PLAIN PRESENT NEGATIVE

hanasanai	*tabenai*	*shinai*
do not speak	do not eat	do not do
will not speak	will not eat	will not do

PLAIN PAST NEGATIVE

hanasanakatta	*tabenakatta*	*shinakatta*
did not speak	did not eat	did not do
have not spoken	have not eaten	have not done

POLITE PRESENT NEGATIVE

hanashimasen	*tabemasen*	*shimasen*
do not speak	do not eat	do not do
will not speak	will not eat	will not do

POLITE PAST NEGATIVE

hanashimasen deshita	*tabemasen deshita*	*shimasen deshita*
did not speak	did not eat	did not do
have not spoken	have not eaten	have not done

EXTRA-POLITENESS

NEUTRAL	RESPECT	HUMBLE
hanasu	*ohanashi ni naru, hana- sareru*	*ohanashi suru*

PLAIN *-TE* FORM[1]

hanashite	*tabete*	*shite*
speak and . . .	eat and . . .	do and . . .
will speak and . . .	will eat and . . .	will do and . . .

POLITE *-TE* FORM[2]

hanashimashite	*tabemashite*	*shimashite*

Note that in the following groups, the ''a'' lines show the plain form of the verb and the ''b'' lines show the polite form.

PRESENT PROGRESSIVE AFFIRMATIVE

a. *hanashite iru*	*tabete iru*	*shite iru*
b. *hanashite imasu*	*tabete imasu*	*shite imasu*
he is speaking	he is eating	he is doing

[1] See Section 17-d-(2), above, for additional meanings.
[2] The polite *-te* form is only used in the most formal conversations. Furthermore, the polite *-te* form is unacceptable in the usages described in 17-d-(2).

PAST PROGRESSIVE AFFIRMATIVE

a. *hanashite ita* *tabete ita* *shite ita*

b. *hanashite* *tabete imashita* *shite imashita*
   imashita he was eat- he was doing
   he was ing
   speaking

PRESENT PROGRESSIVE NEGATIVE

a. *hanashite* *tabete inai* *shite inai*
   inai

b. *hanashite* *tabete imasen* *shite imasen*
   imasen he is not he is not
   he is not eating doing
   speaking

PAST PROGRESSIVE NEGATIVE

a. *hanashite* *tabete inakatta* *shite inakatta*
   inakatta

b. *hanashite* *tabete imasen* *shite imasen*
   imasen *deshite* *deshita*
   deshita he was not he was not
   he was not eating doing
   speaking

PRESENT STATIVE AFFIRMATIVE

a. *Hanashite* *Tabete aru.* *Shite aru.*
   aru.

b. *Hanashite* *Tabete ari-* *Shite arimasu.*
   arimasu. *masu.* It's done.
   The matter The meal is [The work is
   has already finished. in the state
   been men- [The meal is of my having
   tioned to in the state done it.]
   him. [The of my having
   matter is eaten it.]
   in the state
   of my hav-
   ing spoken
   about it.]

PAST STATIVE AFFIRMATIVE[1]

a. *Hanashite atta.* *Tabete atta.* *Shite atta.*

b. *Hanashite arimashita.* The matter had been mentioned to him. *Tabete arimashita.* The meal had been eaten. *Shite arimashita.* The work had been done.

PRESENT STATIVE NEGATIVE

a. *Hanashite nai.* Tabete nai. Shite nai.

b. *Hanashite arimasen.* The matter has not been mentioned. Tabete arimasen. The meal is not finished. Shite arimasen. It is not done.

PAST STATIVE NEGATIVE

a. *Hanashite nakatta.* Tabete nakatta. Shite nakatta.

b. *Hanashite arimasen deshita.* The matter hadn't been mentioned. Tabete arimasen deshita. The meal hadn't been finished. Shite arimasen deshita. It hadn't been done.

[1] Usually translated into English by the past perfect.

PROVISIONAL AND CONDITIONAL

hatarakeba	*tabereba*	*sureba*
hataraitara	*tabetara*	*shitara*
hataraku to	*taberu to*	*suru to*
hataraku nara	*taberu nara*	*suru nara*
hataraite wa	*tabete wa*	*shite wa*
if I work	if I eat	if I do.

18. PARTICLES USED WITH VERBS

The following particles which are used with verbs can also be used with adjectives or the copula. (See also Section 10-g of the Summary of Japanese Grammar for particles used with nouns.)

a. *bakari desu* =

   (1) (following a *-u* form) does nothing but (something); does only . . . :

Sotsugyoo o matsu bakari desu.	I am just waiting for graduation. (I have no more school work to do.)

   (2) (following a *-ta* form) has just done (something); did only (something):

Gohan o tabeta bakari desu.	I have just finished eating.

b. *dake* = that is just about all; that is just about the extent of it; only; just:

Mita dake desu.	I just took a look at it.
Hanashi o suru dake desu.	I am just going to discuss it. (I won't make any decision yet.)

c. *ga* = but; in spite of that fact stated above (when preceded by either the plain or polite forms).

Ikimashita ga aemasen deshita.	I went (there) but I couldn't see him.
Kaimashita ga mada tsukatte arimasen.	I have bought it but it hasn't been used.

d. *ka* = a spoken question mark:

Kyoo wa oisogashii desu ka?	Are you busy today?

e. *kara* =

(1) (following a *-te* form) after doing (something); since doing (something):

Mite kara kimemasu.	I will decide after taking [having taken] a look at it.

(2) (following any sentence-ending form— *-u, -ta, -i*) and so, and therefore:

Omoi desu kara watakuski ga omochi shimashoo.	It's heavy so I will carry it.

f. *keredo(mo)*[1] = in spite of that fact stated before; but; however; although:

Isoida keredo ma ni aimasen deshita.	I hurried, but couldn't make it.
Yonda keredomo yoku wakarimasen deshita.	I read it, but I didn't understand it well.

[1] The use of *mo* is optional.

g. *made* = up to the time of (something)'s happening; until; so far as:

Yamada-san ga kuru made koko ni ori-masu.	I will stay here until Mr. Yamada gets here.

h. *na* =

    (1) (following a plain present affirmative form) don't do (something); note that this is never used in refined speech; instead, *-naide kudasai* is used:

Hairu na!	Don't enter!
Hairanaide kudasai.	Please don't enter.

    (2) (following a sentence-ending form) yeah, that's what it is (used only by men in colloquial speech):

Ii tenki da na!	What fine weather!
Genki da na!	You are in good shape! (You look fine!)

    (3) (following a verb and used with *ka*) should I?; I wonder if I should (used in colloquial speech):

Dekakeyoo ka na?	Let's see. Shall we go now?
Eiga de mo miyoo ka na?	I guess I will see a movie or something.

i. *-nagara* = (following a pre-*masu* form, showing that two or more actions or states take place or exist concurrently) while; in the course of:

Arukinagara hanashi-mashoo.	Let's talk as we walk (to that place).
Hatarakinagara ben-kyoo shite imasu.	He is studying while working (he is supporting himself).

j. *nari* =

    (1) (when used in a parallel sequence) either . . . or . . . ; whether . . . or . . . :

Denwa o kakeru nari tegami o kaku nari shite minna ni shirasemashita.	She informed everybody either by phoning or writing a letter.

    (2) (when *not* used in a parallel sequence) as soon as; the moment (something) has taken place:

Kao o miru nari naki-hajimemashita.	He burst into tears the moment he saw me.

k. *ni* = the purpose of the "going" or "coming" that is expressed (when it follows the pre-*masu* form of a verb):

Kaimono o shi ni iki-mashita.	He went shopping. [He went in order to shop.]

l. *node* = (following a sentence-ending form) and so; and therefore:

Amari tsukareta node sukoshi yasumitai desu.	I got very tired, so I would like to [take a] rest.

Okane o harawanakatta node okutte kimasen deshita.	I didn't send the money for it; that's why it didn't come.

m. *noni* = and yet, but, although:

Yonda noni henji ga nai.	I called her but there was no answer.
Itta noni awanakatta.	Although I went there, I didn't see her.

n. *to* =

    (1) (following a present form) whenever:

Hima da to sanpo shi-masu.	Whenever I am free, I take a walk.

    (2) acts as an "end quote" when it precedes a verb meaning "say," "hear," "ask," "think," "believe":

Itsu kimasu ka to kik-areta.	I was asked [as to] when I would be coming.

    (3) (when it follows a tentative and is in turn fol-lowed by *suru*) to be on the point of doing (something); to try to do (something):

Uchi o deyoo to suru tokoro e tomodachi ga kimashita.	Just as I was about to go out, a friend of mine came (to visit me).

o. *-tari . . . -taru suru* =

    (1) sometimes does (something); at other times does (something else):

Nihon to Amerika no aida o ittari kitari shite imasu.

She travels back and forth between Japan and the United States.

(2) does (one thing) and (another):

Hito ga nottari oritari shite imasu.

Some people are getting on, some are getting off.

p. terminal particles:

(1) *ne* = isn't it? doesn't it?

Erai hito desu ne?

He is a great man, isn't he?

(2) *sa* = sure it is so (used only by men, slang):

Shitte iru sa!

Of course I know it.

(3) *wa, wa yo* = a diminutive used only by women:

Sanji ni denwa o kakeru wa (yo).[1]

I will phone you at three.

(4) *yo* = an exclamatory particle:

Kyoo wa okyakusan ga arimasu yo!

We are going to have a visitor today.

(5) *zo* = an emphatic particle (used only by men, slang):

Naguru zo!

I'll hit you!

---

[1] The use of *yo* is optional.

19. NEGATIVES

a. Used with Verbs

(1) Plain negative present—formed from the base of a consonant verb plus the suffix *-anai,* or the base of a vowel verb plus *-nai:*

Kaku.	I write.
Kakanai.	I don't write.
Taberu.	I eat.
Tabenai.	I don't eat.

Notice that a verb like *kau* [buy] or *warau* [laugh], whose plain present affirmative ends in two vowels, appends an extra *w* before adding *-anai:*

Kawanai.	I don't buy.
Warawanai.	She doesn't laugh.

(2) Plain negative past—formed from the stem of the negative present (the form without the final *-i*) plus *-katta* (like the plain negative past of an adjective):

Kaita.	I wrote.
Kakanakatta.	I didn't write.

(3) Plain negative tentative:
   (a) For a consonant verb, use the plain present affirmative plus *-mai.*
   (b) For a vowel verb, use the pre-*masu* form plus *-mai.*
   (c) For the irregular verbs, use *komai* and *shimai.*

Kakoo.	I think I'll write it.
Kakumai.	I don't think I'll write it.
Tabeyoo.	I think I'll eat.
Tabemai.	I don't think I'll eat.

b. **Used with a Copula**

(1) Plain forms:

... *da*	It is ...
... *de aru*	It is (formal, bookish) ...
... *ja nai* ... *de (wa) nai*	It is not ...
... *datta*	It was ...
... *ja nakatta* ... *de (wa) nakatta*	It was not ...
... *daroo*	It may probably be ...
... *ja nai daroo* ... *de (wa) nai daroo*	It is most probably not

(2) Polite forms:

... *desu*	It is ...
... *ja arimasen* ... *dewa arimasen*	It is not ...
... *deshita*	It was ...
... *ja arimasen deshita* ... *dewa arimasen deshita*	It wasn't ...
... *deshoo*	It may probably be ...
... *ja nai deshoo* ... *de (wa) nai deshoo*	It is most probably not ...

c. **Used with *I*- Adjectives**

(1) Plain forms:

Takai.	It is expensive.
Takaku nai.	It is not expensive.
Takakatta.	It was expensive.
Takaku nakatta.	It wasn't expensive.
Takai daroo.	It may be expensive.
Takaku nai daroo	It is probably not expensive.

(2) Polite forms:

Takai desu.	It is expensive.
Takaku arimasen.	It is not expensive.
Takakatta desu.	It was expensive.
Takaku arimasen deshita. *Takaku nakatta desu.* }	It was not expensive.
Takai deshoo.	It is probably expensive.
Takaku nai deshoo.	It is probably not expensive.

d. **Other negative expressions** (used with negative predicates):

zenzen	not (at all)
hitotsu mo	nothing
dare mo	no one
doko mo	nowhere
nani mo	nothing
dochira mo	neither . . . nor
kesshite	never
Zenzen wakarimasen deshita.	I did not understand it at all.

20. WORD ORDER

There are two very important rules to remember for word order in declarative sentences:

a. A predicate word (the copula, verb, or adjective used as a predicate) is placed at the *end* of the clause or sentence except when a sentence-ending particle such as *ka* (the question-mark particle) or *ne* [isn't it? doesn't it?] is used, in which case the predicate word is placed *immediately before* such a particle.

b. A modifier *always precedes the word or clause it modifies:*

   (1) An adjective or adjectival phrase (a noun plus *no*) always precedes the noun it modifies;
   (2) A prenoun always precedes the noun;
   (3) An adverb or adverbial phrase always precedes the adjective, adverb, verb, or copula it modifies;
   (4) A modifying clause always precedes the noun it modifies.

For example:

akai booshi	a red hat
ano hito	that person
ano hito no booshi	that person's hat; her (his) hat
ano hito no akai booshi	that person's red hat; her red hat
ookina booshi	a big hat
ano hito no ookina akai booshi	that person's big red hat

katta booshi	the hat she bought
kinoo katta booshi	the hat she bought yesterday
kinoo Matsuya de katta booshi	the hat she bought at Matsuya's yesterday
ano hito ga kinoo no gogo Matsuya de katta booshi	the hat which she bought at Matsuya's yesterday afternoon
ano hito ga kinoo no gogo Matsuya de katta ookina akai booshi	that big red hat which she bought at Matsuya's yesterday afternoon
ano hito ga kinoo no gogo watakushi to issho ni itte Matsuya de katta ookina akai booshi	that big red hat which she bought yesterday afternoon with me at Matsuya's

21. QUESTIONS

The word order for questions is the same as for declarative sentences. The question particle *ka* may or may not be added at the end to show that a question is being asked. For instance:

When *ka* is used, it is not necessary to use the rising intonation. The intonation may remain that of a declarative sentence even though a question is being asked. However, when a question is being asked and *ka* is not used, the rising intonation must be employed, and the last syllable is pronounced with a distinct rise in pitch. (See Lesson 13.)

Ikimasu.	I am going.
Ikimasu?	Are you going?
Ikimasu ka?	Are you going?

See the following section for other words that are used in formulating questions.

22. QUESTION WORDS

There are several words that are used to form questions. Study the list to help you grasp more easily what the words are and how they are used.

QUESTION WORDS	MEANING	NOTES
nan, nani[1]	what thing? what? how many?	For the usage of *nan,* see Lesson 32. The meaning "how many?" applies only when the word is used before a counter.
nannin	how many persons?	
ikutsu[1]	what number? how many?	The answer must be a number.
iku-	how many . . . ?	A prefix used only with a counter.
itsu[1]	what time? when?	When used adverbially, it may sometimes be used without a particle.

[1] Notice that this is a noun in Japanese.

Itsu kimashita ka?	When did it arrive?	
Itsu hajimarimasu ka?	When does it begin?	
Itsu ga ii desu ka?	When would it be good for you?	

dare[1]	which person? who?	*dare no:* whose? *dare ni:* to whom? *dare kara:* from whom? *dare to:* with whom?
dore[1]	which thing? which?	Used when there is a choice of more than two.
dochira[1]	which of these two? which direction? which place (polite)?	Used when there is a choice of only two.
dochira e	where to?	
dochira kara	where from?	
dotchi	see above	A variant for the first meaning of *dochira.*
doko[1]	which place? where?	

Doko ni arimasu ka?	Where is it?
Doko de tabemashita ka?	Where did you eat?

---

[1] Notice that this is a noun in Japanese.

Doko kara kimashita ka?   Where did you come from?

Doko ga itai desu ka?   Where does it hurt?

dono	which	A prenoun used when there is a choice of *more than* two. Use *dochira no* when there is a choice of *only* two.
donna	what sort of?	A prenoun used when you are interested in the kind or type of thing being discussed.
doo	how? in what manner?	An adverb.
ikaga	how (polite)?	An adverb; same as *doo* (above) but used in refined speech.

23. SOMETHING, EVERYTHING, NOTHING, ANYTHING

Each of the question words appearing in the first column of this table undergoes a change in meaning when it is used together with one of the particles appearing in the other columns. The new meaning is shown for each combination.

TABLE III

QUESTION WORD	+ ka	+ mo (used with affirmative predicate)	+ mo (used with negative predicate)	+ de mo	+ -te mo
nani, nan = what	*nani ka* = something or other	*nani mo ka mo* = everything	*nani mo* = nothing	*nan de mo* = anything	*nani ... te mo* = whatsoever
dore = which one	*dore ka* = one or the other; anyone	*dore mo* = all, any	*dore mo* = no one, not anyone, not a one	*dore de mo* = whichever it may be; anyone at all	*dore ... te mo* = whichsoever
dochira = which of the two	*dochira ka* = either one	*dochira mo* = both	*dochira mo* = not either one, neither one	*dochira de mo* = whichever it may be, either one	*dochira ... te mo* = whichever
dotchi[1] = which of the two	*dotchi ka* = either one	*dotchi mo* = both	*dotchi mo* = not either one, neither one	*dotchi de mo* = whichever it may be, either one	*dotchi ... te mo* = whichever
doko = which place	*doko ka* = somewhere or other	*doko mo* = everywhere; all places	*doko mo* = not anywhere, nowhere	*doko de mo* = wherever it may be, any place at all	*doko ... te mo* = wherever
dare = which person	*dare ka* = somebody	*dare mo* = everybody	*dare mo* = not anybody, nobody	*dare de mo* = whoever it may be, anybody at all	*dare ... te mo* = whoever

[1] *Dotchi* is more informal than *dochira*.

(continued)

TABLE III (continued)

QUESTION WORD	+ ka	+ mo (used with affirmative predicate)	+ mo (used with negative predicate)	+ de mo	+ -te mo
itsu = what time	*itsu ka* = sometime or other	*itsu mo* = always	*itsu mo* = not anytime, never	*itsu de mo* = whenever it may be; anytime at all	*itsu . . . te mo* = whenever
doo = how	*doo ka* = somehow or other; please; by some means or other	*doo mo* = in every way, very	*doo mo* = somehow; not; in no way	*doo de mo* = however it may be; anyway at all	*doo . . . te mo* = however; one does
dooshite = why	*dooshite ka* = somehow or other, for some unknown reason	*dooshite mo* = by all means, under any circumstances	*dooshite mo* = somehow or other . . . not; however one tries . . . not	*dooshite de mo* = by all means; at all costs	—
ikutsu = how many	*ikutsu ka* = some number, several	*ikutsu mo* = any number	*ikutsu mo* = not many, no great number; not much to speak of	*ikutsu de mo* = however many it may be; any number at all	*ikutsu . . . te mo* = however many one may
ikura = how much	*ikura ka* = some amount	*ikura mo* = any amount; ever so much	*ikura mo* = not much; no great amount	*ikura de mo* = whatever amount it may be	*ikura . . . te mo* = however much it may be one may

24. EVEN IF, EVEN THOUGH

a. Affirmative
Use -te plus -mo:

Ame ga futte mo iki-masu.	I'll [still] go, even if it rains.
Takakute mo kaimasu.	I'll [still] buy it even if it's expensive.

b. Negative
Use -nakute plus mo:

Ame ga yamanakute mo ikimasu.	I will go [anyhow] even if it doesn't stop raining.
Yasuku nakute mo ka-maimasen.	I don't care even if it's not cheap.

c. Permission
Use -te mo ii desu for "you may [you have my permission to]"; use -nakute mo ii desu for "you don't have to [you have my permission not to; even if you don't, it is all right with me]":

Itte mo ii desu.	You may go.
Ikanakuto mo ii desu.	You don't have to go.

d. No matter how, No matter who, No matter how much
Use a question word plus -te mo:

Donna ni yasukute mo kaitaku arimasen.	I don't want to buy it no matter how cheap it is.
Dare ga shite mo kekka wa onaji desu.	No matter who does it, the result will be the same.

Ikura yonde mo imi ga wakarimasen deshita.	I couldn't understand it no matter how many times I read it.

25. HEARSAY

To express the ideas "I hear that . . ." or "They say that . . ." in Japanese:

a. For the Affirmative

Use a plain affirmative form of a verb, an *i*- adjective, or the copula plus *soo desu:*

Kyoo wa Yamada-san ga kuru soo desu.	I hear that Mr. Yamada is coming to visit us today.
Sapporo de wa yuki ga futta soo desu.	I hear that it snowed in Sapporo.
Takai soo desu.	I understand (that) it's expensive.
Tanaka-san wa byooki da soo desu.	I hear Ms. Tanaka is sick.

b. For the Negative

Use a plain negative form of a verb, an *i*- adjective, or the copula plus *soo desu.*

Rajio no tenki yohoo de wa kyoo wa ame wa furanai soo desu.	According to the weather forecast it's not going to rain today.
Yamada-san wa konakatta soo desu.	I hear that Mr. Yamada didn't come.
Takaku nai soo desu.	I hear (that) it's not expensive.

*Furansugo wa joozu ja
    nai soo desu.*

I hear she is not good at
French.

26. SEEMING

You can express the idea of "it seems" or "it
seems to me that ..." in several ways in Japanese:

a. For the Affirmative

(1) Use a plain affirmative form plus *yoo desu:*

*Moo shitte iru yoo
    desu.*

It seems to me that he
    already knows it.

*Chotto muzukashikatta
    yoo desu.*

It seems that it was a
    little difficult.

Minna genki na[1] *yoo
    desu.*

It seems that everybody
    is fine.

(2) Use a plain affirmative form plus *rashii desu:*

*Moo shitte iru rashii
    desu.*

It seems to me that he
    already knows it.

*Ano hito wa Amerika e
    kaetta rashii desu.*

It seems that he has
    gone back to the
    United States.

However, it is more likely that the sentence with
rashii desu will be interpreted with the meaning of
"hearsay" like *soo desu* in Section 25 than with
the meaning of "it seems."

(3) Use an *i-* adjective without the final *-i* or a
    na-adjective without the copula plus *-soo desu:*

---

[1] The copula *da* (present affirmative) becomes *na* before *yoo desu.*

Kurushisoo desu. — It seems that he is finding it painful.

Genki soo desu. — It seems that she is fine.

b. **For the Negative**

(1) Use a plain negative form plus *yoo desu:*

Mada shiranai yoo desu. — It seems that he is unaware of this.

Amari takaku nai yoo desu. — It seems that it is not very expensive.

(2) Use a plain negative form plus *rashii desu:*

Mada shiranai rashii desu. — It seems that he is unaware of this.

Ana hito wa Nihon e konakatta rashii desu. — Apparently [it seems that] he didn't come to Japan.

(3) Use a negative *i-* adjective without the final *-i* or the negative copula without the final *-i* plus *-sasoo desu:*

Kurushiku nasasoo desu. — He is apparently [it seems that he is] not finding it painful.

Are wa Nakamura-san ja nasasoo desu. — That does not seem to be Ms. Nakamura.

27. IMMINENCE

To express the idea ''it appears that . . . will soon happen'':

a. **For the Affirmative**
Use the pre-*masu* form of the verb plus -*soo desu:*

Ame ga furisoo desu ne.	It looks like rain, doesn't it?
Yamada-san wa yame-soo desu.	It looks as if Mr. Yamada is ready to quit.

b. **For the Negative**
Use the pre-*masu* form of a verb plus -*soo ja arimasen:*

Ame wa furisoo ja arimasen.	It doesn't look as though it will rain soon.
Nedan wa yasuku narisoo ja arimasen.	It doesn't look as though the price is going down.

28. OBLIGATION AND PROHIBITION

To convey the idea of obligation or impulsion (expressed in English by "should," "must," "ought to," "have to"):

a. **For the Affirmative**

(1) Use the negative -*ba* form of a verb, an *i*-adjective, or the copula, plus *narimasen* or *ikemasen* [if you don't do it, it won't do; if not (something), it won't do]; or

(2) Use the negative -*te* form plus *wa* plus *narimasen* or *ikemasen:*[1]

---

[1] Notice the use of a double negative.

Ikanakereba narimasen.	
Ikanukerebu ikemasen.	I should (must, have to,
Ikanakute wa nari-	ought to) go.
masen.	
Ikanakute wa ikemasen.	
Yoku nakereba narimasen.	
Yoku nakereba ike-	
masen.	It should (must, has to,
Yoku nakute wa nari-	ought to) be good.
masen.	
Yoku nakute wa ike-	
masen.	

b. **For the Negative**

(1) Use the affirmative *-te* form of a verb plus *wa* plus *narimasen* [if you do (something), it won't do; if it is (something), it won't do]:

Itte wa narimasen.	I should not (must not, ought not to) go.

(2) Use the affirmative *-te* form of a verb, an *i*-adjective, or the copula plus *wa* plus *ikemasen* or *dame desu.*

Koko de asonde wa ikemasen.	You should not (must not, ought not to) play here.
Yasashikute wa dame desu.	It should not be easy.
Kono kaban de wa dame desu.	You should not use this bag. [It should not be this bag.]

c. *Beki desu* [should], *beki ja arimasen* [should not]
Beki is a form left over from classical Japanese.

(1) For the affirmative, use the plain present of a verb plus *beki desu:*

Iku beki desu.	I should (must, have to, ought to) go.
Iku beki deshita.	I should have gone.

(2) For the negative, use the plain present affirmative of a verb plus *beki ja arimasen:*

Iku beki ja arimasen.	I should not go.
Iku beki ja arimasen deshita.	I shouldn't have gone.

(3) For warning or prohibition (seen in public signs only), the plain present affirmative of a verb is used with *bekarazu* [don't][1]:

Hairu bekarazu!	No admission!
Tooru bekarazu!	No trespassing!
Sawaru bekarazu!	Don't touch!

29. PERMISSION

To express the granting of permission, use *-te* plus *mo* plus *ii desu* [you may, it's all right to]:

Kaitakereba katte mo ii desu.	If you want to buy it, you may (buy it).
Uchi e motte kaette mo ii desu.	You may take it home if you wish.
Takakute mo ii desu.	It may be expensive. [Even if it is expensive, it is all right.]

[1] *Bekarazu,* which is a derived form of *beki,* is getting obsolete in public signs. *-Nai de kudasai* [Please do not—] now is preferred.

Kono jisho de mo ii desu. This dictionary will do. [It is all right to use this dictionary.]

30. ALTERNATIVES

In statements setting forth a choice of alternatives, use:

a. **-tari ... -tari shimasu** (the *-ta* form plus *ri* followed by the *-ta* form plus *ri suru*):

Kyoo wa ame ga futtari yandari shite imasu. Today it has been raining off and on.

Ano hito wa chikagoro gakkoo e ittari ikanakattari shimasu. He has been irregular recently in (his) attendance at school.

Nichiyoobi no gogo wa shinbun o yondari terebi o mitari shimasu. On Sunday afternoons I spend my time doing such things as reading newspapers and watching television.

Hito ga detari haittari shite imasu. People are going in and out.

b. **-tari shimasu** (a single *-tari* followed by *suru*):

Eiga e ittari shimashita. Among the various things (I did), I went to the movies. I spent my time going to the movies and doing things like that.

Miyagemono o kattari shimashita. I hunted for souvenirs and did (other) things like that.

31. PASSIVE, POTENTIAL, AND RESPECT

A verb made up of its base plus *-areru* or *-rareru* may be any one of the following: (1) passive, (2) potential, or (3) respect. (Use *-areru* with a consonant verb and *-rareru* with a vowel verb.) The exact meaning of such a verb is determined by the context in which it is used.

a. **Passive**

Watakushi wa keikan ni namae o kikaremash-ita.

I was asked my name by a policeman.

b. **Potential**

Nihon no eiga wa Amerika de mo mi-raremasu.

Japanese movies can be seen in the United States, too. [One can see a Japanese movie in America, too.]

c. **Respect**

Itoo-sensei wa kinoo Amerika kara kae-raremashita.

My teacher, Mr. Ito, came back from the United States yester-day.

The passive of some Japanese verbs—most particularly the passive forms of intransitive verbs—means ''(something) happened when it wasn't wanted,'' or ''I underwent (something),'' or ''I suffered from the interference of (something)'':

Densha no naka de kodomo ni nakarete komarimashita.	We were embarrassed by our child, who cried continuously while riding on a train.
Ame ni furarete sukkari nurete shimaimashita.	We were drenched by the rain.

32. CAUSATIVE

To form the causative of a verb, add *-aseru* to the base of a consonant verb and *-saseru* to the base of a vowel verb. The causative forms of the irregular verbs are: (for *kuru*) *kosaseru,* and (for *suru*) *saseru.*

Causative verbs may be used to express the thought that:

a. X *causes* (makes, forces) Y to do (something), or

b. X *allows* (permits, lets) Y to do (something).

Notice that in each instance the element Y is marked by the particle *ni.*

Tanaka-san wa Yamada-san ni den-poo o utasemashita.	Ms. Tanaka had Mr. Yamada send a tele-gram.
Kodomo ni kimono o kisasete kudasai.	Please have the chil-dren put on their clothes.
Kyoo wa itsu mo yori ichijikan hayaku kaerasete itadakitai desu.	I would like to have your permission to go home one hour earlier than usual. [I would like to have you make me go home . . .]

A causative can be combined with a passive ending. If the causative ending comes first, the combination means "be made," not "be allowed."[1]

Ikaseraremashita.	I was made to go.
Tabesaseraremashita.	I was made to eat it.

33. DESIDERATIVES

The desiderative is the grammatical term for verbal expressions that signify a desire to do something.

a. To say, "I want to do (something)," use the pre-*masu* form plus *-tai:*

Kyoo wa kaimono ni ikitai desu.	I want to go shopping today.
Ima wa nani mo tabetaku arimasen.	I don't want to eat anything now.

b. To express the idea, "one shows that s(he) wants to do (something)," add *-tagaru* to the pre-*masu* form.

Kodomo ga soto e ikitagatte imasu.	The children can't wait to go outside.
Uchi no kodomo wa sono kusuri o nomitagarimasen.	Our child doesn't like to take that medicine. [Our child shows that he doesn't like to take that medicine.]

[1] The combination where the passive ending comes first is possible. In this case, the meaning of the combination does not mean "be made." For example, *naguraresasemashita* means "I made somebody be hit." But such a combination is rare, and awkward.

c. Use the stem (the form without the final *-i*) of an *i*-adjective plus *-garu* to express the meaning that "someone[1] shows outwardly that he feels ...":

Samugarimashita.	He showed that he felt cold.
Hoshigarimashita.	He showed that he wanted to have it.

d. To say, "I want you to do (something) for me," use the *-te* form of a verb plus *itadakitai desu:*

Kono tegami o Eigo ni yakushite itadakitai desu.	I would like you to translate this letter into English for me.
Kore o katte itadakitai desu.	I would like you to buy this for me.

34. TO DO (SOMETHING) FOR ...

a. To say, "Somebody does (something) for me," in the respect form, use *-te kudasaimasu;* in the neutral form, use *-te kuremasu:*

Sonokoto wa Yamada-san ga shirasete kudasaimashita.	Mr. Yamada was kind enough to inform me about it.
Shirasete kudasai.[2]	Please let me know.
Ani ga katte kuremashita.	My older brother bought it for me.

b. Use *-te agemasu* to say "I (or somebody) do (something) for you (him, her)." In the humble form, use *-te sashiagemasu.* You can use *-te yari-*

---

[1] Usually not the speaker.

[2] *Kudasai* is a request form of *kudasaimasu.*

masu when the receiver of the favor is animals or plants. When the receiver of the favor is a person who is inferior to the speaker, such as a child, *-te yarimasu* can be used, but it is not always appropriate. Thus, it is safer not to use *-te yarimasu* when the receiver of the favor is a person.

Sore wa anata ni katte ageta no desu.	I bought it for you.
Anata ni katte sashiage-mashoo.	I'll buy it for you.
Inu ni katte yarimashita.	I bought it for our dog.

c. Use *-te itadakimasu* to say, "I (or somebody) have you (him, her) do (something)" in the humble form, and *-te moraimasu* in the neutral form:

Yamada-san ni katte itadakimashita.	I had Mr. Yamada buy it for me.
Tomodachi ni yakushite moraimashita.	I had a friend of mine translate it for me.
Yamada-san ni yakushite itadaite kudasai.	Please have it translated by Mr. Yamada.

35. MAY, PERHAPS, PROBABLY

To say that "something may (might) happen," add *ka mo shiremasen* after a plain form of a verb, an *i*-adjective or the copula.

Ame ga furu ka mo shiremasen.	It may rain (but I can't tell for sure).
Shiken wa muzukash-ikatta ka mo shire-masen.	The test might have been difficult.

Tanaka-san wa tenisu ga joozu ka mo shiremasen.[1]	Ms. Tanaka may be good at tennis.

36.   IF AND WHEN

a. **The Use of** *to*

(1) Use *to* between two clauses to show that the second clause follows as a natural result of the first clause. The particle *to* in such a case comes at the end of the "if" or "when" clause:

Ame ga furu to anmari hito ga takusan ki-masen.	When it rains, not too many people come.
Kippu ga nai to haire-masen.	If you don't have tick-ets, you can't get in. [If there isn't a ticket . . .]
Atarashii to takai desu.	When it's new, it's expensive.

(2) Note that the predicate before *to* is *always* in the present form regardless of the tense of the rest of the sentence:

Hima da to sanpo shi-mashita.	Whenever I had time, I took a walk.

(3) The predicate before *to* usually appears in the plain present form. When *to* is used for "if" or

---

[1] The copula *da* (present, affirmative) is deleted before *ka mo shire-masen.*

"when," the predicate of the main clause (the one following the clause ending in *to*) must be the *-u* or *-ta* form; it can *never* end in *-masyoo* or *-te kudasai.*

b. **The Use of *-tara***

To introduce a condition or a supposition, add *-ra* to the *-ta* form of a verb, adjective, or copula:

Ame ga futtara iki-masen.	If it rains, I won't go.
Denpoo ga kitara denwa o kakete ku-dasai.	If you get a telegram, please phone me.
Anmari samukattara mado o shimete ku-dasai.	If it's too cold (for you), please shut the window.
Nihonjin dattara dare de mo ii desu.	Anybody who is a native Japanese will do. [If it's a native Japanese, anybody will do.]

c. **The Use of *nara***

Use *nara* with a plain form of a verb, an *i-* adjective, and the copula to express "if."

Byooki[1] nara yasumu hoo ga ii desu.	If you are sick, you had better rest.
Shiranai nara oshiete agemasu.	If you don't know, I'll teach you.
Yasui nara kaimasu.	If it is inexpensive, I'll buy it.

d. **The Use of *-ba***

The *-ba* form is used only for unconfirmed situa-

---

[1]For present affirmative, the copula is deleted.

tions. The *-ba* form is formed in the following ways:

Consonant verb:
Drop the final *-u* of the dictionary form and add *-eba*.

furu   →   *fureba*

Vowel verb:

Drop the final *-ru* of the dictionary form and add *-reba*.

miru   →   *mireba*

Irregular verb:

kuru   →   *kureba*
suru   →   *sureba*

i-adjective:

Drop the final *i* of the dictionary form and add *-kereba*.

takai   →   *takakereba*

Negative of a verb, an *i-* adjective, the copula:

Drop the final *-i* and add *-kereba*.

furanai   →   *furanakereba*
takaku nai   →   *takaku na-*
                                kereba

shizuka ja nai   →   *shizuka ja*
                                nakereba

Ame ga fureba ikimasen.	If it rains, I won't go.
Ame ga furanakereba ikimasu.	If it doesn't rain, I will go.
Mireba sugu wakarimasu.	If I take a look at it, I can readily identify it.
Takakereba kaimasen.	If it's expensive, I won't buy it.
Shizuka ja nakereba ikitaku arimasen.	If it is not quiet, I do not want to go.

e. **The Use of -*te wa***

This expression for "if" is most often found in an expression denoting "must" (e.g., "if you don't do . . . , it won't do"):

Soko e itte wa dame desu.	You must not go there. If you go there, it will be no good.
Okane ga nakute wa kaemasen.	If you have no money, you can't buy it.
Yoku benkyoo shi-nakute wa ikemasen.	If you don't study hard (you must!), it won't do.

37. WHETHER . . . OR . . . , IF . . . OR . . .

a. **The Uses of *ka***

(1) Use *ka . . . ka* in a sentence conveying the meaning "whether or," "if or":

Okane ga aru ka nai ka shirimasen.	I don't know if he has money or not.

Takai ka yasui ka shiri-masen.	I don't know if it is expensive or not.

For present affirmative; the copula is deleted:

Suki ka kirai ka kiite kudasai.	Please ask her whether she likes it or dislikes it.

(2) Use *ka doo ka* to express "whether or not," "if or not,"

Okane ga aru ka doo ka shirimasen.	I don't know if he has money or not.
Takai ka doo ka shirimasen.	I don't know if it's expensive or not.
Iku ku doo ka shiri masen.	I don't know whether she is going or not.

(3) Use *ka* in a sentence having the sense of "either . . . or":

Suiyoobi ka Mokuyoobi ni kimasu.	She will come on Wednesday or else on Thursday.
Yoshida-san ka mata wa Kida-san ni kite moratte kudasai.	Please have either Mr. Yoshida or Mr. Kida come.

38. NOUN-MAKERS

Certain nouns that appear at the end of a clause convert that entire clause into a noun equivalent. For example:

a. *no* = the one (the time, the person, the place); the act of:

Kesa hayaku uchi e denwa o kaketa no wa Tanaka-san deshita.	The person who phoned us early this morning was Ms. Tanaka.
Kinoo mita no wa Amerika no eiga deshita.	The one we saw yesterday was an American movie.
Kyooto e itta no wa Shigatsu deshita.	It was in April that we went to Kyoto. [The time when we went to Kyoto was April.]
Mainichi yoru osoku made hataraku no wa karada ni warui desu.	Working late night after night is bad for your health.

b. *koto* = the act of; the experience of:

Hokkaido e itta koto ga arimasu.	I have been to Hokkaido. [The experience of having gone to Hokkaido exists.]
Nihongo wa hanasu koto wa dekimasu ga yomu koto wa dekimasen.	I can speak but I can't read Japanese.

39. IN ORDER TO

a. To say that "one goes or comes in order to do (something),"

   (1) Use the pre-*masu* form plus *ni* plus a verb of locomotion such as *ikimasu* or *kimasu*:

Mi ni ikimasu.	I am going there to see it.

| *Gohan o tabe ni iki-mashita.* | He went to eat. |
| *Amerika no shinbun o yomi ni kimashita.* | I came to read American newspapers. |

(2) Use a noun describing an action, plus *ni* plus a verb of locomotion:

| *Kaimono ni ikimashita.* | He went out to shop [for shopping]. |
| *Ryokoo ni dekakema-shita.* | He set out on a journey. |

b. To say that "one does (something) for the purpose of doing (something)," the predicate verb can be any verb including a verb of locomotion.

(1) A present-tense verb plus the noun-maker *no* plus *ni* plus a verb:

| *Kono megane wa hon o yomu no ni tsukaim-asu.* | I use these glasses for reading books. |
| *Kono basu wa shitama-chi e iku no ni benri desu.* | This bus is convenient for going downtown. |

(2) A present-tense verb plus *tame ni* plus a verb:

| *Kuruma o kau tame ni okane o karimashita.* | I borrowed some money to buy a car. |
| *Tomodachi o miokuru tame ni eki e ikima-shita.* | He went to the station to see a friend off. |

40. REQUESTS, COMMANDS

There are several ways to express a request, command, or wish in Japanese. Use:

a. *-te kudasai* = **please do** (something)

(1) For the affirmative:

Hayaku kite kudasai.	Please come early. Come early.
Yukkuri hanashite kudasai.	Please speak slowly.

(2) For the negative:

Hayaku konaide kudasai.	Please don't come early.
Yukkuri hanasanaide kudasai.	Please don't speak slowly.

b. *o kudasai* = **please give me**

Rokujuunien no kitte o kudasai.	Give me a sixty-two-yen stamp, please.
Mizu o kudasai.	Please give me some water.

c. *ga hoshii desu* = **I want to have** (preceded by the noun showing the thing desired)

Puroguramu ga hoshii desu.	I would like a program.
Sake wa hoshiku arimasen.	I don't want any sake.

d. *-te itadakitai (no)* desu *(ga)*[1] = I would like to ask you to

Kore o yonde itadakitai desu.	I would like to ask you to read this for me (but do you have time or would it interfere, etc.).
Eigo de kaite itadakitai no desu ga.	Would you mind writing (may I trouble you to write) this in English?

e. *yoo ni shite kudasai* = be careful (not) to, try to

Kono tegami wa hayaku dasu yoo ni shite kudasai.	Please make every effort to send this mail out early.
Kore wa otosanai yoo ni shite kudasai.	Please be careful not to drop this.

f. *-te choodai* = please do (something)
This request form is used in an intimate, informal, or relaxed situation.

Katte choodai.	Please buy it.
Sore o totte choodai.	Please pick it up.

g. The Plain Imperative of a Verb
Each verb has a form called the "plain imperative" which is constructed by adding *-e* to the base of a consonant verb and *-ro* to the base of a vowel verb. The imperative of the irregular verbs is *koi* for *kuru* [come] and *shiro* for *suru* [do].

---

[1] The use of *no* and *ga* is optional in this construction.

Ike!	Go!
Miro!	Look at it!

Take note, however, that the plain imperative is used *only* in "rough" speech, and *should not* be used in everyday conversation.

41. ADVERBIAL EXPRESSIONS

a. Formation of Adverbial Expressions

(1) Many adverbs are formed by adding *-ku* to the stem (the plain present affirmative minus *-i*) of adjectives:

ADJECTIVE		ADVERB	
takai	expensive	*takaku*	expensively
yasui	cheap	*yasuku*	cheaply
yasashii	easy	*yasashiku*	easily
karui	light	*karuku*	lightly

(2) Some adverbial expressions are formed from *na-* adjectives by using *ni* following the *na* adjective.

ADJECTIVAL PHRASE		ADVERBIAL PHRASE	
kantan na	simple	*kantan ni*	simply
benri na	convenient	*benri ni*	conveniently
tokubetsu na	special	*tokubetsu ni*	especially
joozu na	skillful	*joozu ni*	skillfully

b. Comparison of Adverbial Expressions
Adverbial expressions can be compared like adjectives (see Grammar Section 16):

POSITIVE	COMPARATIVE	SUPERLATIVE
takaku – expensively	*motto takaku* = more expensively	*ichiban takaku* = most expensively

c. **Adverbial Expressions of Place**

Use *ni* when the verb is *arimasu* [there], *imasu* [be at a place], or *sunde imasu*. Use *de* for most other cases.

koko ni, koko de	here
soba ni, soba de	at the side, near
mae ni, mae de	before, in front
ushiro ni, ushiro de	behind
ue ni, ue de	on top
shita ni, shita de	underneath
naka ni, naka de	inside
soto ni, soto de	outside
doko ni mo, doko de mo	everywhere (*with an affirmative verb*)
doko ni mo, doko de mo	nowhere (*with a negative verb*)
tooku ni, tooku de	far
chikaku ni, chikaku de	near
doko ni, doko de	where
soko ni, soko de	there (nearby)
asoko ni, asoko de	there (far off)

d. **Adverbial Expressions of Time**

kyoo	today
ashita, asu, myoonichi	tomorrow
kinoo, sakujitsu	yesterday
ototoi, issakujitsu	the day before yesterday

asatte, myoogonichi	the day after tomorrow
ima	now
sono toki	then
mae ni	before
moto	once, formerly
hayaku	early
sugu	soon, presently
osoku	late
tokidoki	often, from time to time
itsu mo	always
nagai aida	for a long time
. . . tari . . . tari shimasu	now . . . now, sometimes . . . sometimes (See Section 30 of the grammar summary.)
mada	as yet, still
moo	already (*with an affirmative*)
moo	no longer (*with a negative*)

e. Adverbial Expressions of Manner

yoku	well, frequently; studiously; hard
waruku	ill, badly
konna ni	thus, so
onaji yoo ni	similarly
hantai ni	otherwise, conversely
issho ni	together
taihen	much, very
yorokonde	willingly
toku ni	especially
waza to	on purpose, expressly

f. Adverbial Expressions of Quantity or Degree

takusan	much, many
juubun (ni)[1]	enough
sukoshi	little
motto	more
hidoku	extremely, excessively
amari, anmari	too, too much, too many
sonna ni	so much, so many

42. THE WRITING SYSTEM

The Japanese writing system contains four types of symbols that are usually used together:

1. One set of 46 phonetic symbols called *hiragana;*

2. One set of 46 phonetic symbols called *kata-kana;*

3. 1,945 ideographic symbols called *kanji;* and

4. The letters of the English (or Roman) alphabet, called *Roomaji,* together with the Arabic numerals, which are called *arabiya suuji* or *san'yoo suuji.*

Each of the symbols in *hiragana* and *katakana* represents *one syllable,* and each of the forty-six basic syllables of the Japanese language is written with a single symbol, whether in *hiragana* or *katakana* (see Tables IV and VIII, which follow), *Hiragana* symbols

---

[1] The use of *ni* is optional.

are considered to be standard, and are most widely used. Katakana symbols are used primarily for (a) writing "borrowed" words (words derived from Western languages), (b) to give special emphasis to certain words within a sentence, in much the same way that italics are used in English, and (c) writing certain onomatopoeic words.

a. The Hiragana Symbols

Study the charts of *hiragana* symbols on pages 383–385. Compare these charts with Chart I of Table I on page 296. (The syllables in parentheses are only for *katakana.*) Note that the *sound* or *syllable* for each symbol appears in the corresponding square of that chart. For instance, at the point of intersection of vertical and horizontal columns 1 in the chart below, the symbol stands for *ka.*

SPECIAL NOTES FOR
THE *HIRAGANA* SYMBOLS

(1) Note that the first vertical row of symbols (headed "O") shows the symbols for the *vowel-syllables only.* In all of the other columns (except the last), each consonant (or semi-vowel) plus-vowel combination has a new symbol as each stands for a different syllable.

(2) Note, too, that there are *two* symbols for the vowel-syllable *o.* The one in column 9 (を) is used *only* to write the particle *o* (the thing acted on, or the direct object); it is *never* used to represent anything else.

(3) Some symbols have a dual function:
   (a) The symbol for *ha* (は) is also used to write *wa* in the following cases:

particle *wa*	これは	kore wa
Konnichi wa	こんにちは	Hello
Konban wa	こんばんは	Good evening
dewa	では	well then
negative of copula	しずかではありません	It is not quiet.

   (b) The symbol used for *he* (へ) is also used to write the particle *e* [to, toward]. The symbol for the vowel *e* (え) (which appears in the 0 column) is used to write all other *e*'s.

(4) Write syllables other than the forty-six basic syllables covered in the above table as follows:

   (a) Syllables listed in Chart II of Table I (see page 297) are written using the basic symbols plus a diacritical mark ('' or °) on the upper right shoulder of each symbol, as in Table VI, on page 387.

The following table shows the number of strokes that are necessary to write each of the *hiragana* symbols. In each chart within the table, the first vertical column shows the completed symbol; the following columns show the strokes that make the symbol. Match these left-hand columns against the symbols in Table IV to read the symbols. The charts are numbered to correspond with the vertical columns in Table IV.

(b) Syllables that have a *y* in the middle, e.g., *kya, kyu, kyo, gya, gyu, gyo*, etc., are written with special combinations of two syllables (see Table VII, page 388). This is true also of the syllables *cha, chu, cho, sha, shu, sho, ja, ju, jo*. Thus, in writing *kya*, you combine the symbol for *ki* with the symbol for *ya*. Note that in forming these special combinations, the symbols for *ki, shi, chi, ni, hi, mi*, and *ri* are used as if they were symbols just for the initial consonant, and not for the consonant-plus-vowel syllable. And so, to write *kya*, you would use the symbol for *ki*, き , which here would represent the consonant *k*, plus the symbol for *ya*. Remember, too, that the second symbol in a special combination must always be one of the following three: *ya* や , *yu* ゆ , or *yo* よ , and this second member of the combination is usually written smaller than the first, and is usually placed slightly right of the center in a text written from top to bottom. Study Table VII for examples of these special combinations, and compare with Chart III, Table I, for sound values.

TABLE IV
THE BASIC HIRAGANA SYMBOLS

		0	1	2	3	4	5	6	7	8	9	10
		vowel	k	s	t	n	h'	m	y	r	w	n
v	1. a	あ	か	さ	た	な	は	ま	や	ら	わ	ん
o	2. i	い	き	し	ち	に	ひ	み		り		
w	3. u	う	く	す	つ	ぬ	ふ	む	ゆ	る		
e	4. e	え	け	せ	て	ね	へ	め		れ		
l s	5. o*	お	こ	そ	と	の	ほ	も	よ	ろ	を	

TABLE V

CHART 0

Vowels	1	2	3	4
a	あ	二	女	女	あ
i	い	小	い		
u	う	二	う		
e	え	汉	え		
i	お	二	好	お	お

CHART 1

k				
a	か	づ	カ	が	
i	き	二	き	き	き
u	く	く			
e	け	小	に	け	
o	こ	こ	に		

CHART 2

s				
a	さ	二	七	さ	
i	し	小			
u	す	二	す		
e	せ	世	せ		
o	そ	ジ	そ		

CHART 3

t				
a	た	二	た	た	た
i	ち	二	ち		
u	つ	つ			
e	て	二	て		
o	と	と	と		

CHART 4

n				
a	な	二	ナ	ナ	な
i	に	に	に	に	
u	ぬ	ぬ	ぬ	ぬ	
e	ね	ね	ね	ね	
o	の	の	の		

CHART 5

h				
a	は	は	に	は	
i	ひ	ひ	ひ		
u	ふ	ふ	ふ	ふ	ふ
e	へ	へ			
o	ほ	ほ	に	に	ほ

CHART 6

CHART 7

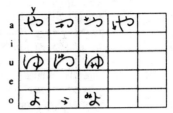

CHART 8

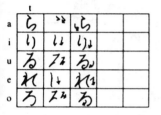

CHART 9

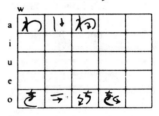

CHART 10

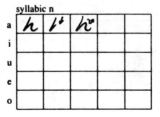

(c) To write a double consonant in Japanese, you *always* use the symbol for *tsu*, っ , for the first letter, *regardless of the sound that is being doubled,* whether *kk, ss, ssh, tt, tch, tts,* or *pp.* Note that the symbol for *tsu,* when it is used in this way, is frequently written smaller than usual and placed to the right of center in a text that is written from top to bottom. In a text written horizontally from left to right, however, the symbol for *tsu* is placed either a little above or below the center. Study the examples below. See how the *tsu* symbol is written in place of the first letter in a doubled consonant, which appears here in bold-face type:

*Cho**tt**o*	ちょっと	a little
*Ke**kk**on*	けっこん	marriage
*I**ss**huukan*	いっしゅうかん	one week
*I**pp**un*	いっぷん	one minute

(d) See the examples of double vowels:

aa (a-a)	ああ	Oh!
*okaasan (o-ka-**a**-sa-n)*	おかあさん	mother
*oishii (o-i-shi-**i**)*	おいしい	delicious
*kuuki (ku-**u**-ki)*	くうき	air
*oneesan (o-ne-**e**-sa-n)*	ねえさん	older sister

There is one exception to this rule: to write *oo*, you almost always use the symbol for the vowel-syllable *u* in place of the second *o*, as illustrated below.

kooshoo (*ko-o-sho-o*)	こうしょう	negotiation
Tookyoo (*to-o-kyo-o*)	とうきょう	Tokyo
moo (*mo-o*)	もう	more, not any more (with a negative)
doozo (*do-o-zo*)	どうぞ	please
doozoo (*do-o-zo-o*)	どうぞう	bronze statue

TABLE VI
HIRAGANA WITH DIACRITICAL MARKS[1]

	1 g	2 z/j	3 d	4 b	5' p	9 v
1-a	が	ざ	だ	ば	ぱ	ゔ゙ぁ
2-i	ぎ	じ	ぢ	び	ぴ	ゔ゙ぃ
3-u	ぐ	ず	づ	ぶ	ぷ	ゔ
4-e	べ	ぜ	で	べ	ぺ	ゔ゙ぇ
5-o	ご	ぞ	ど	ぼ	ぽ	ゔ゙ぉ

[1] ぢ and づ are ji and zu, respectively, just as with じ and ず. Usually, じ and ず are used, except for special cases.

TABLE VII
COMPLETE LIST OF THE
SPECIAL COMBINATIONS

	1	2	3	4	5	6	7	8	9
	k	sh	ch	n	h	m		r	
1.	きゃ	しゃ	ちゃ	にゃ	ひゃ	みゃ		りゃ	
3.	きゅ	しゅ	ちゅ	にゅ	ひゅ	みゅ		りゅ	
5.	きょ	しょ	ちょ	にょ	ひょ	みょ		りょ	
	g	j			b p				
1.	ぎゃ	じゃ			びゃ ぴゃ				
3.	ぎゅ	じゅ			びゅ ぴゅ				
5.	ぎょ	じょ			びょ ぴょ				

b. The Katakana Symbols

All the rules used for writing *hiragana* apply to *katakana* except for the following cases:

(1) Some syllables that are not traditionally Japanese syllables can be used for borrowed words, which are written in *katakana*. Such syllables are shown in parentheses on Table I. They are written as follows:

ti	ティ		*fa*	ファ
tu	テュ		*fi*	フィ
tse	ツェ		*fe*	フェ
			fo	フォ
di	ディ		*va*	ヴァ
du	デュ		*vi*	ヴィ
			vu	ヴ
she	シェ		*ve*	ヴェ
che	チェ		*vo*	ヴォ
je	ジェ			

(2) For the second vowel of a double vowel, use a bar —. In a text written vertically, write | . (When *katakana* symbols are used for giving special emphasis to certain words, a bar is not used. Instead, *katakana* symbols are used in the manner of *hiragana*.)

kaado (*ka-a-do*)	カード	カ ー ド	card
biiru (*bi-i-ru*)	ビール	ビ ー ル	beer
suupu (*su-u-pu*)	スープ	ス ー プ	soup
keeki (*ke-e-ki*)	ケーキ	ケ ー キ	cake
booto (*bo-o-to*)	ボート	ボ ー ト	boat

The following table shows the number of strokes that are necessary to write each of the *katakana* symbols. In each chart within the table, the first vertical column shows the completed symbol; the following columns show the strokes necessary to make the symbol. Match these left-hand columns against the symbols in Table VIII to read the symbols. The charts are numbered to correspond with the vertical columns in Table VIII.

TABLE VIII
THE BASIC KATAKANA SYMBOLS*

	0 vowel	1 k	2 s	3 t	4 n	5 h	6 m	7 y	8 r	9 w	10 n
1. a	ア	カ	サ	タ	ナ	ハ	マ	ヤ	ラ	ワ	ン
2. i	イ	キ	シ	チ	ニ	ヒ	ミ		リ		
3. u	ウ	ク	ス	ツ	ヌ	フ	ム	ユ	ル		
4. e	エ	ケ	セ	テ	ネ	ヘ	メ		レ		
5. o*	オ	コ	ソ	ト	ノ	ホ	モ	ヨ	ロ	ヲ	

TABLE IX

CHART 0

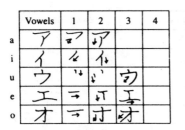

CHART 1

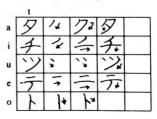

CHART 2

CHART 3

*Note that in *katakana,* as in *hiragana,* there are two symbols for the letter *o.*

CHART 4

n

CHART 5

h

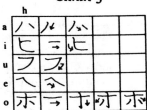

CHART 6

m

CHART 7

y

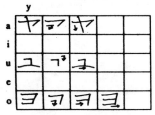

CHART 8

t

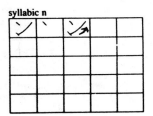

CHART 9

w

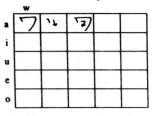

CHART 10

syllabic n

c. Ideographic Symbols (Kanji)

A few of the most frequently used ideographic symbols are shown below. These are called *kanji* or, in English, "Chinese characters," because the vast majority of these characters are of Chinese origin, unlike the *hiragana* and *katakana* symbols, which were created in Japan.

SYMBOL	READING	MEANING AND CONTENT
日	*hi* *nichi* *bi* *jitsu*	the sun; a prototype was a stylized picture of the sun: ⊙ This symbol also is used to write -*nichi* in *mainichi* [everyday], *nichi,* and -*bi* in *Nichiyoobi* [Sunday], and it occurs in many other words pertaining to the sun, day, day of the week, etc. Write this figure in the order shown by the arrows:

↓| ⟆ 月 日

| 月 | tsuki gatsu getsu | the moon; a stylized picture of the moon; its prototype was more like a crescent: ☽ This symbol is also used for many other words pertaining to the moon, such as |

month (as a duration of time) or name of the month, etc.

The order of writing is:

丿 冂 月 月

木 ki
moku
boku

a tree; a picture of a tree; its prototype had the branches and roots more pictorially drawn: 凷

The order of writing is: 一 十 オ 木

一 hitotsu
ichi

one: "one-ness" is depicted by one line, "two" is 二 , "three" is 三 , but beyond three it is not this simple.

The stroke is written from left to right: ⇁

LETTER WRITING

Formerly, letters were written in accordance with rather rigid forms, but today such forms are seldom used except in formal announcements, such as for weddings, births, and deaths. Instead, ordinary personal correspondence is written without adhering to any particular form.

FORMAL LETTERS

a. **Salutation**

(1) In a formal letter, it is customary to begin with one of the following highly stylized salutations:

(a) *Haikei:* corresponds to "Gentlemen," "Dear Sir(s)," or "Dear Madam" [I humbly state . . .].

(b) *Kinkei:* corresponds to "Gentlemen," "Dear Sir(s)," "Dear Madam" [I reverently state . . .], used mainly by men.

(c) *Haifuku* (used only in reply to a letter): "Gentlemen," "Dear Sir(s)," "Dear Madam" [I reply humbly . . .].

(2) The addressee's name does not appear until the very end of the letter, where it is written in the following order:

(a) The family name,

(b) The given name, and

(c) The proper honorific (the most common and useful of which is *-sama,* a formal variation of *-san* [Mr., Mrs., Miss]). (See also the section on complimentary closings, below.)

(3) When a letter in Japanese is written in the English alphabet, it customarily follows the form for an English letter; thus, the addressee's name is used with the honorific *-sama,* and the formal salutation word (see Item (1), above) is omitted.

b. Complimentary Close

(1) First, use one of the following stylized closing remarks:
   (a) *Mazu wa oshirase made.* = Just to inform you (of) the above.
   (b) *Mazu wa goaisatsu made.* = Just to extend my greetings to you.
   (c) *Toriaezu gohenji made.* = Just to answer your letter in a hurry.

(2) Then add one of the following complimentary closings:
   (a) *Keigu.* = Respectfully yours. [I have respectfully stated.]
   (b) *Soosoo.* = Sincerely yours. [In a hurry. Hurriedly.]
   (c) *Kashiko.* = Sincerely yours. [In awe (used by women only).]

(3) After signing your name, place the addressee's name with the proper honorific on a separate line, either flush with the left margin or slightly indented:
   (a) *Yamada Yoshio-sama* = Mr. Yoshio Yamada.

(b) *Yamada Yoshio sensei*[1] = Mr. Yoshio Yamada (used for a minister, priest, doctor, schoolteacher, etc.).

(c) *Yamada Yoshio-dono* = Mr. Yoshio Yamada (*used in official letters*).

(d) *Yamada Yoshio Shichoo-dono* = (Mr.) Mayor Yoshio Yamada (used for writing to someone we would address as "the Honorable"—e.g., a distinguished officeholder: consists of the addressee's name plus his or her official title plus the honorific *-dono* or *-sama*).

---

[1] *Sensei,* unlike *-san* or *-sama,* may be used by itself as a term of address (somewhat like our word "sir"), and consequently is not always appended to the name as a suffix.

BUSINESS LETTERS

LETTER 1

Peter Paine[1]
104
Tookyoo-to, Chiyoda-ku
Marunouchi Hoteru
Heisei 4 nen[2]
9 gatsu 25 nichi

104
Tookyoo-to, Chuuoo-ku
Tsukiji 5-3-2
Asahi Shinbun Sha

Japan Quarterly Onchuu:[3]
   Japan Quarterly ichinenbun no koodokuryoo to shite yonsen yonhyaku nijuu en no yuubinkawase o ookuri itashimasu. Ouketori kudasai.

Piitaa Pein
(Peter   Paine)[4]

---

[1] It is customary to retain the English name of the writer in the Japanese heading.
[2] *Heisei 4 nen* = the fourth year of the Era of Heisei, corresponding to the year 1992.
[3] *Onchuu* is used when the addressee is a group, such as a company.
[4] Normally, the English name would be signed as in the parentheses.

Marunouchi Hotel
Chiyoda-ku, Tokyo 104
September 25, 1992

Japan Quarterly
Asahi Shinbun Sha
Tsukiji 5-3-2, Chūō
Tōkyō 104

Dear Sir/Madam:[1]

Enclosed you will find a money order for ¥4,420 for a year's subscription to your magazine *Japan Quarterly*.

Very truly yours,
Peter Paine

---

[1] In Japanese, it is not necessary to use such a salutation.

LETTER 2

104
Tookyoo-to, Chuuoo-ku
Ginza 4-choome, 2
Sakata Shookai
Heisei 4 nen
8 gatsu 16 nichi

100
Tookyoo-to, Chiyoda-ku
Yuurakuchoo, 1-choome 3
Tanaka shookai Onchuu

Haifuku:
  *Otoiawase no shinamono wa saru 8 gatsu 13 nichi
ni machigainaku kozutsumi de hassoo itashimashita.*
                    *Mazu wa oshirase
                    made.*
                    Sakata Yukio

Sakata and Co.
2, 4-chome, Ginza
Chūō-ku, Tokyo 104
August 16, 1992

Tanaka and Co.
3, 1-chōme, Yūrakuchō
Chiyoda-ku, Tōkyō 100

Dear Sir/Madam:
  In reply to your recent letter, we wish to advise you
that the merchandise was mailed to you parcel-post on
August 13.

                    Very truly yours,
                    Yukio Sakata

INFORMAL LETTERS

a. **Salutation and Content**

(1) Do not use one of the formal salutations described in the preceding section on formal letters.

(2) It is customary to mention the recent weather and climate in your locality.

(3) Inquire into the health of the person to whom you are writing and his or her family.

(4) Go into whatever other topics you want to bring up.

b. **Close**

(1) Instead of using any of the complimentary closing remarks described in Item b(2) of the preceding section on formal letters, close with a stylized remark such as:

(a) *Dewa mata.* = Well, then again.

(b) *Gokigen yoo.* = Wishing you good health.

(c) *Okarada o odaiji ni.* = Keep well. Take good care of yourself.

(d) *Minasan ni yoroshiku.* = Regards to everyone.

(2) Sign your name on a new line.

(3) Place the addressee's name on another line, either flush with the left margin or slightly indented.

c. **Examples**

Study the informal letter and thank-you note that follow.

INFORMAL LETTER

Heisei 4 nen
3 gatsu 15 nichi

Azusa sama:
  Otegami ureshiku haiken shimashita.
  Minasama ogenki no yoo de nani yori ni omoimasu.
  Sate watakushidomo no Kyooto hoomon no koto desu ga Shigatsu no hajime ni jikkoo suru koto ni shimashita. Nishuukan taizai no yotei desu. Minasama ni ome ni kakareru no o tanoshimi ni shite imasu.
  Kanai no Irene mo issho ni mairimasu. Shoobai no hoo mo okegesama de umaku itte imasu. Kore ga tsuzuite kureru to ii to omoimasu. Chotto muri na chuumon ka mo shiremasen ga Azusa san mo Shigatsu ni haittara sukoshi te o nuite issho ni ikuraka asoberu yoo ni shimasen ka.
  Konoaida Nomura kun ni attara Azusa san wa doo shite iru daroo to itte imashita. Kare mo shigoto wa umaku itte iru rashii desu.
  Daiji na koto o wasureru tokoro deshita ga Gurando Hoteru ni heya o yoyaku shite moraemasen ka? Shigatsu itsuka desu. Onegai shimasu.
  Ja kyoo wa kore de shitsurei shimasu. Otayori o matte imasu. Okusan ni yoroshiku.

                                    Jakku
                                    (Jack)

March 5, 1992

Dear Azusa:

I was very happy to receive your last letter. I'm glad to hear that all of you are well.

First of all, I expect to spend two weeks in Kyoto at the beginning of April and I'm looking forward to seeing you and your family.

My wife, Irene, is coming with me. Business is pretty good right now. Let's hope it keeps up. Try not to be too busy during the month of April so that we can have some time together. I suppose that's a little difficult for a busy man like you.

The other day Nomura asked about you. His business is going well.

I almost forgot the most important thing. Can you reserve a room for me at the Grand Hotel for April fifth? You'll be doing me a great favor.

I'll stop writing now. I hope to hear from you soon. My best regards to your wife.

Yours,
Jack

THANK-YOU NOTE

Yamada Fujiko-sama:
  *Kono tabi wa taisoo rippa na okurimono o choodai
itashimashite atsuku atsuku orei mooshiagemasu.
Hanga ni wa watakushi mo higoro kyoomi o motte ori
sono ue ni kondo itadakimashita no wa kyakuma ni
kakete yoku choowa itashimasu no de hontoo ni
yorokonde orimasu. Arigatoo gozaimashita.*
  Mazu wa on-rei made.

Robaato Sumisu
Robert Smith

Dear Fujiko Yamada,
  I should like to thank you for your delightful
present. I have long had an interest in wood-block
prints, and I'm glad that the one you gave me matches
the other things in my parlor perfectly.
  Thank you ever so much.

(Sincerely yours,)[1]
Robert Smith

[1] Note that in Japanese there is no formal closing in a note of this
kind.

ADDRESSING AN ENVELOPE

For a letter using the Roman letters:

Peter Paine
3-2 Oiwake-chō
Bunkyō-ku, Tōkyō 112

     602
     Tanaka Tarō Sama
     Kyōto Daigaku Igakubu
     Sakyō-ku, Kyōto-shi

In Japanese writing and using a Japanese envelope:

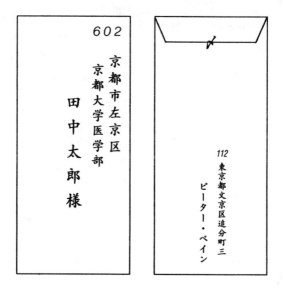